INSTITUTIONAL VIDEO

PLANNING, BUDGETING, PRODUCTION, AND EVALUATION

CARL HAUSMAN
NEW YORK UNIVERSITY

INSTITUTIONAL VIDEO

PLANNING, BUDGETING, PRODUCTION, AND EVALUATION

WADSWORTH PUBLISHING COMPANY
BELMONT, CALIFORNIA
A DIVISION OF WADSWORTH, INC.

Senior Editor: Rebecca Hayden
Editorial Assistant: Nancy Spellman
Production Editor: Jerilyn Emori
Designer: Andrew H. Ogus
Print Buyer: Randy Hurst
Copy Editor: William Waller
Technical Illustrator: Susan Breitbard
Compositor: TypeLink, Inc.
Cover: Vargas/Williams Design

Printed in the United States of America   85

1 2 3 4 5 6 7 8 9 10 — 94 93 92 91 90

Library of Congress Cataloging-in-Publication Data

Hausman, Carl
    Institutional video : planning, budgeting, production, and
evaluation / Carl Hausman.
        p.   cm.
    ISBN 0-534-12786-X
    1. Television in management.   2. Industrial television.   3. Video
recordings — Production and direction.   I. Title.
HD30.34.H38   1990
384.55'6'0973 — dc20   90-33824
                                                            CIP

ABOUT THE AUTHOR

Carl Hausman (M.A., Antioch University) is a well-known writer and practitioner in the communications media. He is author of *The Decision-Making Process in Journalism* (Nelson-Hall) and coauthor, with Lewis B. O'Donnell and Philip Benoit, of *Modern Radio Production; Announcing: Broadcast Communicating Today;* and *Radio Station Operations: Management and Employee Perspectives,* all published by Wadsworth. Hausman is coauthor, with Philip Benoit, of *Positive Public Relations* (Liberty/McGraw-Hill); and he is author or coauthor of five other books.

A former commercial television reporter and anchor, Hausman has produced a variety of institutional videos. He designed and originated Syracuse University's television news service, producing a daily program carried by WTVH Television, Syracuse's CBS affiliate, and was responsible for other university-related videos shown on network television. As an independent writer, producer, and announcer, Hausman has produced videos for many industrial and business firms; some of his scripts are reproduced in this book.

He also brings a performer's perspective to *Institutional Video*, offering advice on selecting and coaching talent. Hausman has been the on-camera or voice-over narrator on institutional presentations for firms such as Digital Equipment Corporation, Data General Corporation, and Greater Media Cable, Inc.

Hausman, Mellon Fellow in the Humanities, Department of Journalism and Mass Communication at New York University, has taught media production and writing courses at Emerson College in Boston and Clark University in Worcester, Mass.

PREFACE

There's a revolution going on in the world of video, albeit a quiet one. Thousands — by last count, tens of thousands — of corporations and nonprofit institutions are using video as a major component of their communications and training efforts. Many graduates of college communications programs are finding out about this silent revolution. Not only are institutional jobs plentiful, they pay better than traditional broadcasting positions, offer civilized working hours, and often allow newcomers to find employment virtually wherever they want it, even in major metropolitan areas.

Now that the secret is out, colleges and universities are offering an increasing number of courses and sequences aimed at educating the institutional video producer. The course titles are varied (Corporate Video, Professional Video, Nonbroadcast Television, and so forth), but the goal is essentially the same: to show how video production skills can be applied in an institutional setting.

That, of course, is the purpose of this book. *Institutional Video* is designed to help the reader gain an overview of the field as well as to understand the specifics of how the video department operates within an organization, how institutional programs are planned, produced, and evaluated, and how advancing technologies are changing the scope of the profession.

The 15 chapters of this book are divided into four parts.

≡ Part 1 deals with the overall concepts of institutional video, examining who uses video and why. It also discusses the workings of video departments, both in-house divisions and those that serve as outside contractors.

≡ Part 2 explores all aspects of planning the video program, including chapters on analysis and design, scripting, budgeting, basics of learning theory, and evaluation.

≡ Part 3 is a guide to production. It includes a much-needed chapter on choosing and directing amateur and professional talent, as well as comprehensive chapters on the techniques specific to institutional studio production and institutional field production.

≡ Part 4 focuses on specialized applications of institutional video. For example, interactive video is detailed. Emerging technologies, such as computer-created graphics and modern methods of teleconferencing, are also explained.

But this is not a hardware or a gimmick book. Its overarching purpose is to show how the institutional video specialist uses the tools of the trade to communicate and thus achieve corporate or institutional goals.

I have assumed that most readers of this book have a basic knowledge of television production. However, because some students take institutional video courses without a full menu of basic production prerequisites, some of the more technically oriented descriptions in the text are prefaced by a brief review and explanation of production basics.

I also realize that instructors often need to tailor a text to meet their individual needs; therefore, the chapters are designed so that they can be assigned out of order and understood in isolation. To ensure that each chapter is comprehensible on its own, terms must sometimes be briefly redefined or cross-references made to other chapters.

It is my hope that this book will meet the needs of emerging professionals planning to enter the exciting world of institutional video. If this work does succeed, it is largely due to the efforts of Senior Editor Becky Hayden, the editorial and production staff at Wadsworth, and the many professionals who contributed their advice. I also owe many thanks to the reviewers who patiently waded through the manuscript and offered their comments and suggestions: Joseph R. Chuk, Kutztown University; Don M. Flournoy, Ohio University; Barton L. Griffith, University of Missouri; Michael J. Havice, Marquette University; William D. Jackson, Middle Tennessee State University; Wes Marshall, University of Arizona; Robert Musburger, University of Houston; David H. Ostroff, University of Florida; and Michael J. Porter, University of Missouri.

CONTENTS

CONTENTS

PART 3
EXECUTING THE VIDEO PROGRAM

PART 1

INSTITUTIONAL VIDEO: USERS AND THEIR GOALS

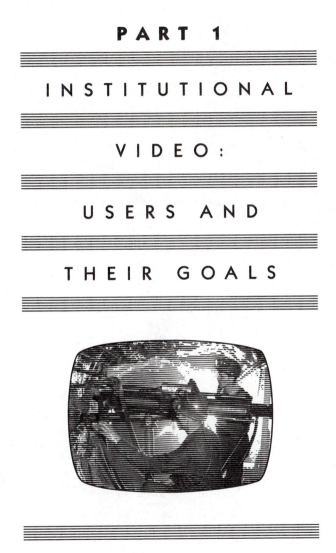

8

CHAPTER 1

══════════════════════

WHO USES

══════════════════════

VIDEO —

══════════════════════

AND WHY?

══════════════════════

≡ At the Neiman-Marcus department store in Dallas, customers watch a promotional sales video in the jewelry department, a lavish production featuring interviews with the performers Angie Dickinson and John Forsythe.

≡ Computerland, a giant retail chain, has its own television network, appropriately called CLTV. The network, fed to individual stores via satellite, offers sales training and staff motivation. CLTV also makes time available for vendors (who often have their own TV networks) to demonstrate new hardware to the people who will be selling it.

≡ A mock McDonald's restaurant in Elk Grove, Illinois, doesn't serve up hamburgers from its kitchen — it dishes out training videos, with over 100 served yearly.[1]

Television has become an essential tool of businesses and other organizations. Video, which is what TV is commonly called by professionals, is among the fastest growing fields in the communications industry. Although it is prone to periods of leveling off, this emerging profession seems to have an unlimited potential for growth.

THE NEW PLAYERS IN TELEVISION: BUSINESS AND EDUCATION

According to industry observer Judith Stokes, 25,000 nonbroadcast businesses were producing videos in 1988, with that number projected to double by 1995.[2] These figures translate into an exciting new job market for people trained in communications, in general, and institutional video, in particular. In addition to providing new jobs, institutional video — programs produced for use by a business, college, or other institution — often provides *better* jobs, with higher starting salaries and more stability, than comparable entry-level positions in traditional broadcast TV.[3]

WHY INSTITUTIONAL VIDEO IS GROWING

Although there are many factors behind the emergence of nonbroadcast video, two considerations are supreme: cost and convenience.

Television equipment is not cheap and probably never will be, but the initial capital expense involved in setting up a TV production facility is drastically lower than it was 10 or 15 years ago. This change is partially a result of simplified, solid-state technology. A high-quality video tape recorder, or VTR, of 1970 vintage was a massive device the size of two refrigerators with a price roughly equivalent to that of a modest suburban home. Today, an investment of only a few thousand dollars can buy a versatile, high-quality, easily portable recording unit. Similar savings can be found in cameras, editing gear, and studio equipment.

The huge and hugely expensive VTR of the '70s had another problem that made it impractical for most business and industry: It required a highly trained broadcast engineer to calibrate it and keep it running. Working those behemoths was no joy, either; producers trained in that era remember with no special fondness that the operating controls of the VTR were nightmarishly complex. A similar problem confounded users of almost all TV production equipment: Without exception, the equipment was big, bulky, and temperamental and required specialized technical training to operate. Shooting on location (doing a "remote") involved a virtual moving van and an army of technicians to set up the equipment and fix the inevitable breakdowns. Shooting in the studio involved less lifting but similar complications.

Despite those drawbacks various institutions began to realize that video was worth the effort. Teachers and professors came to appreciate that video could do things that standard classroom techniques could not. The instructor of a large lecture class found that the close-up views necessary for understanding a particular assembly process, for instance, were easily captured on video. No longer would students have to file past the lecture table for a fleeting glance at the tiny object in question. Videotape and conveniently mounted monitors solved the problem.

Some businesses braved the expense and inconvenience of early video and made training tapes. In addition to appreciating television's utility, they found that most people *liked* watching it and were more inclined to sit attentively through training or motivational video presentations than through lectures. Better yet, planning departments began to realize that it was not particularly cost-effective to have the same employee, often a senior officer drawing a high salary, parrot the same lecture week after week, year after year.

Pioneering organizations grew with the times. The equipment became cheaper, better, more portable, more consistent, and vastly easier to use. Today, video is within reach of virtually all organizations.

SUCCESS STORIES: HOW TELEVISION HAS PAID OFF

Managers of all types of organizations are using video to meet varying goals. In some cases those goals call for the medium to pay off immediately on the balance sheet; this can happen, for example, when teleconferencing brings a reduction in travel expenses. Sometimes, the benefits are less quantifiable but still tangible, such as increases in company morale or better relations with customers. These benefits are detailed in this section.

Easing Logistics   Teleconferencing, addressed in Chapter 14, has proved a dramatic budgetary success. With the costs of corporate travel rising sharply, savvy managers have found that face-to-face meetings via video are not only cheaper but also sometimes more productive. The Eastman Kodak Company, for example, maintains a teleconferencing network. Teleconferencing is not limited to big business. Educational institutions have found the technology useful, especially when distributing classroom instruction through ad hoc networks among schools and colleges.

Another logistical advantage is that videotapes can be used at any time that is convenient for the viewer — during the day or night, at work or at home. Videotape players are now widely available, and a home or office not equipped with a VCR is rapidly becoming the exception, not the rule.

Providing Consistent Training   Many successful businesses have grown by using uniform procedures and standard methods of operation. But in the age of franchising, far-flung operations sometimes find it difficult to ensure that training methods remain consistent from location to location.

Institutional video has significantly aided in the effort to standardize training. It is especially useful to restaurant chains, which typically rely on a consistent product as the linchpin of advertising and sales efforts and also must cope with relatively high worker turnover. Domino's Pizza is one such organization. Domino's found that distribution of training tapes (and later, as the organization grew, distribution of training videos by satellite) assured uniform standards of employee education.[4]

Bolstering Morale   It's no secret that employees perform better when they feel that they are a valued part of the organization. This factor was a prime motivator in the long tradition of "house organs," the colloquial term for printed magazines, newsletters, and newspapers distributed within organizations.

Only recently has the full potential of in-house communication been realized. House organs have developed into sophisticated tools for management-employee communication and are no longer characterized by being restricted to "bowling and baby" articles. Today, employee publications deal with the "hard news" of a business: personnel issues, new products, and leadership goals as well as with morale-boosting features that build a sense of community.

As publications grew up, so did in-house video. Institutional video provides a direct conduit from top management and an alternative to the grapevine and rumor mill. It ensures that the message from the top is not lost in translation through memos and layers of bureaucracy. For example, C. J. ("Pete") Silas, chief executive officer of the giant Phillips Petroleum Company, frequently appears in shirtsleeves on video programs, making an effort to address the bad news as well as the good. Company officials feel that this direct approach means that employees not only get the message, they get it with a minimum of rumor and distortion.[5]

Helping the Sales and Marketing Effort   Television is the great entertainer among the mass media, and businesses and organizations are using this capability to entice and hold an audience. Increasingly, college recruiters travel with a videotape illustrating the institution's appeal much more evocatively than any brochure. Point-of-sale video displays in stores highlight various pieces of merchandise. Many firms utilize video as a mechanism of public information, generating recognition and goodwill by getting their message to the public.

VIDEO AT WORK

The uses of video vary according to the task, and as a result the planning and production techniques vary, too. Although this statement may appear obvious, the hard fact is that finding the correct way to utilize video is no easy task, and the entire video effort may be at stake if the video department's time and talent are squandered on inappropriate projects.

Some video managers call that the "Hey, kids, let's put on a show" syndrome, referring to the inclination to use video just because it's there and, ostensibly, because it's fun. But video is expensive and time consuming, and as we'll see in Chapter 3 ("Analysis and Design"), successful video requires a well-targeted plan of attack before the first sheet of copy paper is loaded into the typewriter or the first lens is uncapped.

In short, the video effort must provide a return on the investment in order to survive. It must, in some way, produce a tangible or at least identifiable benefit to its sponsoring agency.

TYPES OF PRODUCTIONS

Let's examine three basic types of productions in terms of how they produce a benefit and what purpose they serve.

Video as a Management Tool As we have seen, video is a direct link from the top of an organization to the rest of the branches, and is an effective pruner of the corporate grapevine. Dampening rumors is a particularly vital task in times of crisis, and most executives will tell you that business is a series of crises.

Many managements have come to realize the power of video in reaching employees with information on company policies, progress reports on the firm's finances, or holiday greetings to employees. Enlightened executives have even taken, as of late, to accepting training in ways to improve their performance on camera.[6]

Instructional Video   A videotape or, as is common in some training applications, a video disc is infinitely patient. It can be recued to demonstrate the same activity countless times, and because it is usually under the control of the learner, the apparatus is entirely nonjudgmental. That is, the replay mechanism makes no assumption as to the "proper" rate for a viewer to absorb the information and does not become exasperated when a repeat performance is requested.

Video is also helpful in training situations because many demonstrations simply cannot be given as a live display to a group. It may be impractical or impossible, for example, to continually stop and disassemble a machine that you are training people to repair. Also, close-up views may be difficult to achieve when demonstrating small items to a large audience without the use of audiovisual aids.

Marketing and Public Relations   Video is a powerful tool for convincing buyers or swaying public opinion. In some cases it is used as a high-tech press release. That is, instead of sending written information to broadcast or cable television stations, that news is provided in a videotape. Other public relations and marketing functions are often accomplished today by "cross-networking," or exchanges, among the emerging in-house networks. In an example cited earlier a vendor of a computer product rents time on a computer retailer's private video network in order to demonstrate the product the retailer will be selling.

VIDEO'S PLACE IN INDUSTRY: SOME WEAKNESSES

Video is not the universal solution to all management, training, and marketing problems. For example, video is highly unlikely to totally replace face-to-face business meetings, nor should it. A popular aphorism in business is that you only really get to know someone once you're "close enough to smell his breath." Most experienced producers and performers realize that it is easier to deceive a camera, with the aid of coaches, directors, and editors, than it is to fool a person in the same room. And although many video meetings allow for extensive conversation and feedback, the technology does, by its very nature, tend to eliminate small talk.

That can be an excellent feature, but it can be a problem, too. Small talk, social interaction, and conversation about shared experiences are integral to the way we make judgments and establish relationships with people who may be very important in our organizational dealings.

Just as video is not a cure-all for management problems, it is not necessarily effective in all kinds of training. Sometimes, the denser, more easily accessible facts contained in a printed manual are the only practical way to communicate information. For example, a video "manual" on emergency first aid would not be entirely practical. Although first aid techniques can be demonstrated very clearly on video in advance of emergency situations, when a person is choking, it is not the time to be spooling through a videocassette trying to find an illustration of the Heimlich maneuver.

Another weakness of video in training lies in the fact that it is not particularly adaptable to the individual needs and problems of the trainee; in other words, the video playback unit is simply not human and cannot tell if the trainee is nervous, threatened, exhausted, or hostile.

Moreover, although video is a superb tool for marketing and public relations, it does have its limitations. For one thing, sending out video press releases can be incredibly expensive and not very productive. The success rate (placements in the news media) will probably be considerably less than that for a printed release. One reason is obvious: Printed releases can be used by newspapers and therefore can reach more individuals on a cost-per-unit basis. Another problem is that many television stations will not broadcast taped footage provided by an organization, either as a matter of news department policy or, more commonly, because there is just no time to use it in the cramped TV newscast. (However, an organization can elect to produce a program and pay for the air time; in that case there are few restrictions other than that the program must be of decent technical quality, must be in reasonably good taste, and must not promote something the owners of the television station deem illegal or immoral.)

Another marketing consideration also involves cost, but in a slightly less direct way. Viewers have become accustomed to the production values of commercial television, and thus they have increasingly high expectations of institutional video. If a company's video is produced with the intent of matching broadcast production values (not always a given, as we'll see in later chapters), it must be an excellent piece of work. And if it's that good, it's probably going to be expensive.

These are not blanket indictments of video. Rather, they are cautionary notes if you are interested or involved in a field with great, but not unlimited, potential.

THE EMERGING SPECIALIST IN INSTITUTIONAL VIDEO

Just how do we measure the potential of institutional video? It is difficult to accurately gauge the number of jobs available in the field. Any assessment is outdated virtually as quickly as it is printed. But we do know that surveys, such as a thorough study conducted by Linda Lee Davis of the University of Kansas, show institutional video to be a rapidly expanding field with some surprising advantages over broadcast television.

We also know that there is a surge in educational curricula designed to prepare students for entry into institutional video, or, as the field is sometimes called, "private video," "organizational video," or "industrial video." Another term gaining popularity is "professional video."[7]

Professional organizations involved in nonbroadcast media are also gaining in stature. The International Television Association (ITVA), for example, has become a worldwide organization. A recent convention drew more than 1,800 attendees, including representatives from 10 international affiliates, including Australia, New Zealand, and Japan. There are many other relevant professional organizations, including the International Association of Business Communicators (IABC), the International Teleproduction Society (ITS), and the Society of Motion Picture and Television Engineers (SMPTE).

THE PEOPLE OF INSTITUTIONAL VIDEO

Professionals in institutional video can be divided into two distinct groups: in-house employees and employees of independent production houses. Sometimes those production companies are branches of cable or broadcast TV stations or networks.

Although institutional video departments and production houses used to be staffed primarily by former employees of broadcast outlets, that is no longer the rule. Many staffers enter institutional video directly, sometimes after college training specifically preparing them for a career in the field.

TYPICAL JOB STRUCTURES

In many cases the professional in the field of institutional video is from the mold usually known as the "producer," meaning, usually, someone trained in the use of all television equipment and capable of directing technical crews. Sometimes, the producer is a one-man or one-woman band; more commonly, the producer is part of a department of several persons. It is unusual to find very large staffs, say, 15 or more, employed in an in-house video department, although such departments are often every bit as sophisticated as broadcast outlets; outside contractors also frequently have advanced facilities (Figure 1.1).

When organizations have extensive or complex video demands, much of that work is contracted to outside production agencies rather than done in house.

Indeed, contracting for out-of-house production personnel is a growing trend in video units of all sizes. It will be discussed in the next chapter, which will also provide fuller detail on how video departments are usually structured and operated.

At this point, though, it's worth remembering that although production skills are certainly valued in the world of institutional video, organizational skills are emerging as prime qualifications, too. With more work being contracted out of house, companies are seeking those with the ability to find and manage outside staff, draw up budgets, and juggle the contributions of many participants (while keeping those contributions on schedule).

REQUIRED BACKGROUND AND QUALIFICATIONS

A college degree is rapidly becoming a necessity for work in corporate television. Employers in all fields commonly use a degree to narrow the field, despite the fact that many talented people are arbitrarily eliminated from contention.

Mere possession of a degree, however, is not always enough to gain professional employment in the communications media. A degree plus experience is ideal, but Davis's study shows an increasing willingness by video department managers to hire recent graduates; 75 percent said they would consider hiring such newcomers.[8]

The Davis study also indicates that a degree in corporate TV would be the most desirable credential. Next in order of desirability are degrees in radio and TV journalism, communications, public relations, magazine and newspaper journalism, English, and other disciplines. The *skills* most valued in the survey were production skills, interpersonal skills, writing, and video photography, in that order.

A CAREER IN INSTITUTIONAL VIDEO: THE SURPRISING FACTS AND FIGURES

Working conditions, job location, and pay are all worth considering in choosing between employment in institutional video and broadcast TV.

Working Conditions   As a general rule entry-level positions in the commercial media usually involve long and irregular working hours and offer job security roughly equivalent to that of a career in Latin American politics. The Davis study

(a)

(b)

D. Max McCormick edits a production at Boston Edison's in-house facility
(a). The skyline seen on two upper monitors is an animation logo used
in the company's productions. Independent production houses often
feature the latest in high-tech equipment. WAVE, Inc., in Worcester,
Massachusetts (b), uses sophisticated half-inch broadcast-quality video
technology and is able to process video digitally, utilizing computer-
generated effects.

Photo (b) by Jonathan Kannair.

found that working hours were significantly shorter in the realm of institutional
video than in broadcasting and that job tenure was greater.

Location   Newcomers to broadcasting typically get their first jobs in small markets. This is the traditional rite of passage of broadcasting, and those who wish to
work their way into large markets are generally confronted with no option but to
tolerate frequent moves from city to city, making incremental advances in market
size, salary, and job responsibility.

Though entry-level broadcast positions in large markets are highly coveted, in
truth those jobs rarely involve doing anything meaningful. To make matters
worse, "gopher" positions in big-city TV don't necessarily lead to anything more.

Institutional video, on the other hand, offers many starting opportunities in
major cities. If big-city life is deemed an attraction, institutional work may be the
best alternative.

This assessment is not intended to demean small- or medium-market broadcasting. Many exceptionally talented people, especially those who highly value the
quality of life found in small cities, simply do not choose to move to larger metropolitan areas. Also, the talent pool is so large and the number of jobs so small that a
measure of luck, the factor of "being in the right place at the right time," is certainly an element in advancement to large-market work. The competitive world of
broadcast media does not always equitably reward talent and hard work.

Money   Davis's study considered many factors relating to pay, but in summary
she found that starting salaries were better in institutional video than in broadcast
television. Entry-level jobs in corporate video tended to carry salaries in the range
of $16,000 to $18,000 a year.

Newcomers to the field of broadcasting are often horrified by the salary structure. A detailed survey by the *Washington Journalism Review* in 1986 confirmed
that employees in major-market television stations were earning pretty good salaries, whereas their counterparts in small markets were toiling for abysmal remu-
neration. Using newspeople as an example, consider that in the smallest TV markets general-assignment reporters earned an average of $14,693 a year. Radio

journalists earned considerably *less*. And remember that *these were not starting salaries*; they represented the pay of *current employees.*

In fact, salaries prompted the author of the *Washington Journalism Review* survey to muse that should the reader be interested in the news business and like outdoor work, perhaps selling newspapers on the street might be the best option. The average salary of a news vendor at the time of the survey was $15,647.[9]

Another factor not reported but certainly applicable is that institutions with in-house video departments tend to be large and would be likely to have much better benefits, such as health insurance and vacations, than small-market broadcasting stations.

Jobs in institutional video are not there for the taking. With current trends in corporate retrenching, the institutional market has tightened, and with more work being sent to independent production houses, there is a tighter market for in-house employees. Still, institutional video represents a viable career path that offers welcome opportunities to professionals trained in media production.

SUMMARY

≡ Institutional video, often called corporate video or professional video, is enjoying rapid growth as a profession. Two reasons are the decreasing cost of equipment and the increasing simplicity and portability of that equipment.

≡ All types of businesses and institutions have found that video is more than just a status symbol or entertaining frill; it pays off in various ways.

≡ Among those payoffs are the facts that video is an excellent management tool, allowing for better contact between management and staff, and a fine training device as well. Video is also a strong public relations tool.

≡ Using video is not the best option for all situations, however. Its use must be evaluated in light of the particular circumstances. Misused video can be clumsy and expensively wasteful of time and effort.

≡ Although many organizations have complete in-house departments, work is often contracted out. This means, in practical terms, that the video professional must be an organizer as well as a producer.

≡ As a professional career institutional video has many advantages over work in broadcasting. In general, starting salaries, working conditions, and job security are better in institutional work.

FIGURE 1.1

13

EXERCISES

1. Speculate about how video might be a benefit to the management of a nationwide hamburger chain. The hypothetical restaurants are profitable as a whole but are suffering from uneven food quality and service from location to location. The most difficult aspect of correcting the problem is that individual owner-managers are rebelling at central management's requirement that they strictly adhere to a standard menu, food-preparation methods, and a particular accounting system. How can TV help? Be specific. Write three or four paragraphs.

2. Using the same format and reasoning process, pose a possible use of video in this situation: An auto-parts company, which dismantles thousands of cars and has literally millions of parts in its inventory, is trying to increase its business base. Specifically, it wants to reach do-it-yourself consumers — shade-tree mechanics, as they're called. Currently, the clientele is limited primarily to professional mechanics. There's another problem: The owner of the business wants the public to realize that this is not a slapdash junkyard but a major firm with a multimillion-dollar payroll and a fully computerized inventory. How can video help? To whom would this tape be shown?

3. Video is not, as discussed in the chapter, an ideal vehicle for all situations. Briefly list three circumstances under which you think video might be inappropriate, and explain why.

NOTES

1. Cited by Gail Ablow and Christian Cooper, "Who's Who and What's What in Corporate TV," *Videography* (March 1986): 31.

2. Quoted in "It's Showtime for Business," *Nation's Business* (April 1989): 54.

3. Linda Lee Davis, "Corporate Television: The Lure of a Non-Broadcast Career," *Feedback* (Fall 1987): 37–42.

4. "Domino's Gets Satellite Network," *Video Manager* (September 1987): 1, 25.

5. See "Excellence in Corporate Video," *Educational Industrial Television* (December–January 1988): 30.

6. One notable point is the increasing recognition of the need to perform well on camera and the fact that such topics frequently appear in management-oriented magazines. For one such summary see Vincent Vinci, "Effective Videotape Presentations," *Sky* (September 1988): 140–148.

7. See "A National Survey of 'Professional Video' Programs in Higher Education," conducted for the International Television Association and its Mid-Missouri Chapter, by Michael J. Porter and Barton Griffith. Information on this study is available from the authors at the Department of Speech and Dramatic Art, 200 Swallow Hall, University of Missouri-Columbia, Columbia, MO 65211.

8. Davis, "Corporate Television," 38.

9. Figures from "Where the Money Is: You'll Love the Work—But How Soon Will You Starve?" *Washington Journalism Review* (March 1986): 12–17.

CHAPTER 2

THE VIDEO

DEPARTMENT

The ways in which institutional video departments operate are as different as the types of programs they produce. However, one constant can be used to evaluate the functions of a video department: It exists to provide a benefit to the overall organization. At the same time, it consumes some resources of the organization. In general, any business or institution will want the video department to *produce* more than it *consumes*. Some broadcast-trained producers tend to view the production of a program as an end in itself. But institutional video largely exists in a corporate culture, an environment with its own rules and peculiarities. Thus, video producers working within the corporate culture must balance production and consumption.

Much of this chapter addresses the ways in which an in-house department operates. The chapter also examines how independent production houses are gaining ground in the battle for institutional business.

THE WORKINGS OF A VIDEO DEPARTMENT

The video department, whether it works completely in house or augments its work with outside help, must somehow produce a profit, indirect or direct, to its sponsoring organization. As a practical matter few if any departments regularly turn a profit for their sponsoring firms; indirect benefits therefore assume great importance.

TYPICAL STRUCTURES

The design of the video effort usually takes one of three forms. The first is an in-house department specifically dedicated to the organization, which is typically created when management sees an ongoing need for video. In such a case the return on the company's investment can be increased morale or more smoothly functioning operations. Those returns constitute an indirect profit.

Organizations often favor in-house video production because management feels that it will have greater control over the department and eventual product than if all the work were given to outside contractors. Perhaps most significantly, in-house video departments can be depended on to produce a regular schedule of video. It has become an accepted maxim that video produced only in reaction to crisis does not significantly help in the management effort.

The second typical structure is an in-house department producing both for the organization and for outside customers. It can provide what business managers would surely see as the best of both worlds: an intangible return (goodwill, enhanced management) coupled with tangible revenue (studio-rental and production fees from outside clients).

A problem with in-house video operations is that state-of-the-art editing suites sit idle much of the time. It's usually not possible, or desirable, to produce enough raw tape to keep editors constantly in motion. As a result the proud owners of such equipment increasingly rent the facility to outside clients. Marshall Field and Company, a 25-store chain noted in the video industry for its predilection for very-high-quality video gear, is doing just that. After finding that the editing room was unused for about 75 percent of the work schedule, management opened the doors to renters.[1]

Finally, independent production houses are often hired by an organization to participate in some or all of the production process. Using outside services obviates the need for building facilities and hiring staff.

Interestingly, the choice between in-house and out-of-house services is often resolved by geography. In major metropolitan areas office and production space is at premium and independent production equipment and personnel are plentiful, so out-of-house contracting may seem a more logical alternative. In rural or isolated areas the opposite may be true.

Both in-house departments and independent production houses usually augment their staffs with free-lance writers, performers, crew members, and other production personnel.

This last option — supplementing in-house staff with outside help — accounts for the seemingly superhuman productivity of many in-house video departments. The production unit at the General Foods Corporation was able to produce 60 programs, including instructional and motivational videos, in one year with a staff of five. William Hoppe, manager of the company's video center in White Plains, New York, points out, though, that such productivity would be impossible if the center were not located near New York City.

Drawing on a pool of about 50 free-lancers and eight production companies, along with an unlimited supply of talent provided by agencies, General Foods produces about a third of its total output of videos by farming out the projects. Roughly another third of the programs are handled by contracting some work with outside producers and hiring free-lance help. The remaining third are accomplished in house.[2]

Program output varies widely, of course, depending on the complexity of the programs. A major documentary may tie up considerable personnel and expenses, whereas simple product announcements may be accomplished with few resources. When all users of video, large or small, are surveyed, the figures usually show most departments turning out fewer than 50 programs a year. But most departments in major organizations can turn out very high numbers of productions, perhaps between 50 and 200 a year. The video production center at the Chesapeake and Potomac Telephone Company, for example, produced 162 programs in 1986.[3] The media services department of Wang Laboratories produced 125 programs in 1987.[4]

TYPICAL LINES OF RESPONSIBILITY

Both the video department's place in the overall institutional structure and the internal structure of the department itself vary widely. In business organizations the video department (or the audiovisual department) is often located under the supervision of the office usually called *public relations*, *institutional relations*, or *corporate*

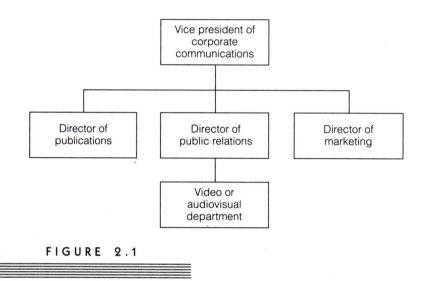

FIGURE 2.1

In some cases the video or audiovisual department is regarded as an arm of the public relations department, which reports to a vice president. Note that these blocks can be interchanged. For example, marketing is sometimes the superior department, with corporate relations reporting to it.

communications. Corporate communications is sometimes a distinct entity beneath the aegis of public relations and above video production. In such a case corporate communications may be responsible for production of all media output, including newsletters, press releases, and the company magazine.

The public relations department in any large corporation may report to a vice president, often a vice president for marketing. Sometimes, the public relations function is given vice-presidential status. Some corporations have a *vice president for corporate relations* or, if the firm does business with the government, a *vice president for institutional and governmental relations*. Figure 2.1 shows how such a video department might fit within a corporate bureaucracy. Note that this is presented as one possible example, but there are many others.

Chains of command are frequently similar in nonprofit institutions. The video department is commonly placed under the director of *public relations*, who is usually under the supervision of the office or individual in charge of *development*. Development usually entails fund-raising as well as public relations; in universities and many other nonprofit organizations the chief development officer is often a vice

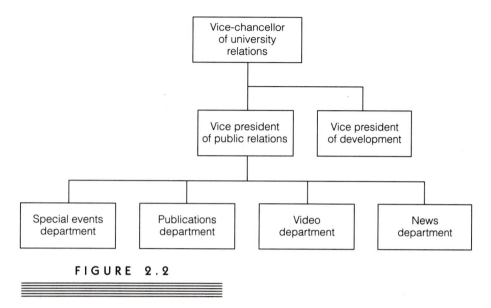

FIGURE 2.2

In this structure the vice-chancellor is in overall charge of development and public relations. The video department reports to the public relations executive. The chief development officer is shown at a lateral level with PR in this example but is sometimes in a supervisory position.

president. Figure 2.2 shows how such an organizational structure might work in a university.

Although video departments are often connected to the public relations function, video is sometimes viewed as a *training* function, and when that is the case the video department is placed under the supervision of the training department, which in turn is generally supervised by the office in charge of *personnel* or *human resources*.

Another exception to the typical hierarchy occurs in very large organizations where video production is not centralized but is assigned to various units. In such cases the head of the video department (who may also be its only member) reports directly to the chief of the operating unit, who is often an executive in charge of product development, sales, or manufacturing.

Lines of responsibility within departments usually flow from the overall department head, who is often called the *video manager*. When the video department comes under the aegis of a personnel function, the director is often known as the *director of training* or some similar title.

TRADITIONAL LINE ORGANIZATION

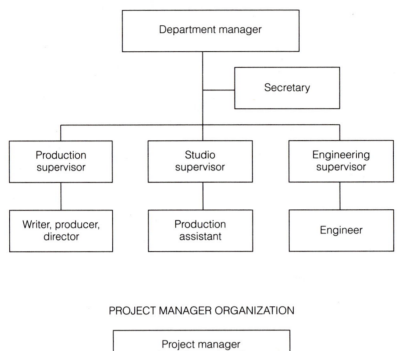

PROJECT MANAGER ORGANIZATION

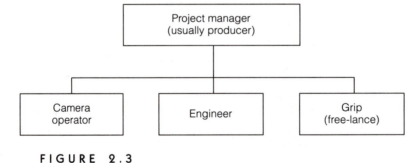

FIGURE 2.3

An example of the typical structure of a video department (top). The lower part of the figure shows the "project manager" type of organization, an ad hoc arrangement by which people involved in a particular project form their own working units.

It is not uncommon for video departments to have a *director of engineering*, who is in charge of technical matters, a *director of production*, overseeing scripting and overall concept, and a *studio supervisor*, who is in charge of the hands-on aspects of production. These people report to the video manager. That is how many departments, such as the Deere and Company staff, are organized (Figure 2.3).[5]

The top part of Figure 2.3 shows a relatively simple layout, but the organizational tree can become much more complex; in some cases there will be directors of graphics, crew chiefs, art department heads, and so forth.

Irrespective of the depth of the organization it is important to note that military-type chains of command do not always work well with creative enterprises. Therefore, it is sometimes necessary to create ad hoc working arrangements, under which an individual producer will pick his or her temporary "subordinates" and will assume the role of a *project manager* (see Figure 2.3).

Incidentally, it is worth noting that the type of program produced by the video department is often affected by the department's location in the corporate hierarchy. For example, if the video unit is in the human resources department, staff members may be more heavily involved with production of training tapes. Thus, they probably need more familiarity with instructional design than if the video unit were housed in marketing and public relations.

VIDEO AND THE CORPORATE PECKING ORDER

Although video departments play an undeniably important role in the marketing, training, and public relations efforts of institutions, it is unfortunately also the case that many institutional leaders have little or no understanding of the video function. The situation is steadily improving, but video professionals all too often feel that they are outside of the "decision loop" in the corporate culture; that is, they are not given an adequate voice in the way judgments are made and funds are allocated.

Some veterans in the field speculate that this problem may date back to school days. Ray Carpenter, a longtime audiovisual consultant, points out that "being assigned to the audio-visual club had about as much prestige as the job of clapping blackboard erasers. Historically, AV personnel have been necessary and functional, but not very well understood."[6]

In short, it is incumbent on video personnel to realize that they exist within a corporate culture, a culture that may not recognize production specialists as anything beyond drones who change bulbs in a slide projector. Although steps to remedy this misconception are beyond the scope of this book, many industry trade publications run regular features on methods for the video or audiovisual department to market itself internally, making its presence clearly known and understood within the corporate culture. Educating others about video is a vital function, and it should be taken seriously by anyone who wishes to participate in corporate decisions and possibly be promoted to a position beyond the realm of the production studio. Also, it should be clearly understood that in-house video units must conform to other aspects of the corporate culture, including dress codes.

HOW THE VIDEO DEPARTMENT INTERACTS WITH INSIDE SPECIALISTS

One "marketing" function that is directly within the purview of this book is the method by which the video department deals with inside specialists, the people who request department assistance. These specialists are often executives of the organization's training department, marketing arm, or sales wing. Sometimes, a request will come directly from a manufacturing division.

These executives are *clients*, who will have a considerable input into the scripting of the programs produced and will probably take an active role in their production. Dealing with inside specialists usually involves having video department personnel take the following steps:

≡ Determine how an idea will be handled, from conception to production: Who will be involved in the production? When will the production be done? How will it be presented in terms of length and format?

≡ Work directly with the client to assess what the program is intended to accomplish and how that goal will be met.

≡ Determine the feasibility of both the program as a whole and its elements, weighing such factors as the cost versus the possible benefits, the practicality of video as a medium for the message, and whether, in sum, the idea and its components are realistic.

These functions, of course, are at the core of the entire production process and are treated as separate chapters in this book. For now, I will briefly introduce the concepts and quickly show how they relate to the basic function of a video department.

AN IDEA FROM CONCEPTION THROUGH PRODUCTION

Although charting the progress of an idea from conception through production *before production begins* may seem hopelessly ambitious, that's precisely what the video department must attempt. Why? First of all, people and equipment must be scheduled well in advance. Location "shoots," for instance, often involve plane and hotel reservations. Editing means booking a busy suite of equipment. Secondarily, the video project manager must plan for the *interaction* of the varying schedules. For example, the desired announcer may be available only on certain days, which may not coincide with the time when the executive in charge of script approval is available.

The project manager must plan for these eventualities. Some managers use a so-called critical path structure (Figure 2.4). This visualization has the advantage of helping the project manager determine which time links are most critical. He or she may, for instance, use such a diagram to decide that the music can be shoved back to another date but that the script approval date cannot be changed, because such a delay in approval would hold up the whole project.[7]

WHAT THE PROGRAM IS SUPPOSED TO ACCOMPLISH

The job of the video manager is, in essence, to translate the client's idea into video. But with that job comes the responsibility of determining whether the idea is well suited to video in the first place, whether a video program can be produced effectively within the allotted budgetary and time constraints, and whether the proposed solution really meets the actual problem.

What the head of a manufacturing department may consider to be a problem caused by a deficiency of *training*, for example, may instead be caused by a deficiency in worker *morale*. A video producer should do enough detective work to ensure that the stated problem is the real problem.

SIMPLIFIED CRITICAL PATH STRUCTURE

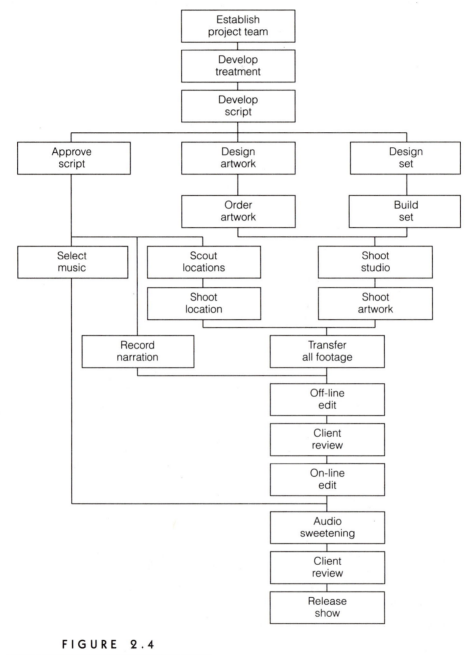

F I G U R E   2 . 4

A critical path structure for tracking projects and personnel.

The process of design and analysis often begins with a phone call from a department head. Sometimes, those callers are asked to fill out a proposal form. Proposal forms are unique to individual organizations, but Figure 2.5 represents a distillation of the features of many such forms.

It is unquestionably difficult to be placed in the position of dissuading a client from putting a message into video, and it is also occasionally problematic to persuade the client that a much different approach from the one originally envisioned is required. But that is, indeed, a responsibility of the video project manager.

Such topics will be addressed in Chapter 3, "Analysis and Design," and relevant illustrations of follow-through on initial concepts will be shown in Chapter 5, "Scripting."

DETERMINING THE FEASIBILITY OF A PROGRAM

Another way in which the video department interacts with inside specialists is to offer an informed opinion about the overall feasibility of a program. Usually, two factors are weighed: the inherent *practicality* and the *costs*.

Practicality of Video   As mentioned, video is not always the best option for communication of information. A written manual or a newsletter might serve the required function more efficiently. (Chapter 3 will provide guidance on judging whether a project is a good candidate for successful video production.)

Cost versus Benefit   The ways in which a video department interacts with inside specialists are significantly affected by the financial structure of the organization. Some video departments are given a set budget for the year and are expected to field as many requests as possible within that budget. In other cases video departments operate on a charge-back system, meaning that they bill in-house clients just as an outside production house would. Billings are typically significantly less, of course, because the in-house department doesn't operate on the same profit structure as an independent contractor.

Under a set-budget arrangement the in-house video producer must often reject projects simply because not enough money is available. A charge-back system places the decision back in the lap of the person making the request: Is a documentary on the new plating system worth $20,000 to the company's Plating Services Marketing Division?

PROPOSAL FOR VIDEOTAPE

Request made by: _____

Department: _____

Title: _____

Phone: _____

Please provide us with some brief information about your proposed project.

1. What is the basic subject of the program you would like produced?

2. What is the purpose of the program?

3. Can you briefly describe the scope of the program?

4. Will your department be able to provide us with a script?
   If yes, who will write it?

5. Do you want background music?

6. Do you want us to hire a professional narrator? If not, who will do the narration?

7. Where will the taping be done? Can you ensure access to the shooting sites and props?

8. What is your deadline?

FIGURE 2.5

A proposal form for a video production.

The emerging trend in the dilemma of cost versus benefit is that in-house departments are moving away from involvement in a large number of small projects and toward a smaller number of major and presumably well-planned productions. This trend is documented by a number of surveys, including one showing that average spending on productions doubled between 1981 and 1985.[8]

HOW THE VIDEO DEPARTMENT INTERACTS WITH OUTSIDE VENDORS

No tendency seems more immediately apparent than the move toward increased use of outside vendors. *Vendors* are independent production houses and individual free-lancers who sell their services, and sometimes rent their equipment, to the in-house video department.

Part of the reason for this trend is the growing sophistication of in-house producers, programs, and technologies and the resulting need for ever-costlier and more sophisticated equipment and increasingly highly trained personnel. Three major categories of outside vendors fulfill these requirements: *rental houses, independent production firms*, and *free-lancers*.

DEALING WITH RENTAL HOUSES

Rental houses fill the need for high-quality apparatus by buying state-of-the-art equipment and renting it to customers. Although not generally well known to the general public, rental houses have for years done a thriving business leasing high-tech film and video equipment to producers. Today, large firms such as Camera Mart, of New York City, Tritronics, Inc. (TTI), of Burbank, California, and Video Replay, of Chicago, find video systems to be the rental medium of choice and corporate customers to be the prime users of rental services.[9]

You can locate rental houses by reading trade journals, by checking in the phone book under such categories as "Audiovisual Rental and Supplies," or — perhaps the best option — by asking associates for recommendations. Rental houses are obviously a good choice when you will need certain pieces of equipment only once or twice or for an unusual application. A good example is extra lighting instruments needed for a one-time shoot in a cavernous room.

Note, too, that rental houses, which make their reputations by having the very latest in high-tech apparatus, often sell off *slightly* outdated equipment at bargain prices. Keep this in mind when considering the purchase of hardware.

Although many in-house video departments do not rent equipment per se, almost all "rent" equipment and expertise by hiring independently contracted production houses and free-lancers.

SUBCONTRACTING WITH INDEPENDENT PRODUCTION FIRMS

According to a survey of more than 2,000 institutional video users, conducted by Knowledge Industry Publications, 39 percent of respondents use outside production services to augment their own operations.[10] Outside contractors are also hired by firms that have no in-house department, a factor not included in the above-cited statistic. It would appear that independent production houses are an increasingly indispensable portion of the business of institutional video.

Independent houses, however, often do other types of video assignments, including TV commercials. Commercials are usually more lucrative than institutional video, so that many (certainly not all or even most) independent houses regard institutional video, often called "industrials" in the trade, as a less attractive option than advertising.

Should you be in a position of contracting with outside production houses, pay attention to this caveat. Check the references of the production house with other institutional clients to be sure that you will not be given short shrift should a lucrative advertising contract drop into the house's lap. Also, ask to view previous industrials to ensure that the firm is capable of handling an institutional production. It is an obvious mistake for an independent house to assume that experience in producing commercials translates into producing institutional video; the two media simply are not the same in structure and content. This mistake is, nonetheless, frequently made.

Hourly costs for services of independent houses will be listed on a "rate card," but be sure not to base your decision entirely on hourly rates. Some houses that charge high hourly rates can actually finish the job and hand you a smaller bill than the house with the lower rates. Their higher rates may reflect better equipment and more experienced personnel.

WORKING WITH FREE-LANCERS

Free-lancers market a particular skill to clients but work for themselves. In-house producers frequently use free-lance scriptwriters, sometimes use free-lance crew personnel, and almost always use free-lance "talent," or actors.

Free-lancing is a full-time occupation for some, but many other people moonlight. Full-time free-lancers often charge what appear to be very high rates. This is not a criticism; free-lancers have overhead just like any other business and must charge accordingly. Fifty dollars an hour is not at all an unreasonable price for a proven professional. In most cases the free-lancer must pay for word-processing equipment, health insurance, heat and light for the working area, telephone, and so forth. Easily half of the free-lancer's hourly rate can go toward covering overhead. Keep in mind, too, that you are paying for a skill that has been developed through many years of formal education and professional experience.

Free-lancers also provide production services. Some camera operators supply their own camera and other equipment. Although this is an appealing offer, do be sure that the camera is adequate. First, of course, you want your tape to look good. Second, if the free-lancer's work is to be edited with other footage, the technical qualities of the respective footages must match.

You should ask for a sample of the camera operator's work, usually called a "reel," a term that is a holdover from film days but is still applied to tapes. Ask if the footage you are viewing was shot with the camera to be used in your production.

Other crew members work on a free-lance basis, too. Lighting and audio specialists free-lance; you can often recruit students and others interested in learning TV production as general-purpose helpers.

Free-lancers who moonlight can often bring considerable expertise, but they do come with some unwanted baggage: Since they are beholden to their primary employer, unexpected work assignments can play hob with your schedule. Moonlighters are often restricted to working evenings and weekends. This is not always a problem, because a great deal of shooting is done during those periods. It's not always possible to tape during normal working hours when your location is in full operation.

When dealing with any outside contractor, it is important to gather as much information as possible. A video department head shopping for outside production services, for example, should take a trip to the production house. Constance Truesdale, vice president of marketing and operations at Computer Generated

Imagery, Inc., a production and postproduction firm in Ontario, New York, recommends looking for a clean, well-organized facility, on the theory that if the production house cares about its image, it will care about its clients'. She also offers these considerations to the head of a video department when evaluating the need for outside assistance or equipment:

≡ Consider farming out work if purchasing special equipment is impractical because it will not fit into the design of the existing facility. Also, consider going out of house if there will not be a continuing need for the equipment.

≡ One attraction for management of going out of house for specialized help is the fact that skilled staff members, such as editors with experience on one-inch systems, can command sizable salaries. Will there be a continuing need for such employees on the company's payroll?

≡ Be sure to gather as much information as possible about out-of-house vendors. Ask for brochures, staff resumes, and samples of previous work.[11]

SUMMARY

≡ Most video departments exist in a corporate culture. Thus, they are expected to provide a return, either directly or indirectly, on the organization's investment.

≡ Some video departments produce all their own material, but many augment their output with services from free-lancers or independent production houses. Some in-house departments rent out facilities to clients in order to maximize their use during off hours.

≡ In the corporate world the video production department is often located under the public relations or marketing function in the corporate hierarchy. Public relations is increasingly known as "corporate communications." In nonprofit institutions the video department will usually be found under the development or public relations office.

≡ Responsibilities of an in-house video producer are planning the time and equipment schedules for a production, analyzing the intended goals of the proposed program, and determining if those goals are valid and achievable.

≡ The video department must often rely on specialists from out of house, including equipment rental houses, independent production firms, and free-lancers.

≡ Price is not the only consideration when choosing contractors. An outside contractor may charge higher rates because the house has better equipment and personnel; the eventual bill, therefore, may actually be lower.

≡ Free-lancers have expenses, too. Skilled professionals charge and deserve a reasonable hourly fee.

EXERCISES

1. Today is January 2. You must deliver a training tape about a new computer system by February 15. The expert who will provide you with content for scripting and who must approve the script will be away and unavailable January 10–14 and February 1–9. The announcer who will provide the introduction and closing to the show (but who will not provide the on-camera instruction or narrate over the video) will be unavailable after February 7. You will tape at the computer center, which operates Monday through Friday from 9 to 5:30. The center is very busy in the mornings, and it has requested that you not tape during those hours.

    Construct a production schedule based on these details. Feel free to invent details of the tape itself. In fact, use one typewritten page to furnish those details (what specifically will be demonstrated, how the show will be structured, and so on). But concentrate on developing a realistic schedule. List all the tasks that you think need to be done and the dates at which you believe you can do them.

    Hint: Try to think outside of self-imposed boundaries in order to create the most efficient schedule. For example, do you need to wait until the very end of the production schedule to tape the announcer? Could the announcer's script be approved and recorded as soon as possible, before the script-approval bigwig leaves? How about the computer center? Would shooting on weekends be possible?

2. If possible, profile a local in-house production department. Write a three- or four-page paper describing the organization of the department. During your

interview with staffers of the department, pay particular attention to gathering information about the *informal*, ad hoc arrangements utilized in production.

3. Instead of, or in addition to, exercise 2, write a similar paper about a local independent production house. During your interviews be sure to gather information on the mix of work undertaken by the house. What is the relative percentage of "industrials" to commercials? Which do they favor? Do they even like doing industrials? Why or why not?

NOTES

1. Sammy R. Danna, "In-House Operation Reaches Out for Profit," *Educational/ Industrial Television* (May 1987): 27–29.

2. "Matching Video Facilities to the Tasks at Hand," *Educational/Industrial Television* (May 1987): 13–26.

3. William A. Edmunds, "Marketing Your Facility In-House," *Video Manager* (May 1987): 19, 20.

4. Figure obtained by a research assistant, Jodi Walsh, during an interview at Wang Laboratories, November 1988.

5. From Michael D. Shetter, "People, Equipment and Time: A Case Study of Managing These Elements in a Growing Television Facility," *International Television* (September 1984): 70–78.

6. Ray Carpenter, "Focusing the Image," *Audio-Visual Communications* (April 1982): 69.

7. Shetter, "People, Equipment and Time," 70–78.

8. Bill Eldred, "The Cutting Edge: Training the Corporate TV Producer," *Videography* (March 1986): 77–79. The statistic cited by this article and cited secondarily in this chapter was supplied by D. J. Brush Associates.

9. Ric Gentry, "Rental Houses: At the Vanguard of State-of-the-Art," *Videopro* (July–August 1984): 44–48.

10. Judi Stokes, "Outside Sources Utilized," *Video Manager* (February 1987): 1, 29.

11. Summarized from Constance Truesdale, "The Dollar Dilemma: Expand Your Facility or Contract for Outside Services," *Educational/Industrial Television* (May 1987): 24, 25.

PART 2

PLANNING

THE VIDEO

PROGRAM

CHAPTER 3

ANALYSIS

AND DESIGN

Why should a video program be produced? That is a tantalizingly straightforward question but one that can be extraordinarily difficult to answer. First, an institutional video producer must ascertain the matter of feasibility: *Can* the particular problem be solved or the need be met by video? And if so, *how?*

Those two questions must be answered before the first camera is uncapped. This chapter focuses on the tasks related to determining the feasibility of a proposed program, making an initial analysis of the needs the program will meet, and fashioning an initial program design.

FEASIBILITY

Not every idea needs to be communicated by television, and television cannot solve every problem. Television is not a medium that can be all things to all people in all situations. Indeed, an important role of the producer of institutional video is to convince certain clients *not* to commit their ideas to television. There are four reasons:

1. An in-house video department has limits on resources and personnel. Allocating those resources to unrealistic production goals limits the department's chances for success in the areas in which it can shine.

2. Video departments, both in house and out of house, are judged by the effectiveness of their products. It is a mistake to take on any and all program concepts regardless of their suitability to the television medium, because the producer will be judged by the misses as well as the direct hits.

3. Television simply does not do a very good job of illustrating certain concepts. The operation of complex computer software, for example, might be better demonstrated by a tutorial run by the computer (an actual computer program), perhaps in combination with an indexed workbook. Television presentation of this and other intricate subjects usually cannot communicate the information adequately, because there is too much material to be summarized.

4. Sometimes, the situation does not call for a video or, for that matter, any other type of media presentation. For example, a department supervisor may insist that a training tape is necessary to instruct personnel in the proper method of filling in a payroll form. The problem, though, may lie in the form itself. Perhaps it is inscrutably designed or is not being distributed to the proper employees. A needs analysis can determine whether the problem involves a shortcoming in training methods or a deficit in other areas.[1] These decisions, of course, should be made in concert by the subject expert and the media-use expert.

Before undertaking an analysis of the need, weighing such questions as those posed in item 4 of the list, it is wise to first weigh the production considerations illustrated by item 3. Does the proposed presentation lend itself well to TV?

STRENGTHS OF VIDEO

The technical strengths and weaknesses of television are instrumental in the producer's decision whether to produce in the first place. Among the strong points of television (good television, that is) is that it engages the viewer. Because it uses sight, sound, and motion, it is an effective tool for tapping emotions. Many people find it to be a more compelling format than reading or listening to a lecture. However, watching does not always translate to learning. Producers must ensure, to the best of their ability, that learning is taking place.

Video also provides the benefits of a speaker addressing the viewer — but is not subject to the same foibles as a live presentation. A television tape is accurate every time it is played, assuming it was accurate when it was produced. Tapes are not subject to colds, bad moods, boredom, or traffic jams. Television is a tireless worker.

A television camera is superbly effective in capturing close-up detail. Hospitals, for example, have found that video is often a better alternative to the traditional operating-room observation theater; students, interns, and residents can view the procedure clearly, as opposed to squinting down from an observation deck. Along the same lines, the latest generation of high-tech gear can combine with traditional video to produce extremely effective demonstration and training tapes. Surgeons, for example, utilize tiny cameras mounted, believe it or not, on their headbands. These camera and light units (Figure 3.1) are used to tape deep-cavity surgery, a type of operation that was previously impossible to tape using standard video gear.[2]

WEAKNESSES OF VIDEO

TV is not without its drawbacks. A producer of institutional television would be wise to bear in mind that video is not a good medium for listing items or explaining a complex series of actions. Grocery stores long ago learned that television was not a particularly effective vehicle for advertising their weekly specials. There's simply too much information to present in television's linear format. (Interactive video is another story; see Chapter 11 for details on how it can be used to present multiple options.) Producers of training videos are coming to appreciate this fact, and they are becoming more confident in recommending that certain presentations are better candidates for print.

Another drawback is that video is not tangible or always easy to consult. Printed instructions for operating computer software, for example, can be carried in a pocket. Television instructions, though, are not so easily handled, stored, and retrieved. Information conveyed by video is, in the parlance of education, less "dense" than printed information. More information can be packed onto a printed page that takes one minute to read than into a minute's worth of video.

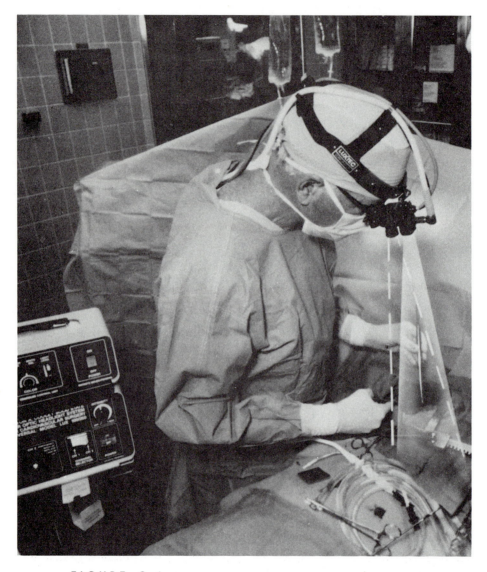

FIGURE 3.1

Because it is difficult for surgeons in training to view operations in deep cavities, a firm known as Luxtec, which specializes in fiber-optic technology, has developed a camera mounted on the surgeon's headband.

Courtesy Luxtec Corporation, Sturbridge, MA.

Video is also expensive and difficult to produce. Consider this example: A writer of a corporate newsletter who needs an interview with an executive at a remote location needs only to pick up the telephone. But a corporate video producer must travel in person, often with a crew, to conduct the interview. Equipment and crews can sometimes be hired by telephone, but results can be spotty. If a specific amount of money is available for the project, choosing between video and print often boils down to deciding between a very good newsletter and a mediocre video program.

A closely related point is that viewers' expectations are often unrealistically high. Most viewers are accustomed to the production values of commercial television, an arena of enormous resources. As a result low-budget programs — and compared with commercial television produced for the major networks, almost any in-house production is low-budget — suffer by comparison. It is not uncommon for high-level managers in an organization to become alarmed at the relatively unexciting fare produced in house, especially when these managers, who are often ignorant of the standard expenses of television, feel that they are dedicating enormous resources to the video department.

CHECKLIST: DOES VIDEO SUIT THE JOB AT HAND?

Consider the pros and cons of the prospective task, and form a realistic frame of reference. Fielding any and all tasks thrown your way will generally be counterproductive. Attempting to produce a product poorly matched for a television presentation will often result not only in a poor program but also in damage to your department's reputation.

You may not always have the option of turning down a project, but in many cases you can explain to management why the proposed topic would be better handled by another medium. In some cases a compromise may be in order. A video demonstration of a complex series of actions can be supplemented by an illustrated brochure, for example. The following questions, although not definitive, provide a starting point from which to evaluate whether TV is the best option.

Can the Program Support a Simple Theme? Will there be an unwavering point of view throughout the program's entire content? This is generally more a question of politics than of aesthetics. Institutional television programs are frequently created by committee, and committees can hopelessly fragment the straightforward thematic unity required by video. Be as sure as you can, before you make commitments, that you won't wind up refereeing between one manager who wants a sales motivational tape produced in a closely simulated sales situation and another executive who wants a glitzy Madison Avenue strategy. The two ideas probably can't be melded into a unified whole, and you are bound to end up pleasing no one.[3]

Is the Task Logistically Feasible?   The demands of travel and personnel time are relatively straightforward to calculate, but they are not the only considerations. For example, does the proposed program call for a large amount of outdoor shooting over an extended period? Three weeks in autumn can make a startling change in the backdrop, so under certain circumstances a job such as this might better be postponed until spring. Consider as many other variables as you can imagine: Can the factory floor be lighted well enough to produce a decent shot of a large-scale manufacturing process? Can all the props for a demonstration of a new product line be gathered at one place if the program is to be set in the studio? Remember, one product might be a wall-size shelving unit.

Is extensive preparation necessary, as might be the case for a training tape on engine repair? Engines have to be thoroughly cleaned and sometimes partially painted in order for clear detail to show.

Is Television the *Best* Choice for This Presentation?   If it seems as though the idea could better be presented through another vehicle, then it probably can be. Do, of course, remember that some functions of corporate video are simply archival, meaning that you are just making records and that there is no true distinction between "good" and "bad" TV.

In addition to considering the strengths and weaknesses of television mentioned earlier, it's also worthwhile to scrutinize the motivations of corporate executives when deciding whether an idea merits a television production. Unfortunately, appeasement of someone's ego is sometimes the motivating factor in the decision to use TV. That, of course, is a poor reason to produce unless your fundamental job is appeasement of that person's ego. Of course, if bad television is the result, this strategy can still go awry.

Each proposal must be judged on its own merits, but keep in mind that the following scenarios often make for bad TV:

≡ *Lectures that involve nothing more than what could be presented in a standard face-to-face presentation.* Although a 15-minute lecture is not necessarily dull, it usually is because few amateur television performers have the skills necessary to carry it off.

≡ *One-camera, low-budget coverage of affairs or events.* Requests to simply "get some film" of a conference or trade show, with no other production values or support, usually result in something similar to a bad home movie of your Uncle Ralph's barbecue.

≡ *Quickly arranged interviews.* The idea of getting someone on tape "because he's in town" or "because we'll be there anyway" is seductively appealing to those who haven't tried it already. Interviews require preparation, both of the people involved in the interview and of the site itself. Yes, experienced television news crews can produce credible interviews on short notice, but keep in mind that those interviews are short segments for insertion into a larger, heavily produced program. An unframed 20-minute interview will suffer by comparison. Also, remember that catching interviews on the fly is the brunt of a TV news crew's job, and most crews have become very good at it. In most cases you won't be able to match their experience or technical support.

Are There Technical Obstacles to the Intended Presentation? Don't forget that television is one link in a chain of communication. Many good programs have been ruined by the fact that the end product simply wasn't shown correctly. For example, consider the failure of one highly detailed presentation of a close-up technical operation. It was a fine training tape when viewed by a nearby observer, but it was intended to be presented to a large group viewing monitors from a long distance. The members of the group simply could not see the presentation clearly enough. Consider, too, the dismal failure of teletext, the displaying of printed information on a television screen. Many teletext ventures, including one in which I was involved, failed after stunningly lukewarm receptions by the viewing public. Many reasons have been offered for these failures, but one that makes intuitive sense is that people are simply not comfortable reading from a TV screen. The distance of their chairs from the screen, for example, may be fine for viewing standard TV but not appropriate for text. Screen size was a variable not adequately considered; what might be perfectly readable on a large set is difficult to follow on a small one.

One final caution: If there is any question about how something will appear on screen, shoot some test tape. One particularly catastrophic industrial tape featured, or rather *was to have featured*, a demonstration of laser-beam technology. But the lab's lasers, bright and brilliant to the naked eye, were all but invisible to the television camera.

Can the Intended Idea Be Expressed on an Emotional Level?   Video need not always consist of heart-rending fare, but it is the vehicle of choice for messages carrying a strong emotional content. Strictly intellectual exercises, such as a straightforward exposition of facts, are just as easily consigned to a printed document. Although television can certainly inform, it is unexcelled at motivating, instilling confidence in an organization, and making viewers feel a part of the institution.

In sum, video is not always the best alternative when choosing a medium. In-house producers exercise their judgment, based on experience and the rationale discussed above, to analyze whether television is the right vehicle and, if so, how to go about making an effective program.

ANALYSIS

Analysis is generally a three-step process. It involves *identifying a need, taking an inventory of available resources* and uncovering resources that may be hidden, and *gauging the intended effect* of the program.

IDENTIFYING A NEED

The strongest presentations are often those constructed to fill the most specific needs; frequently, video is not only the logical alternative but also the only economically feasible alternative. As an example, consider the problem faced by the owner of Tom Foolery's restaurant, Tom McCabe. His Westboro, Massachusetts, establishment, one of the largest restaurants in the state, must train about 300 new employees a year, almost one new employee per day. These new workers require consistent, accurate training. In addition, motivation is an important factor. Restaurant employees need to understand that they must work as a team in order to perform complex daily operations. Finally, an experienced employee, usually a manager, was needed to train an inexperienced worker. Add up the hours involved in training 300 new employees per year and you'll see that this involved an enormous commitment of time and money.

Video matched the restaurant's needs exceptionally well:

NEED	BENEFIT OF VIDEO
Consistent training	Information is repeated faithfully each time the tape is played. An enthusiastic presentation, stressing the importance of the job, is given each time.
Holding attention	Dialogue, music, and dramatic scenes all contribute to holding the new employee's attention. The video is never nervous or distracted, as was the case with managers who were trying to juggle training and several other duties.
Cost-effectiveness	The video, basically a one-time cost, replaces a long-term investment in dedication of management time.
Motivating workers	Music, narration, and action combine to provide an inspirational tone, one that is expected to inspire teamwork among new employees.
Providing broad overview	The most important factor in training is convincing the new employee that he or she is part of a team and that individual job performance affects the performance of others. Video presentations can jump from scene to scene with great speed, familiarizing the worker with the restaurant much more efficiently than an initial tour on foot.

The television format did, then, seem to meet the needs of the client. In fact, the tape matched needs so well that its use was featured in *Restaurant Business Management*, a trade publication that presented the idea as a possible model for other restaurants. The script for this tape will be reprinted in Chapter 5.

In the needs-analysis stage, it is not essential that every detail be anticipated. Simply identify what you hope the intended tape will accomplish, and keep this objective clearly in mind throughout the process of scripting and production. In the words of one management expert, "If you have nowhere to go, you will certainly get there."[4]

DISCOVERING RESOURCES

One method of achieving excellence in production is maximizing available resources — in other words, making the most of what you've got. Because virtually all productions operate under some sort of budgetary constraint, it is essential to discover the "hidden resources" at your command.

One possibility is to determine whether the department with which you are working can lend you personnel. A "production coordinator" familiar with the workings of the department or operation to be featured in the tape can be of enormous help. If that person is assigned to you full time for the duration of the shoot, so much the better. Do be wary, however, of people who attempt to exercise undue control over your operations.

You can also ask if any stock footage is available from other sources and if you can obtain rights to that footage. As an example, a producer of a tape for an auto parts recycling firm needed to illustrate and demonstrate the advantage of buying a previously assembled car fender as opposed to manufacturing a new one. The process of disassembling a fender in order to show the component parts was daunting: a daylong shoot, at best. But an executive of the firm remembered seeing an industry-association film with an animated disassembly sequence. Rights were obtained, and the film was integrated smoothly into the final tape.

The department or firm for which you are shooting may be able to help with logistics. The same auto parts firm had a private plane from which terrific aerial shots were taken. (The script for this program is reprinted in Figure 5.1.)

Do any of the employees have acting or broadcast experience? You may be surprised at the number of people who have appeared in commercials or have done amateur theater. It's usually best to ask a disinterested third party for recommendations, though. Once you have directly asked a worker about acting experience and he has told you he is a great actor, it's difficult to back out of the situation when you find out he's not.

In any case be certain that you ascertain the precise limits under which on-camera or off-camera help will be made available to you. Your plans can be scuttled if someone who has played a featured role in the first two days of shooting is suddenly made unavailable on the third day, when her final scene was to have been shot.

GAUGING THE INTENDED EFFECT

After-the-fact measurement and evaluation are another critical area of video, dealt with in Chapter 7, but some preshooting evaluation is also essential. The process of gauging the intended effect amounts to reevaluating what the program is supposed to do and whether, now that some facts have been gathered, it is really going to serve its intended purpose.

Some examples will clarify the concept. Suppose you have been asked to prepare a videotape for training employees to use a new piece of machinery. In the process of analysis and design you discover that the executive who asked for the production appears most interested in describing how fast and powerful the machine is. Although his point is certainly valid, it is hardly the key to training operators. The orientation must be designed to fit the audience.

Alternately, perhaps the orientation is right but the intended audience is wrong; it would be perfectly legitimate to produce a video extolling the speed and power of a new manufacturing machine if it were a training tape for the firm's sales representatives, who would inform potential customers of the cost-saving benefits of the company's highly efficient production gear. The lesson is to determine the intended audience, and slant the presentation toward that audience. Consider the audience's educational level, motivation, and any other relevant factors.

Here's another case: Assume you are planning a tape to motivate salespeople to increase orders on a new line of office furniture. The stated objective is to fire up the sales force and convince them that this fine product can line their pockets with commissions. But in the analysis and design of the program you find that the executives are more interested in having you shoot every detail of the furniture.

At this point you should wonder what the actual objective is. Is it to produce a tape that demonstrates how all the doors open, how all the carts roll, and how all the computer-paper storage areas work? If so, fine: Showing sales representatives how to demonstrate the items is an absolutely legitimate function of institutional video. But your original objective was to *motivate*. Which is the real objective? Find out. If not, the eventual impression may be that you, in the words of one disgruntled sales manager, "wasted time demonstrating equipment to salespeople who know that gear like a Marine knows his rifle." Determine the real objective, and follow it.

INITIAL PROGRAM DESIGN

It is time to consider what is involved in assembling the skeleton of a program. Before the script is written, it is necessary to determine the program format, how information will be obtained, and at what level the material will be presented.

PROGRAM FORMAT

Programs may take the form of a documentary, a lecture, an interview, an interactive program, a drama, or a combination of any of these. Each format has its own advantages and disadvantages.

Incidentally, when undertaking the first tentative steps in determining program design, don't forget the distribution and viewing environment; this will have a major impact on the type and content of the material. Will viewers be able to stop and start the tape? Will they take the tape home with them? Will they be given time off from work to view the program? All these factors can affect your choice of format.

Documentary   The documentary has a news format, almost always using voice-over narration and carrying a cohesive theme.

≡ *Advantages of the documentary format.* The documentary is, when done properly, a very efficient method of production. It is generally taped with a single camera; when scripted with efficient editing in mind, a documentary can be remarkably simple in structure. Documentaries tell a story, generally with a strong point of view, which draws the viewer into the program. Also, documentaries can be reedited and updated if necessary.

≡ *Disadvantages of the documentary format.* Viewers accustomed to seeing documentaries on commercial television and public TV are used to good productions. If you choose this format, be aware that you will be held to high standards. Also, documentaries are very dependent on a coherent script. You will need a scriptwriter with a good news sense as well as a firm grasp on production values.

Lecture   Many in-house presentations are "chalk talks." The speaker stands before a board or sometimes uses an overhead projector, with shots of the projection televised.

≡ *Advantages of the lecture format.* Lectures are certainly among the cheapest and logistically least complex of all formats. Because of the simple production values there is also little that can go wrong. Also, the simplicity of the structure allows the producer to concentrate on the basic production values: excellent lighting, precise camera shots, and clear scripting.

≡ *Disadvantages of the lecture format.* In the wrong hands televised lectures can be deadly dull. Lectures are talent-intensive, meaning that the speaker can make or break the program. There is also a limit to how long even the most polished lecturer can sustain a program. However, do not rule out lectures arbitrarily. Good talent can make this format surprisingly effective.

Interview   In the institutional field interview programs are generally staged to resemble those on commercial television. A host interviews guests on a variety of relevant topics.

≡ *Advantages of the interview format.* If you have a studio, this type of presentation can be relatively inexpensive and simple to produce. Also, it is a good tool for making viewers feel part of the operation. That is one reason why so many major firms are telecasting regular interviews with top managers.

≡ *Disadvantages of the interview format.* The success of such a program is largely dependent on the skill of the host as well as on the on-air competence of the interviewees. An interview program is often difficult to control; these shows tend to wander and lose thrust if not tightly reined. They can also lack visual appeal. An imaginative producer, though, can compensate by utilizing cover video illustrating the subject about which the speaker is talking. The producer can also help the participants by rehearsing them, working them through a general outline of the program.

Interactive Program   With an interactive program the viewer has some control over how it proceeds. The word *interactive* refers both to a format and to a style. Although interactive video is, in large part, a format unto itself, it also uses the other formats already mentioned to present information.

At the very simplest level the viewer of an interactive videotape can shut it off or rewind it when he or she wants. In its most sophisticated incarnations an interactive presentation can involve many branches, with viewers choosing actions and witnessing the consequences of their choices.

≡ *Advantages of the interactive format.* It is an excellent vehicle for training. Computers drive the video devices; if you're not familiar with a computer-controlled program, you can think of it as similar to a sophisticated arcade game. One reason why interactive programs are so popular is that computers are infinitely patient tutors. Organizations ranging from private industry to the U.S. Army are making heavy use of interactive design.

≡ *Disadvantages of the interactive format.* This is not the type of program you can turn out in a week; think in terms of months or maybe a year. Also, the processes of programming the computer software that runs the presentation and manufacturing the disc that contains the video are expensive. Lastly, writing interactive scripts is a complicated affair, involving a great deal of planning and assuming familiarity with the interactive concept.

Dramatic or Semidramatic Structure   The dramatic format uses acted scenes, with performers usually assuming characters other than their own. There is some sort of forward-moving plot line. Some presentations are entirely dramatic, meaning entirely fictive. In other cases only certain scenes are dramatized, with the rest of the program being produced as a documentary or, perhaps, using other format elements.

≡ *Advantages of the dramatic structure.* Drama is one of the most compelling of all vehicles. Properly executed, it is unsurpassed at maintaining audience interest. Elements of drama can be adapted to almost any format. For example, documentaries typically feature the dramatic staging of events.

≡ *Disadvantages of the dramatic structure.* Bad acting can be *horrifyingly* bad. A great deal of craft is necessary to create the illusion of assuming another character. The task is made easier when people play themselves, but that is still no guarantee that they will turn in a credible performance.

METHODS OF GATHERING INFORMATION

The next step in developing the program is gathering information to flesh out the desired format. What sources of information will you tap for the presentation, and how will you compile material? Gathering information is not simple under any circumstances, and it can be considerably complicated in the institutional environment.

One immediate problem is that you will be working with specialists. They may not have the desire or the capacity to make their specialty comprehensible to you. There is only one solution: Keep digging, even when your actions do not place you in a favorable light. The specialists may consider you hopelessly dull-witted, but press on nonetheless. Use the argument that "if you can explain it to me, it can be explained to anybody."

Other factors enter into the specialists' realms. Aside from the level of their knowledge, experts in a firm have very different outlooks on the relative importance of their specialties. Research and design personnel may feel that their contributions are the very foundation of the organization. Marketing employees are convinced that the organization would not exist without their particular expertise. Maintain your perspective.

When actually gathering information, stock up on printed material. An excellent place to start is your local public library. One producer was assigned the task of covering research into particle physics. He was absolutely baffled by the explanations of the scientists. Help came from a collection of articles from general-interest magazines, located through *The Reader's Guide to Periodical Literature*, an index available in almost any library. Next, he asked the scientists if they had received any previous press coverage. They were able to provide him with an armload of newspaper clippings, comprehensible even to TV producers. Some organizations have institutional archives. Take advantage of this facility. If a librarian is assigned to the archives, he or she may be of enormous help.

Once you have mastered the basics, the actual gathering of script information can be relatively easy. In-person interviews are often most productive at this stage. Once you have an idea of the total concept, you can ask more productive, incisive questions.[5]

UNDERSTANDING AND COMMUNICATING UNFAMILIAR IDEAS

Perspective is an odd and shifting attribute of the human mind. You can quickly lose it after plunging into a project. After spending a week interviewing and gathering information about a company's retirement plan, you may actually be more of an expert than some members of the employee benefits department. In that case it is critical to remember that most of the audience for your informational program will be starting at a lower level than your present one. If *they* had spent a week researching a retirement plan, they wouldn't need to watch a tape. Structure your plans for the show with this and several other principles in mind.

First, just as it is important to not start at too high a level, do not start too low. Audiences can be bored or insulted by presentations that are too basic. Determining the proper level is difficult, but supervisory personnel can usually give you an estimate of the intended audience's level of knowledge. If time and circumstances allow, it may be better to speak directly with members of the target audience. Supervisory or management personnel do not always really "know" their personnel. Doing this can also help the producer understand the language level of the audience as well as their particular likes or dislikes.

Do not load down your audience with too many new concepts at one time. Television is a linear medium; that is, information is presented in series, and viewers cannot go back and refer to previous explanations, unless the program is interactive. A writer composing a brochure can list five new terms under one heading and then explain each one. A television producer will have better success explaining each term immediately after it is introduced. For additional details on effective techniques of training through video, see Chapter 4, "Essentials of Video Instruction."

Finally, do not go from point A to point D while forgetting about B and C. Here is an actual excerpt from a presentation to computer novices interested in desktop publishing:

> The computer is like your own personal print shop. Instead of sending copy to a typesetter, as shown by this diagram, we set it ourselves. We go around the print-shop, as shown by this diagram. And all this is made possible by the new generation of WYSIWYG software and 386, 16-bit processors.

Unfortunately, this approach is all too typical. The insultingly simplistic introduction is somehow intended to placate the audience's desire for basic information and allow the presentation to move to the realm of technobabble. Obviously, no one in the audience knew what WYSIWYG software was. They were neophytes, and the entire presentation was predicated on that fact. Remember, the basics are never enough. The *intermediate steps* in development of the knowledge are just as important.

Finding the right level at which to present information shares a common thread with all the other concepts introduced in this chapter: Audience analysis is much easier to accomplish beforehand instead of after production has begun. An industry axiom holds that one hour spent at the desk can save a full working day in the field, and that may often prove to be literally the case. Although analysis and design may not be the flashiest components of institutional video, they are among the most labor saving.

SUMMARY

≡ Video is an extraordinarily powerful medium, but it is not all-powerful. Although it can be an excellent motivator and a fine visual trainer, it is not the best medium for certain tasks, such as communicating detailed and intricate sets of instructions.

≡ Video is expensive. Even relatively high-budget institutional productions can fall far short of the production values that viewers have come to expect from watching commercial television.

≡ Good institutional video fills a need. The more closely it fills that need, the better.

≡ Video is a team effort. Involvement of others in the institution must be maximized. Find out how the department or organization with which you are working can help you. Be sure you get firm commitments.

≡ Have a clear objective of what you want the program to accomplish. Don't wander from this objective or allow yourself to be diverted.

≡ Many program formats are available to the producer. They include the documentary, the lecture, the interview program, and the dramatic or semi-dramatic program. Shows often contain elements of each.

≡ Although experts can offer invaluable technical advice, they often have trouble communicating with the general public and are sometimes swayed by company politics. It is important for the producer to gain an overall perspective and use objective interviews and fact gathering.

≡ Determine as closely as possible the skill, knowledge, and preparedness level of the audience, and gauge your program design accordingly. Do not gauge it too low; a roomful of experts will be insulted by a simplistic treatment. Likewise, don't aim too high; if everyone in the audience were an expert, there would be no need for training tapes.

EXERCISES

1. Pick a subject on which you are very well informed, be it politics, music, or stereo systems. Write a two-page description of how you would demonstrate, in a video presentation, an interesting part of your topic (how to choose the right speaker for your amplifier, for example) to people who have very little knowledge of the topic. You need not include such details as camera shots or narration. Simply give an overview of what you would do. Include the basic thrust of the program, the types of shots necessary, and the goal of the program. Be sure to summarize what viewers will be able to do after watching the program that they could not do before.

2. Write the same summary, but this time gear it toward people who have almost as much knowledge on the subject as you do. Go into much greater specific detail on a narrower portion of the material.

3. Of the formats listed in this chapter, choose which structure you would use for the following assignments. Briefly explain why, and give some details of how you might use that format.
   a. a video presentation designed to give workers an introduction to top managers and convince them that management cares about them
   b. a tape designed to help personnel employees conduct better job interviews (Hint: Is there a better alternative than just explaining the techniques?)
   c. an explanation of a 401-K plan, a financial strategy designed to help employees save money and share in profits
   d. a program about an exciting new substance manufactured by your company that will be a component of a new space shuttle

NOTES

1. For an incisive discussion of one method of determining whether a problem can or should be addressed by video, see "Using Focus Groups: Putting the Audience to Work," *Video Manager* (April 1987): 9, 10.

2. See "Health Care Video: Cost Containment in Living Color," *Educational and Industrial Television* (March 1988): 16–23.

3. For further discussion of this and similar scenarios see "Screwed-Down Scriptwriting," *Audio-Visual Communications* (November 1985): 16–18.

4. From J. Neal McCorvie's "The Great Management Truths," *Small Systems World* (July 1984): 40. Another truth particularly relevant to the video producer: "Set your strategies. You cannot be all things to all customers. Fish where the fishing is best, and you will eat better than those who try to fish everywhere at once."

5. Interviewing is a craft in itself. Although practice is the only sure way to develop this skill, there are many good books that make the process easier. Among them are Shirley Biagi's *Interviews That Work* (Belmont, CA: Wadsworth, 1986), and Ken Metzler's *Creative Interviewing* (Englewood Cliffs, NJ: Prentice-Hall, 1977).

CHAPTER 4

━━━━━━━━━━━━━

ESSENTIALS

━━━━━━━━━━━━━

OF VIDEO

━━━━━━━━━━━━━

INSTRUCTION

━━━━━━━━━━━━━

Video is an appealing medium; of that there is no question. Most people like video, and they watch a great deal of it. But — and this is an important point for an institutional video producer — *watching* is not the same thing as *learning*.

As we have seen, many of the video programs produced by firms and other institutions are, to various extents, instructional. Since producers are not necessarily educators, well-intentioned (and well-produced) programs sometimes do not effectively impart knowledge.

This chapter examines three basic areas: how people learn, how an instructional program is designed, and how producers evaluate whether instructional video really works.

HOW PEOPLE LEARN

There is a huge body of literature on learning theory, and obviously it cannot be summarized in this brief chapter. Should you have the opportunity to take formal course work in education, do so, because you can gain valuable exposure to the principles involved in conveying information. Also, various readings (some listed in the suggested readings at the end of this book) can provide insight into the process.

It is a fundamental mistake to assume that a videotape is a complete teaching tool. No device is a comprehensive method for conveying information in such a way that the receiver can retain and recall it. For example, you can learn from a textbook. But what happens if you do not understand a particular paragraph or need further explanation of how a specific point relates to your field of study? In most educational settings you ask an instructor, a presumed expert who can add context, perspective, and additional insight.

As an additional example consider the fact that anyone who has attempted to learn a physical skill, such as a proper backhand in tennis, from a videotape knows that there is no way to receive useful feedback. Although the tape may be worthwhile in many aspects, only an experienced tennis player can view your stance and inform you that you are not standing far enough to the side of the ball to allow for a proper swing.

This is not to denigrate the value of video, of course. The tennis video can do things that the human instructor cannot or will not do. If you want to view 100 demonstrations of the proper way to toss the ball in serving, you can do so with your VCR. Your tennis pro probably won't be so cooperative. So, accepting that video does certain things better than others, we will briefly examine the strengths and weaknesses of television in relation to the specific requirements of instructing.

RETAINING AND RECALLING INFORMATION

To (vastly) oversimplify some basic principles of learning theory, we can assume that there are three types of learning: cognitive, psychomotor, and affective.[1]

1. *Cognitive learning* generally means absorbing and recalling facts and figures as well as gaining an understanding of fundamental principles. A cognitive objective of an instructional tape might be that "the viewer

will be able to recall the functions of a video tape recorder and list the controls that activate those functions."

2. *Psychomotor learning* entails developing physical skills, or what are sometimes called manipulative skills. A psychomotor objective for a videotape could be that "the viewer will, after viewing the tape, be able to perform basic operations on the video tape recorder."

3. *Affective learning* concerns values, attitudes, and motivation. An affective objective of an instructional videotape could be that "the viewer will realize the importance of the videotape operator in our organization and be inspired to do the best job possible."

Note that each category of learning is tied into the objective of the program. The word *objective* will surface frequently in any discussion of instructional video, because instruction is most powerful when it is focused on specific objectives. That concept was explained in Chapter 3.

REACHING AND INVOLVING A VIEWER

To reiterate an idea raised in the last chapter, video does not do everything equally well, and that caveat applies to instructional video. Cognitive learning can, at some levels, be difficult via television. If the cognitive learning involves many words or numbers, then printed learning material or high-resolution color slides could, under many circumstances, be more practical or could be used to augment the videotape.

Video is a powerful tool for many psychomotor-learning assignments, because the medium can accurately convey motion. As with the example of tennis video, though, any program attempting to convey psychomotor learning should be backed up with person-to-person instruction.

It is hard to beat video for affective-learning tasks. The combination of pictures, words, and music, edited into a powerfully paced whole, is unexcelled in motivating and inspiring. As a cognitive medium, however, video does not usually provide the same depth of information as does printed matter. For example, a sales promotion tape might be most constructive when backed up with brochures that clearly detail the specific benefits of the product or service.

The logical conclusion from these points is twofold and is largely a matter of common sense. First, almost all conceivable instructional tasks are a combination of cognitive, psychomotor, and affective learning. Therefore, an instructional producer must determine the rough proportions of each type of learning in order to set objectives for the tape. A producer may ask: "Is the primary goal of this tape to inform or to inspire?" With that question answered, the producer can focus the message.

Second, there are few if any instructional tasks for which use of only one medium is the best choice. Ideally, an instructional videotape should be used in conjunction with other learning strategies. A printed worksheet of calculations, for example, could be used to supplement the cognitive learning of a tape designed to teach arithmetical operations. Follow-up, person-to-person instruction is a valuable addition to any type of learning strategy.

ATTENTION SPAN

The need to keep a viewer's attention is hardly a new concept, nor is it unique to instructional video. There are some points particularly relevant to the instructional producer:

≡ As will be mentioned in the discussion of editing in Chapter 9, the most evocative scripting and editing cannot keep a viewer's attention at the 100 percent level throughout the program. Think in terms of peaks and valleys; after you present a cluster of information (peak), you need a period of rest and reflection during which the viewer can digest the information.

≡ Although there is no standard length for a video presentation, we all know instinctively that people have limited attention spans. Instructional presentations simply cannot be produced on the scale of network miniseries. People can absorb only so much information, and if you lose your viewers, they may not be able to "tune in" again if the information they missed is essential to understanding later material.

≡ Do not feel uncomfortable about injecting entertainment into an instructional tape as one method of keeping viewers' attention. If you are capable of lightening the tape with some humorous scenes, go ahead. This strategy must be followed within the boundaries of taste and reason, of course, but some humor, if it is good humor, can be useful. Studies of children's television, for example, have shown that humorous elements in instructional programs are an important stimulus to the thinking process.[2]

DESIGN OF AN INSTRUCTIONAL PROGRAM

Some fundamental principles of learning theory underlie the design of an effective teaching tool. Those principles include *keying the presentation* to the intended audience, *providing a thorough introduction*, *presenting information* in a slow, step-by-step process, *reviewing*, and *demonstrating skills* and *testing*.

KEYING THE PRESENTATION

The producer must, of course, know to whom the message is addressed and what kind of learning is to be imparted to the viewer. When addressing the question of the intended audience, the producer asks questions such as these:

≡ What is the viewers' educational level?

≡ Under what conditions will they view the tape?

≡ What are their motivations for wanting to learn the material?

≡ Is there one distinct audience or many audiences? How do we meet all those needs?

The producer who is attempting to determine what kind of learning is to be imparted might ask these questions:

≡ Is the main thrust of the program imparting information, teaching an operation, or motivating viewers? (These are cognitive, psychomotor, and affective goals, respectively.)

≡ How might the videotape be supplemented? Is classroom instruction the best supplement? What about printed material?

≡ Is the type of learning expected appropriate for video? How can video best be used to achieve these goals?

If you are reading chapters in this book out of order, see Chapter 3 for specific details of analysis and design as they relate to identifying audiences and imparting information.

INTRODUCING THE TOPIC

The viewers must understand precisely what it is they are going to learn. By the same token the producer must understand the intent of the tape. If you cannot sum up the goal in a few words — "This tape will show the viewer how to prepare a hamburger as quickly as possible with a minimum of waste" — your presentation is already in trouble.

Be sure that the introduction is *very explicit* about the goal of the tape. What may seem clear to you (because you are neck-deep in the project) may be obscure to the viewer.

PRESENTING THE INFORMATION

Remember that people learn at different rates, so you must keep the information flowing at a reasonably leisurely pace. Take your time in presenting new information. After researching and writing the script, you may be something of an expert in the area presented, but your viewer needs time to absorb the material.

Present information *from the perspective of the viewer*. Shots of equipment operations, for example, are best done from eye level with a field of view approximating normal vision. Although a highly magnified, vertical shot may be impressive, it may not mean much to the viewer. If such a shot is the only way to illustrate a point, be sure to provide cues to the viewer. Show an establishing shot, for example; then have the narrator say, "Now, we're going to show a magnified view from directly above the unit . . ."

Why should you make an effort to keep the viewer involved? Why did I just write a rhetorical question? Why are you still reading? Because rhetorical questions draw the reader or viewer into the presentation. Questions keep people involved, even if their reaction is not directly solicited. So do not be reluctant to occasionally use questions in narration: "What would you do in this case? [pause] One possible way to remedy the situation is . . ."

REVIEWING THE INFORMATION

Reiterate the information in stages. Do not wait until the end of the program for review. Internal summaries are useful for two reasons. The most obvious reason is that they reinforce what has just been presented. Secondly, a review provides a mental break for the viewer and is a natural segue, or transition, into the next topic. You might, for example, design a review segment like this:

> We've just seen the proper method for removing the access panel: Shut off the electricity, remove the two locking screws, and slide the panel upward until it locks in place. Now that the panel has been removed, we can see the main power unit. It is this unit that we need to disassemble next.

You will, of course, want to have some sort of overall review at the end of the tape, but do not neglect internal summaries. They work.

DEMONSTRATING AND TESTING

The moment of truth comes when viewers of the tape are asked to demonstrate the skills or knowledge they have acquired. This step may take the form of testing — can the viewer do the assembly alone? — or may simply be an extension of the instruction — the teacher will help the student use the principles shown in the tape for practice on the machinery.

Sometimes, an actual written test is in order, especially when the tape has presented essentially cognitive material. Irrespective of the testing or demonstration method you choose, be sure to play fair: Tell viewers that they are going to be tested before they watch the tape. In addition to simple fairness, this information is a powerful motivator. Generally, people are more attentive when they know that they will be responsible for demonstrating what they have learned. (If you are reading chapters out of order, you may wish at this time to refer to Chapter 7, "Evaluation and Measurement," for information on testing and other methods of judging a presentation's success.)

EVALUATION OF
INSTRUCTIONAL VIDEO

In addition to the methods of evaluation and measurement presented in Chapter 7, some specific considerations pertain to instructional video. Among them are *clarification of roles*, *determination of levels of understanding*, and *ensuring the accuracy of the message*. If these concepts, which are presented in terms of methods of evaluation, appear to strongly resemble *goals*, that is no coincidence. Goal setting and evalua-tion are inextricably linked, and as we've seen, they are an ongoing process. Effi-cient production does not involve setting goals, producing the entire program, and then checking to see if those goals have been met. Instead, it involves setting pre-liminary goals, evaluating those goals, redefining the goals, evaluating how current scripting and production efforts are meeting those expectations, and so on.

CLARIFICATION OF ROLES

Researchers in the field of organizational training and communications find that *role ambiguity* is one of the major roadblocks in motivating workers to perform well. If workers do not clearly understand what is expected of them, if duties are not explicit, and if methods of evaluation are not precisely explained, performance will suffer. It is often postulated that workers who are unsure about what exactly is expected of them are less satisfied with their jobs, undergo greater stress, and are less likely to remain with a firm.[3]

Here is one area where the video or audiovisual department can make a power-ful and concrete contribution to both the productiveness and the well-being of employees. As a consultant involved in the presentation of information, you will have the opportunity to clarify the roles of employees. You will also be in a position to assist supervisors in providing clear, precise guidelines for *exactly* what is ex-pected of workers in various situations. When speaking with a department super-visor, push for clarity: "What are the major expectations you have for people doing this job in your department? Can you prioritize those expectations? How are peo-ple evaluated? What mechanisms are in place for handling problems?"

Good training materials should always minimize role ambiguity. Use this crite-rion both for setting goals and for evaluating your production.

LEVELS OF UNDERSTANDING

When evaluating or setting goals (or, in the ideal situation, when doing *both*), determine if you are providing the correct level of understanding to the intended viewer. A chef needs a deeper level of understanding of food and its preparation than does a frycook in a fast-food restaurant. A chef, for example, must be inti-mately familiar with grades of beef and know the uses of particular cuts of the animal. But does a part-time worker flipping hamburgers need that depth of knowledge? No, of course not; in fact, if grading procedures and cut selection were included in the part-timer's training tape, that would cause a measure of role ambiguity. ("Why," the frycook might ask, "am I being shown this? Do I need to cook burgers of different grades for different lengths of time? Am I supposed to do something about picking burgers from the right cuts?")

Evaluate the depth problem at the inception of the project, and monitor it closely through scripting and production. As we saw in Chapter 3, it is seductively easy to wander into deeper waters than first intended once you become familiar with the subject matter.

ACCURACY OF THE MESSAGE

Providing an accurate message means not only getting the facts straight but also *ensuring that essential information is not lost in the translation* from trainer to trainee. This can become a major problem when attempting to communicate complex instructions. Supervisors, for example, are often chagrined that subordinates "don't follow instructions" when the problem is that those subordinates do not understand the instructions.

Surely you can identify with problems stemming from, let's say, papers or exams that you felt had been graded unfairly. It is safe to say that in some cases you probably were graded unfairly, in that the instructor did not make the directions clear enough. College instructors, for their part, frequently catch themselves giving incomplete or misleading directions on tests; when more than half the tests come back with "off-the-wall" answers to a particular question, even the most obdurate instructors will usually admit that their phrasing was confusing.[4]

As a producer of instructional video, you may be called on to produce a tape that "fixes" problems involving employees who "don't follow instructions." One strategy that may help in evaluating this dilemma is to stage a role-playing situation in which the supervisor gives *you* the standard set of instructions that she gives to employees. You then paraphrase and repeat back to her what you think you heard. You may be astounded at the difference in versions.

Use your discoveries to plan and evaluate ways to accurately convey the message from supervisor to employee.

Above all, remember that instructional video is not something done just for the sake of doing it. It is also not a quick fix to a complex problem, nor is it something that can serve all the organizational needs of an institution. Always allow for feedback and reinforcement, either through formal evaluation, testing, person-to-person instruction, collateral educational materials (brochures, slides), or the exciting new technology of interactive video, which is the subject of Chapter 11.

SUMMARY

≡ Watching is not the same thing as learning. As a producer you must be aware of this fact and take steps to ensure that your audience is actually learning from the tape.

≡ It is generally accepted that a training tape should not be the only aspect of a learning program. A tape rarely solves a training problem by itself.

≡ There are three basic types of learning: cognitive, psychomotor, and affective.

≡ When producing instructional material, you must be aware that viewers' attention can wander. Among the techniques for keeping their attention are presenting material in clusters, keeping segments short, and injecting some entertainment into the program.

≡ It is very important to key the presentation to the audience. You must identify the viewers and understand their motivations.

≡ An effective presentation has a clear introduction, reasonably paced information, clear internal summaries, and some sort of mechanism whereby viewers are tested or their newly acquired skills are demonstrated.

≡ Some specific points to keep in mind when producing an instructional video are whether the program clarifies roles, is pitched toward the proper level of understanding, and carries an accurate message.

EXERCISES

1. Choose a subject with which you are quite familiar; a good example might be using a videocassette recorder. Prepare a rough script that demonstrates at least three separate operations. Do not worry about correct script format, since that is yet to be addressed in this book. Instead, simply provide a description of the video shots (what the viewer will *see*) in the left-hand column of your script and the narration (what the viewer will *hear* — instructions read by the announcer) in the right-hand column. Be sure (since this is really the

point of the exercise) to provide two internal summaries and transitions. Remember:

a. demonstration of operation 1
b. summary and transition
c. demonstration of operation 2
d. summary and transition
e. demonstration of operation 3

2. Write a paper, the length and depth of which will be determined by your instructor, on the methods of instruction used by a particular business. You might, for example, choose banking, hotel management, or law enforcement. This assignment will be made easier if you choose a subject that is a major in your particular college, since there will be a wide selection of periodicals and books in the library. Do not limit your examination to audiovisual instruction. Explore the gamut of training methods. Why is training done? What specific problems are trainers in the field attempting to meet? Is training successful? How is success measured? What media seem to work best? (Hint: You will find a surprising amount of information in the particular industry's trade journals. Ask your librarian for help in locating them. Also, you might ask a student or a professor from the particular field you are investigating for leads or information.)

3. Most of us are quite familiar with dead-bolt locks, commonly found on exterior doors, but in some cultures that type of lock is unknown. Assume you are preparing a *video-only* presentation demonstrating a dead-bolt lock and its operation to someone who has never seen one. Remember, the viewer does not speak your language, so you cannot use narration or written graphics. Prepare a storyboard, a rough drawing of each shot, for your presentation. (If *you* are not familiar with dead bolts, visit your local hardware store. Remember, a dead bolt is not the same thing as the wedge-type lock that slides open and slips back into the strikeplate when you shut the door. You may want to communicate that difference somehow in your storyboard.)

NOTES

1. See Steve R. Cartwright, "Training Program Design," *Audio-Visual Communications* (April 1986): 55–57, 65. For a more comprehensive theoretical discussion of these categories of learning theory consult Fred Percival and Henry Ellington, *A Handbook of Educational Technology* (New York: Kogan Page, Nichols, 1988): 55–59.

2. See T. R. Ide, "The Potentials and Limitations of Television as an Educational Medium," in *Media and Symbols: The Forms of Expression and Education*, edited by David E. Olson (Chicago: National Society for the Study of Education, 1974): 330–356.

3. See Karl J. Krayer, "Using Training to Reduce Role Conflict and Ambiguity," *Training and Development Journal* (November 1986): 49–52.

4. As an example, I once wrote a question on a journalism final exam dealing with the legalities and ethics of reporting on the hypothetical case of the chairman of a local arts council who was arrested for a petty crime. The analysis of the case rested on the fact that this was a public employee, but that status was not explicitly stated. I did not tell the test takers that the head of an arts council is often a public employee or that arts councils can distribute public money. The question was obviously flawed and worthless as a testing device; fortunately, the responses on the test clearly indicated that the fault was mine, not the test takers'. Situations are not always so clear-cut, though, which is why a good trainer must be a good analyzer of communications.

CHAPTER 5

━━━━━━━━━━━━━━━━━━━━━━━━

SCRIPTING

━━━━━━━━━━━━━━━━━━━━━━━━

Writing for a *viewer* is far different from the process of writing for a *reader*. A scriptwriter works with sounds and pictures as well as words. The art and science of scriptwriting involve melding the production techniques of the medium with the expository techniques of the writer.

This chapter summarizes the basics of scriptwriting. It focuses on the fundamentals of writing for the eye and ear and explains the mechanics of laying out a script. In addition, we'll explore some of the aesthetics of scriptwriting, including principles of drama, suspense, and characterization.

WRITING FOR TELEVISION: THE FUNDAMENTALS

Scriptwriters are caught in something of a tug of war when they sit down to commit words to paper. They're faced with the problem of producing clarity without dullness, excitement without cuteness.

"Scriptwriting," points out one free-lancer, William L. Hagerman, "should not be noticed. Copy that calls attention to itself usually detracts from the intent of the script — to inform and instruct. Cleverness and witty phrases may attract listeners, but the style must not overshadow the image."[1]

With that goal in mind — writing that is crisp and exciting but that does not call attention to itself — let's look at the basic concepts involved in creating a script: writing for the eye, writing for the ear, and thinking beyond the boundaries of print communication.

WRITING FOR THE EYE

Good scriptwriters think visually. They invent the visuals first and then create words to reinforce those visuals. Scriptwriting is a learned skill, one that is developed by seeing ideas translated into video and gauging the relative strength or weaknesses of the interpretation. But certain basic techniques can be of immediate benefit to the scriptwriter who wants to learn to think visually.

First, your story will be told by a series of scenes. When beginning a script, identify what those scenes might be. If you have access to a VCR, fast-forward in search mode through a well-produced, network-quality commercial. Watching the speeded-up commercial, you gain a quick overview of the scenes and how they are edited together to form a cohesive whole. Consider this hypothetical scenario of a commercial:

≡ *Scene 1* might be an opening shot of a man meeting a woman by the office water cooler. It's a wide shot, showing us the setting. We need to know this setting in order to believe that the characters are real people, to understand something of their occupations and motivations, and not to feel as though the characters are simply suspended in place and time.

≡ *Scene 2* might show the man talking to the woman. We need a tighter shot in order to be introduced to them, to see their expressions. Note how this camera movement toward the subjects mimics your typical field of view when, say, you meet someone at a party. Scene 2 concludes with the woman abruptly walking away.

≡ *Scene 3* could be a close-up of the man; we need to be close to read his expressions and emotions as he realizes that he has committed some sartorial or hygienic violation. Let's assume dandruff is the culprit. Scene 3 concludes with a close-up of our horrified subject discovering flakes on his shoulder.

≡ *Scene 4* could begin with a dissolve indicating a change in time or location, to a medium-close shot of our man in his shower, enjoying the fresh, tingly feel of Extra-Strength Whatever.

≡ *Scene 5*, perhaps, takes us back to the office water cooler, where the previously ill-fated conversation is repeated. We zoom in on the faces of the man and woman as they converse happily, unencumbered by the stigma of dandruff flakes. The camera moves in very tightly on their smiling faces.

Notice that in this hypothetical example the idea is conveyed entirely without dialogue. Now view the taped commercial that you have selected, and notice how the scenes alone make sense and convey an idea.

A second technique for the beginning scriptwriter is to think of the *meaning* of shots. Camera angles and the size of shots convey ideas. A close-up shot suggests intimacy; a long-range shot suggests emotional distance. A very wide "introductory" shot is valuable because heads suddenly popping into the screen are disconcerting. Keep in mind that television shots mimic the way our field of vision works. The next time you walk into a room, for example, notice that your eyes are drawn to the floor. This is an inescapable human instinct; we're compelled to check out the surface on which we will walk to make sure it is safe. Likewise, viewers want to see the environment into which they have been thrust before meeting the characters face to face. (Be aware that this is not a sanctified rule; you can start on an extreme close-up, for example, to produce a visually startling effect. Just be sure that's what you want.)

Third, think of communicating ideas with the *pace* of edited shots. Fast cuts communicate excitement; long scenes separated by dissolves portray low-key action, or indicate a change in time or place.

Include *variety*. The eye becomes bored by similar shots and, sometimes, confused. Use a good mix of long shots, medium shots, and close-ups. Be sure, though, that each shot serves a logical purpose. Don't make it apparent that you are changing shots for the sake of change.

Finally, don't waste the viewer's time. All aspects of the program should serve a purpose. Each shot should *communicate* something. In a similar vein be sure that whatever you show on screen can be visually understood by the viewer. Institutional training tapes, for example, often focus very tightly on, let's say, close-ups of a mechanism within a larger machine. Unrelenting close-ups of pulleys and gears, though, soon lose much meaning. Cut back to a longer shot from time to time to reinforce the context and location of the close-up subject.

WRITING FOR THE EAR

Assume that you are listening to a radio newscast. Which of these phrases do you feel creates a more compelling image?

> A tractor trailer tipped and broke open today on Highway 104. Chemicals went all over the road surface.

> A tractor trailer flipped over and ruptured today on Highway 104. Chemicals spewed across the road surface.

The second example paints a more vivid word picture. The verbs are stronger, carrying more action and creating a moving image in what radio buffs like to call "the theater of the mind." That theater is where the audio components of a script are played out.

Even though a television presentation contains video, the audio must be written for the ear, meaning that all audio components must be clear, uncomplicated, and vivid. There are several fundamental techniques for writing for the ear.

First, write in short sentences with an uncomplicated structure. Your prose need not be formulaic; in other words don't strive for a certain number of words per sentence. But do keep sentences brief. Too many clauses in a sentence can confuse listeners, who can't go back to review the sentence if they don't completely understand it. Likewise, don't use words such as *former* or *latter*, because a listener obviously can't refer back.

Second, use strong verbs and adjectives. Weak words can make your script seem limp. They are also usually less accurate than strong words and phrases. For example:

Weak: This action *helped the program function again.*
Strong: This action *rejuvenated* the program.

Weak: This famous inventor *was really interested in* the idea of putting cameras into the hands of consumers; he experimented day and night.

Strong: This famous inventor *was obsessed by* the idea of putting cameras into the hands of consumers; he experimented day and night.

Weak: We were *faced with* the problem of using an *old, very inefficient facility*.

Strong: We were *confronted by* the prospect of using a *decrepit* facility.

A third technique is not to stray from a central idea or theme. Remember that those listening to a narration are not able to follow the information with the accuracy of readers. It is therefore paramount that you avoid losing the listeners. They must understand the material at all times and remain in the flow of the narrative.

What is "flow of the narrative"? Simply stated, it means that a scriptwriter tells a story that must move from beginning, to middle, to end. You can accomplish this movement by introducing an element in the beginning, reintroducing it in the middle, and making that element a part of the conclusion. The element referred to might be a central character, a problem that must be solved, a ticking clock showing that the characters are working against time, or any and all of the above. Some of these elements, in fact, are used in a script that will be introduced shortly.

Finally, use word transitions. A transition is a technique that links one segment of written material with another segment. In this way the viewer isn't suddenly yanked off path — out of the flow of the narrative — even if the topic does change. As an example, notice how the two previous paragraphs are linked. The words *flow of the narrative* are repeated; the effect is to make the two paragraphs a cohesive unit, even though they address different topics.

THINKING BEYOND THE BOUNDARIES OF PRINT COMMUNICATIONS

Although it appears obvious that writing for the visual media is different from writing for a reader, restatement of that fact is a worthwhile exercise. Scriptwriters — good scriptwriters — routinely take a step back from their work and examine it to ensure that it's a script, not an article. Two questions can help put this in perspective:

1. Does the narration *sound* natural when read? Do read it out loud. Be sure that it is conversational.

2. Do the scenes convey a message, even without the sound? Scan down the list of shots; they should communicate some idea even without the dialogue.

MECHANICS OF SCRIPTWRITING

Scripts for institutional video are usually written in two columns, with video instructions in the left column and audio in the right. Technical instructions, written into the script, give the proper viewpoints of cameras and also indicate other technical operations, such as bringing up music or other sound effects.

Although there are certain basic conventions, each organization has its own method of scripting. Since there is no universal right or wrong, you will have to pick up the particulars on the job.

LAYOUT OF A TYPICAL SCRIPT

The two-column script, the typical format for most presentations except drama, uses the left-hand column to indicate the visual components, with audio at the right. Figure 5.1 shows a typical example. (The abbreviations are explained in a later section of this chapter, "Technical Instructions.")

A dramatic script (Figure 5.2) usually has the characters' names centered, and dialogue below. Directors add in their own notes on specific shots and actions they wish to incorporate into the shooting. Although dramatic scenes find frequent use in institutional video, scripts formatted in this way are not as popular as the two-column script. But it does appear that the dramatic script, sometimes called a "Hollywood script," is gaining in popularity in the realm of corporate video.

Occasionally, the two-column script has time cues inserted. These cues may be the actual time the show is to have run by this point in the script or an indication of time remaining in the show. They are especially useful in newscast-type programs or interview shows, which are run live or recorded in one take and must end at a precise time. Sometimes, inserts must be made at exact times, but this is uncommon in corporate video.

VIDEO	AUDIO
CU of wheel of car, spinning, then slamming to stop	SFX CAR CRASH
COVER SHOT of wrecked car being put on tow truck CU of cop writing on clipboard	ANNCR: The accident report will say that this car is totaled . . . But when we say a car's a total wreck, it means that the cost of repairing it is greater than the current value of the car. It doesn't mean that it's totally ruined.
TIGHTEN UP on car being towed away	There are plenty of usable parts in this wrecked car. In fact, this auto is now a container for used parts. Those parts can be recycled . . . a trend that is saving money and energy. In the next few minutes, we'll see how this trend helps you, the consumer.
CG over montage of shots of auto parts being sorted, hands flipping through inventory book, customer picking up used part CG: Linder's Inc. Presents Auto Parts Recycling: A Resource, A Bargain	MUSIC (THEME) UP FULL
LS of heavy equipment digging into ground (edited from industry film)	ANNCR: A resource? Yes, if you consider the amount of energy expended to manufacture a car from scratch—roughly the same amount of energy that car will consume in a year.

FIGURE 5.1

A video script done in two-column style.

Written by Carl Hausman. Reprinted courtesy Linder's, Inc.

CU of customer buying assembly	A bargain? Yes, auto parts recycling saves money for everyone—and we'll see how as we follow the chain of events following the arrival of a wrecked auto at Linder's in Worcester, Massachusetts, one of the nation's largest auto parts recyclers.
CUT to LS (looking down) of customer leaving	
CUT to AERIAL SHOT	
AERIAL SHOT	Linder's is a 40-acre complex, where a staff of 60 specialists disassemble wrecked autos and make the best possible use of each component.
CS of auto being brought into yard. Company worker or official looks over car.	The first step in the process is determining which parts of the auto are salvageable.
Sequence of cuts of various operations: removing engine, workers with torches taking assemblies off, etc., matched with audio of Linder's official explaining process	LINDER'S OFFICIAL (DESCRIBES HOW THIS PARTICULAR CAR WILL GO TO SEVERAL DIFFERENT OPERATIONS, INCLUDING REMOVAL OF ENGINE, REMOVAL OF SALVAGEABLE ASSEMBLIES, AND RETURN OF THE SHELL TO THE YARD, WHERE THERE ARE STILL WORTHWHILE PARTS AVAILABLE)
CU of individual part w/tag no. CUT to card in catalog. CUT to person at terminal.	ANNCR: Just having the parts in stock isn't enough. To ensure the most cost-effective use of various parts, Linder's has a complete inventory, monitored by a state-of-the-art computer system.
Shot of company jet taking off, shot from runway	And, since it's not always possible to wait for all necessary parts to come in, Linder's officials roam the country to keep the inventory properly

	stocked . . . traveling to auctions and insurance company sales.
Customers at front counter	But we promised you an explanation of how all this saves you money.
	First, let's look at the direct benefit to the consumer of used auto parts.
Assembly sequence of fender (Edited from industry film)	Think of how much time, effort, and money go into assembly of this fender. It consists of 21 individual parts, all of which have to be painstakingly assembled.
	MUSIC UP
MCU of worker loading fender assembly on truck	MUSIC UNDER ANNCR: The customer who's bought this assembly has saved a considerable amount of money by not having to pay for a totally remanufactured part.
CU of order-taker on phone	ORDER-TAKER: An engine for a '71 Saab? Yes, we have that in stock.
MCU of mechanic rebuilding engine	ANNCR: Another advantage to the consumer is the inherent savings stemming from easily obtained used parts . . . from door handles to an entire engine.
CU of engine being tested, perhaps with oscilloscope	At Linder's, used parts are carefully tested, rebuilt if necessary, and are often of better quality than a new part . . . Remember, the used part you purchase has already proved its reliability. Remember, everyone drives on used parts.

FIGURE 5.1, continued.

CS of fork lift removing engine from inventory shelf	The size of Linder's inventory also means that virtually any part can be supplied, without the wait associated with ordering a new part.
MLS mechanic and customer in local shop; mechanic slams hood of auto	MECHANIC: We can save you quite a bit of time and money by ordering a used transmission from Linder's, and it'll be as good or better than new.
CU of mechanic looking for number on Linder's calendar, dialing phone	ANNCR: Saving money by buying used parts pays off, whether the part is ordered through a mechanic or purchased directly by a consumer.
MCU of Linder's order-taker	In fact, mechanics often prefer to order a used part from Linder's, because they avoid the
CS of transmission being located, loaded	delay in ordering a new component from the manufacturer . . . and also please their customers by keeping repair costs low.
XCU of hand polishing car, pull back to show whole auto, worker handing keys to customer. (This should be luxury auto.)	By the way, autos don't always have to be recycled piece by piece . . . Often, stolen or vandalized cars are turned over to recyclers by insurance companies; they are refurbished and
Auto drives away	sold whole, often at a price considerably below wholesale.
Another auto swerves out and the two almost collide.	There's one other advantage to used parts, one that affects everyone because . . .
Near-collision HELD IN FREEZE FRAME (if electronic freeze not available, photo transparency will be used)	accidents do happen, and they happen to everyone. And everyone pays the resulting costs in insurance premiums.
OVER-THE-SHOULDER SHOT of insurance company spokesman	But the savings inherent in widespread use of recycled auto

being interviewed
(NO AUDIO)

parts can help keep a lid on in-surance costs.

ZOOM IN to MCU of insurance spokesman, name and title SU-PERED LOWER THIRD

INSURANCE COMPANY SPOKES-MAN (EXPLAINS WHY USE OF RECYCLED AUTO PARTS CUTS COSTS, AND WHY INSURANCE COMPANIES GENERALLY FAVOR THE IDEA)

So the next time you think in terms of used auto parts, don't think of a junkyard.

CS of engine being pulled

PULL FOCUS BACK, SUPERIM-POSE CG

Think of a nationwide four-billion-dollar industry that is working to . . .

CG: Save Energy, Natural Re-sources
-(add)-

save energy and natural re-sources, . . .

Reduce Costs of Auto Repair to Consumers
-(add)-

reduce costs of auto parts to con-sumers, . . .

Reduce Insurance Premiums

and keep a lid on insurance pre-miums.

LS of Linder's building

And when you think of Linder's, think of a modern, progressive firm that's been a leader in auto recycling for over 60 years. Think of a company that has . . .

800 Engines
-(add)-
1,000 Transmissions
-(add)-
4,000 Parts Vehicles
-(add)-
Backed by 60-Day Guarantee

over 800 engines in stock, more than 1,000 transmissions, over 4,000 parts vehicles, and the northeast's largest selection of repairable vehicles, all backed by a 60-day guarantee.

MUSIC UP AND UNDER

THROW FOCUS FORWARD to front of Linder's; ZOOM IN to door; grandmotherly type,

Yes, auto parts recycling helps everyone. Not only does it save energy—equivalent to an esti-

FIGURE 5.1, continued.

holding auto part, opens door, holds up part, smiles to camera	mated 80 million barrels of oil a year—but it makes quality auto repair affordable to all of us.
Linder's logo and address Production credits	MUSIC UP FULL
Fade to black	MUSIC FADES
End	End

(HAMMOND SITS AT A RESTAURANT TABLE. THERE IS A HALF-FULL BOTTLE OF SCOTCH ON THE TABLE ALONG WITH A PITCHER OF WATER AND SEVERAL GLASSES. A BRIEFCASE IS LEANING AGAINST A LEG OF THE TABLE. MONROE ENTERS. HAMMOND AUTOMATICALLY STANDS—A HABIT—AND NODS. BOTH MEN STARE; NO PLEASANT-RIES WILL BE EXCHANGED. HAMMOND GESTURES TOWARD A CHAIR, AND MONROE SITS OPPOSITE HAMMOND.)

MONROE:

Word of this won't get out?

HAMMOND:

The owners of this place are paid to be discreet. Our production unit rents this private room full time. We meet contacts here almost every day, and there have never been any leaks.

MONROE:

I'd like to get down to business.

HAMMOND:

Fine, but as I told you over the phone, you're wasting your time. Pleas from involved parties never result in a story being pulled. That's Journalism 101. We're going to run with the story next week. If you have some additional comment you'd like to make, we can probably accommodate you. But the story runs.

FIGURE 5.2

A dramatic, or "film-style," script from the play *The Chosen Few*.

Written by Carl Hausman.

FIGURE 5.3

Storyboarding gives the producer, client, and crew a visual representation of the script. This section of storyboard is taken from the script in Figure 5.1.

CONSTRUCTION OF STORYBOARDS AND TREATMENTS

It is important for the producer and director to closely visualize the shots in advance. A *storyboard* (Figure 5.3) incorporates drawings that approximate what will be seen on the screen. Storyboards are used more commonly in scripting commercials than in most institutional presentations, although the format does have its uses. Storyboards are particularly applicable to situations in which a precise visual is important, such as a shot of a product. The storyboard is an indication to the director of exactly how the product will be pictured. Storyboards are also quite useful when selling a proposal for a program to executives who are not versed in the vocabulary of television. They will find a storyboard a useful tool for visualization, much more accessible than a two-column script.

A *treatment* is a condensed version of the story to be told and the approach to be used. It is useful at the decision-making stage. A treatment may range from a paragraph to several pages. There is little agreement on the standard length and format of treatments, even among screenwriters and playwrights, who deal with treatments frequently. In general, though, a treatment outlines the plot and identifies, as fully as possible, scenes, props, and talent.

Because the format is flexible, a treatment allows the writer to hone the approach and arrange and rearrange the contents; if it doesn't work, no great effort is lost. When dealing with committees or other bodies that must give approval, it is much easier to alter a treatment than to rewrite a script.[2]

People who read treatments are encouraged to respond more fully to the *concept* of the treatment, rather than picking at the individual words in a script. Treatments can even take the form of a memo (see Figure 5.4). This type of treatment can be an excellent starting point. In fact, if it is approved, it will be a reasonably simple matter to begin translating the concept into a script.

TECHNICAL INSTRUCTIONS

The TV script has its own vocabulary. As you may remember from previous course work or training, the following are used to indicate the size and position of the shot:

XLS	extreme long shot (not a common shot)
LS	long shot
MS	medium shot
CU	close-up
XCU or ECU	extreme close-up
2S, or 2 SHOT	shot of two persons, usually side by side
COVER SHOT	either a wide shot showing the entire locale, used to orient the viewer, or a shot used to cover an edit when you must go from one scene to another and the result would appear awkward if you could not "cover" it
KNEE SHOT WAIST SHOT BUST SHOT CHEST SHOT	shots of a person with the named body part as the lower boundary
OS	over-the-shoulder shot

TO: Tom
FROM: Carl
RE: Narrative description of proposed video tape production

    I feel the overall objective in this presentation is to show that working in the restaurant is a team effort and that every person's job has an effect on overall functioning.

    We have decided, as I understand it, to try to accomplish three things:

1. As stated, stress the importance of teamwork.
2. Motivate employees to be effective players on that team.
3. Give an overall perspective: a brief introduction to the different jobs in the restaurant, the various procedures used to prepare the meals, and the responsibilities of personnel. This perspective, as I understand it, is the "basic training" that new employees now receive before moving on to their specific assignments.

    This tape should accomplish these objectives with a semi-dramatic format. I don't see a central character fitting in here; instead, let's orient the presentation both toward the food, showing how it is produced, and toward the people who produce it, showing that their cooperative efforts are just as important as the food.

    I envision opening with a shot of two customers being served in the dining area. Then the narration will indicate that the show will shift back in time, exploring all the work that went into preparing the meal.

    We'll show a full week's worth of work. To indicate the time frame, we superimpose a digital clock over the scene in the restaurant, showing the time as 12:15 P.M. Friday. Then we dissolve to the actual opening of the tape: music, theme, and title.

    Now the progression starts. The time jumps back to Monday, 7 A.M. Narration says something to the effect that "planning for that lunch began, in some cases, a week ahead; some long-range planning, as we'll see in a moment, started months in advance." This will orient the viewer. Now we're free to play scenes in sequence. The scenes showing long-range planning that I would suggest showing/recreating/dramatizing are:

- maintenance getting the restaurant in order for the week
- manager putting together schedules for week
- taking inventories
- planning menus
- financial planning

FIGURE 5.4

Treatment in the form of a memo.

Now we use the digital clock to move to Friday morning. We'll cue the viewer. Perhaps narration such as: "Each day in the operation of a restaurant is a result of planning and teamwork. Let's take a look at the day's work involved in serving that open steak sandwich during Friday's lunch."

Digital clock now shows 7 A.M. Friday. We dramatize several sequences showing how employees' jobs mesh into the serving of that open steak sandwich we showed at the beginning of the tape. Let's trace the ingredients, showing what each person does to contribute to that meal. We can show:

- steward signing for order of lettuce and potatoes first thing in the morning
- broiler cook preparing meat
- prep cook cutting potatoes
- prep cook sorting lettuce
- managers doing sauce check
- slicing onions, breading, etc.

Next we move out into the serving area to show how waiters and waitresses prepare for the afternoon rush.

I'd like to do the interview segment here, because we've built up some dramatic tension—we're waiting for the lunch to be served—and now is a good time to suspend the action and address points that don't logically belong in the dramatization, such as the history of the restaurant and management goals.

We will close the interview with a discussion of the teamwork issue, which will segue back to the serving scene. We close with a dramatization of the meal undergoing final preparation and service to customer. We close on a shot of an employee and bring up the theme, "We're Better Together."

I'll be interested in your reaction. If you find that this description matches your ideas, we can move along to preparation of the first draft of the script.

The following are used to indicate camera movements. These commands are not always inserted into the script; the director may add them later.

ZOOM	tighten (zoom in) or loosen (zoom out) the shot by changing the focal length of the lens
DOLLY	physically move the camera in or out
PEDESTAL	vertically raise or lower the camera
TRUCK	move the camera sideways
TILT	point the camera up or down

The following commands indicate transitions:

FADE   mix in the shot from black or gradually go to black from a
               scene (It means only this; you do not "fade between"
               camera shots.)

DISSOLVE   overlap the images of two camera shots, gradually replacing
               the on-screen image of one shot with the other

CUT   instantly move from one camera shot to the other

The following commands refer to the use of other sources, such as:

SOT   sound on tape, or a videotape played back with picture and
               sound (Sometimes SOF, sound on film, is used, even when the
               piece is on videotape.)

VTR   essentially the same thing: take the output of the video tape
               recorder (Sometimes this means "take only the visual image.")

SFX   sound effects

VO   voice-over, or a narrator's voice accompanying the video

CG   character generator — the device that prints characters on the
               screen

SUPER   abbreviation for superimpose, meaning to place one image
               (usually a graphic) over another image

Again, the use of these abbreviations varies, so don't be surprised if you see
scripts that do not use them exactly as they are described above.

AESTHETICS OF SCRIPTWRITING

Yes, scriptwriting for institutional television does have an artistic side. The scenes
must accomplish varying missions. Usually they must motivate, guide the viewer in
performing various operations, impart general information, or persuade the
viewer to understand and adopt a certain point of view.

EXAMPLES OF EFFECTIVE COMMUNICATION

You'll recall that it is critical for a script to accomplish all these missions while maintaining focus — while meeting the need for which the program was requested in the first place. The primary objective of the restaurant tape is to give new employees an overall view of operations and how their particular job — be it dishwasher, waiter, or cook — fits into the overall scheme of things.

The treatment detailed how this concept was approached in general terms. Now, here's the finished script.[3] Explanatory comments about the script are printed in italics. First, the introductory segment:

VIDEO	AUDIO
Plate being set down on table by waitress	NARRATOR: A customer has been served an open steak sandwich at Tom Foolery's restaurant in Westboro, Massachusetts.
SLOW ZOOM into plate; clock SUPERED: 12:15 P.M. Friday	In the next few minutes we're going to explore what's involved in preparing and serving this meal.
MONTAGE of restaurant shots	And we'll see that there's more to restaurant operations than taking an order and popping some food in the oven. Serving a meal, and pleasing a customer, is a complex job, a job that requires teamwork and planning.

Now, the main introduction: theme and title.

Title up over montage	THEME UP

Next, the dramatizations of long-term planning.

To black clock: 7 A.M. Monday; up on maintenance man vacuuming. Manager walks by doing inspection.	THEME UNDER VACUUM CLEANER SFX
	NARRATOR: Planning for that Friday lunch began, in some cases, a week ahead; some long-range planning, as we'll see in a moment, started months in advance.
	The week begins with cleaning and inspection of the restaurant.

MANAGER: ASKS MAINTENANCE MAN TO CLEAN SPOT ON CARPET AND BEHIND BAR

CU of clipboards above manager's desk, pulling back to show manager in conversation with kitchen manager

NARRATOR: Scheduling and ordering involves knitting together the entire inventory and the complete roster of 135 employees.

MANAGER: Two things I noticed about the inventory and schedule . . . First, we've got a three-day weekend coming up—Monday's a holiday—so we've got to order more meat on Friday. Friday's going to be a really busy day because of the holiday, and I see that Frank is scheduled to work his station alone. He's still pretty new, and I think he needs some backup Friday.

LS of inventory room, with employee taking inventory of silverware

NARRATOR: Here are some of the facets involved in preparing for a meal. For example, the kitchen manager is taking an inventory of the steak knives. Steak knives get thrown away and stolen. Think about what would happen if a customer ordered an open steak sand-wich and there was no knife to cut it.

MCU manager, who is wearing sweater and heavy sports coat, examining and tasking exotic frozen drink

MANAGER TO BAR MANAGER: It's pretty sweet even for a summer drink . . . I think a little less sugar would improve it.

NARRATOR: Even in December, we're preparing the summer menu.

CUT to ECU, tilt down menu

Why? Because it takes months to develop, test, and price items for the menu, which is changed twice a year.

CU of the adding machine; PULL BACK to show comptroller working at ledger

Long-range financial planning is critical to a restaurant's continued growth.

Comptroller picks up phone, punches intercom connection, talks into phone.

COMPTROLLER: Tom? I've costed out adding stir fry to the menu next year. The biggest expense is going to be a tilting skillet, and that item runs about $4,000. Now, the projected return on that is . . .

Comptroller points to calendar; ZOOM IN on calendar.

NARRATOR: Each day of operation at the restaurant is a result of planning and teamwork. Let's take a look at the work involved in serving that open steak sandwich on noon, Friday.

We make a transition to the early-morning hours on Friday. Note how sound effects (the cricket noises) are useful to establish place and time. The scene was actually shot in mid-afternoon, with the camera iris stopped to simulate early-morning lighting. Cricket noises came from a sound effects record.

To black clock: 7 A.M. Friday; steward and delivery person

CRICKET EARLY-MORNING SFX

STEWARD: This lettuce is wilted, so I won't accept this crate. The rest of the produce is all right, but I want to do a count on the 90-count potatoes.

Steward opens box, begins count.

NARRATOR: A 90-count box of potatoes is supposed to contain, of course, 90 of them, graded by size. The steward checks on the count from time to time, because even if we are shorted 5 potatoes a box, an order of 85 boxes a week means that we get shorted over 400 potatoes per week—more than four 90-count boxes worth.

Steward signs for order, closes door on loading dock.

The steward is the first step in the process of procuring, preparing, and serving a meal.

What else is involved? Well, let's trace the ingredients that make up an open steak sandwich.

The tape is stopped as new ingredients are added. Editing will make the ingredients pop onto the plate — an easy special effect.

Video of:
7-ounce portion of steak
Garlic bread
French fries
Tomato and lettuce
Onion ring
Tomfoolery sauce

NARRATOR READS INGREDIENTS

Back to kitchen scene, now . . .

Clock: 10:15 A.M. Friday

| Broiler cook placing meat in trays; covers with oil and spice | NARRATOR: Here, the broiler cook prepares the meat for cooking and preps his station. |

Prep cook cutting fries

A prep cook cuts 120-count potatoes for french fries . . . The potatoes have previously been baked, briefly, to release some of the sugars in the potato, which causes the fry to be sweeter and have a better texture. Incidentally, this is the hard way to make a french fry. The easy way—the way most restaurants do it— is to buy prepared fries that are molded or extruded from a potato mixture.

Broiler cook coating garlic bread

After cutting the bread and preparing the garlic sauce, the broiler cook prepares the garlic bread for the oven.

Prep cook picking lettuce

The lettuce that goes on the plate is thoroughly inspected, and unattractive leaves are picked out and thrown away.

Prep cook slicing tomatoes

Tomatoes are also inspected and sliced.

Cook preparing Tomfoolery sauce

The special Tomfoolery sauce will also be served with the meal. Sauce preparation is very important, and the management staff runs checks on all the sauces several times a day.

Managers doing sauce check

MANAGER: This tastes metallic . . . Somebody left a ladle in it. Let's throw it away and make a new batch.

CU of prep cook slicing onions

NARRATOR: The final item on the plate, the onion ring, is one of the most difficult to prepare. It's a process that involves cutting only the largest rings of a giant Bermuda onion. After the

Soaking and breading

rings have been soaked and the membrane removed, a three-step breading process takes place. This is the hard way to make an onion ring, too, but it pays off in appearance and taste.

WIDE SHOT of kitchen	The prep cooks are charged with the responsibility of most of the preparation of the items. Line cooks will be in charge of actually cooking the items when the order is placed.
PAN to line cooks prepping stations	
To black clock: 11:15 A.M. Friday	While line cooks prepare their stations for the coming lunch rush, the servers meet with a manager.
Meeting in dining room	
Manager holds up special brought out by kitchen manager.	MANAGER: Here's a special today. (DESCRIBES SPECIAL)
PAN faces of servers.	There was a big storm yesterday, and the fishermen couldn't get out, meaning that we didn't get part of our fish order this morning, so the haddock items are off today's menu.
CUTS between manager and servers	Finally, there's probably going to be a big rush today, so I want the bussers to be especially alert about helping the servers if they really get in the weeds. Yesterday I saw customers seated without silverware, and the bussers didn't back up and get some. This can't happen.

Some other subjects have to be discussed. This seems to be a logical place to break the action and go to an interview segment.

Tom McCabe speaking; video under narrator's audio	NARRATOR: Efficient service is part of the whole package that pleases a customer and makes a restaurant successful. Tom Foolery owner Tom McCabe describes some of the aspects of the restaurant and its people.
Tom McCabe's name and title SUPERED	[Tom talks for three minutes, dealing with these topics: 1. brief history of restaurant, and why it was conceived to be the way it is today
COVER SHOT matched with audio	2. discussion of ambience of restaurant, decoration, etc. 3. wrap-up discussion of teamwork issue, which will make logical transition back to waitress and kitchen scene]

Now, back to the restaurant for the conclusion of the story.

To black clock: noon, Friday.
Waitress taking order
Puts into computer

NARRATOR: An order for an open steak sandwich has just been placed. The waitress punches the order into a computerized system . . .

Window person picks up order from his terminal.

which automatically places the order into the kitchen.

Window person calls out order.

ECU of ear of broiler cook; PULL BACK to show him place meat and buns in broiler.

The window person is responsible for coordinating all the orders in the kitchen . . . He calls out the order, and each line cook is responsible for picking up the part of the order that will be his or her responsibility.

Quick shots of line cooks making fries, rings, other COVER

THEME UP, MIXED WITH WILD AUDIO

Expediter checks order.

The expediter is the last person in the kitchen to check the order . . . He makes sure that all the garnishes are correct, that the order is complete, and that it is properly cooked.

Window person calls out that order is up and calls for seafood chowder.

Stew ladled out

The window person makes sure that all items come up at the same time . . . In other words, if a party of two orders an open steak sandwich and a bowl of seafood chowder, which is already prepared and simmering, he orders the chowder at the last possible minute, to be sure it doesn't sit on the counter and cool off.

Waitress sets order down.

ZOOM IN on open steak sandwich.

Shot of dishwasher

This meal is a product of teamwork . . . Everyone's contribution is equally important, from the dishwasher who provided sparkling pots, plates, and utensils . . .

Kitchen manager with clipboard

to the kitchen manager who did the ordering . . .

Hostess smiles to camera.	and the hostess who greeted the customers and made them feel comfortable as soon as they walked in the door.
	THEME BUILDS
CUTS, increasing in tempo, showing various employees	Vocal up . . . .
	Vocal . . . .
	Vocal . . . .
Final shot of employee	Vocal . . . .
Credits	THEME UP AND OUT

The script approaches the concept from several different directions but always with the same purpose in mind: to orient employees and show them that their jobs are important. Motivation, for example, is the primary goal of the owner's interview. There is some instruction in the operation of the restaurant; such instruction would seem to be much more lively in dramatized fashion than in a flow chart contained in a new employee handbook. Much general information is imparted, but it is structured in such a way that the viewer is not loaded down with too much detail at one time. For example, descriptions of various jobs are generally given within dramatized scenes, such as the scene showing the steward counting the potatoes.

USES OF DRAMA AND SUSPENSE

Dramatic scenes are used frequently in institutional television. For example, many job-training tapes include acted versions of events. A producer of a tape instructing personnel managers how to conduct better interviews would be wise to reenact such scenes. It lends a human touch and brings the viewer into the flow of the program.

Suspense, or making the audience expect that something is about to happen, is also integral to many productions. Initiating suspense can be as simple as making the audience wait to see the result of an action. An example might involve stopping the re-creation of a job interview just before a decision is apparently going to be made. Then the audience can be kept hanging while other information is imparted.

VERISIMILITUDE

Verisimilitude essentially means having the appearance of truth throughout the presentation. It is important for a scriptwriter to ensure that what happens on the screen squares with reality.

One of the most frequent lapses of verisimilitude involves acted scenes in which people say things they just would not say normally. Extended explanations are a common offense. People simply do not give detailed recitations of the workings of their computer system to a casual guest.

Science fiction writers, to take another example, can fall victim to verisimilitude problems, even when operating in the realm of fantasy. A bad piece of science fiction often involves one character giving a detailed exegesis of the workings of his antigravity vehicle to a passenger. Think about it: Do you explain the controls of your car to people who ride with you?

CHARACTERIZATION

The people who populate your script must never be cardboard cutouts. They must be real, even if they are imaginary. Grant Williams, an independent writer and director for corporate TV and the former manager of the creative media department for the Georgia-Pacific Corporation, offers this advice for creating believable characters: "In writing drama, whether it's for the big screen or the company tube, there is one thing that is all important: The character. It is the character who weaves the story. . . . If you have strong characters, you have the making for a strong program."[4]

Williams advises the scriptwriter to pick a central character whose point of view will be followed. Bringing that character to life involves creating some guidelines for developing a character representative of your audience. But that's not enough: "To get to know your character, you have to make a number of choices," Williams says. "You have to know who that person really is, and from where and what he or she came. Begin by writing a biography of your character, and start from the very beginning."[5]

Writers in all genres utilize this approach. By constructing elaborate biographies of characters, they can bring them to life, making them living, breathing entities and not simply vehicles to move the narration forward.

Do recognize, though, that video scriptwriting is different from novelization. Characters really do not have to be psychologically complete; instead, they must be *functional*. But of course a functional character must be a realistic character, and that's the importance of creating some perspective by which to evaluate whether a character's actions are logical and reasonable within a given context.

SUMMARY

≡ Scriptwriting must be imaginative but not self-conscious. It should not call attention to itself.

≡ It is the writer's obligation to write for the ear, meaning writing that is meant to be heard and not read.

≡ Similarly, a scriptwriter must write for the eye, meaning that video must be created in a series of scenes that creates meaning visually.

≡ A script for institutional television usually has video descriptions in the left-hand column and audio in the right.

≡ Dramatic scripts have the dialogue written entirely across the page, with character names and technical directions above the dialogue.

≡ Storyboards, script coupled with visual representations of scenes, are sometimes used in corporate video. Treatments are commonly utilized.

≡ Scripts tell a story and, if appropriate, move a central character through the story. It is not always necessary to have a central character, though.

≡ Good scripts can motivate, provide instruction, impart general information, persuade, or all of the above.

≡ Scripts, even if the topic is dramatized or largely fictional, must carry the ring of truth. Characters and incidents should present an atmosphere of reality.

EXERCISES

1. You have been assigned the task of writing an institutional video presentation designed to offer preretirement information to employees nearing retirement age. Create a central character, and write a biography of him or her. Include name, date of birth, education, occupation of parents, early life,

military service, and the like. Add anything you can invent, as long as it squares with reality. Try for about 250 words.

2. Do you feel this person is looking forward to retirement? What worries or positive expectations might this person have? Explain in about 250 words, and be sure to refer to the characteristics you detailed in exercise 1.

3. Pick a subject in which you are very knowledgeable, be it bowling, sewing, or fly-tying. Write a two-page typewritten treatment of an instructional tape, a tape which is geared toward people with little knowledge of the subject.

NOTES

1. William L. Hagerman, "Scriptwriting: Write and Wrong II," *Audio-Visual Communication* (December 1986): 35.

2. For information on coping with this situation see "Scriptwriting for a Committee," *Video Manager* (February 1987): 12, 34.

3. Script written by Carl Hausman; reprinted courtesy of Tom McCabe, Tom Foolery's, Inc.

4. "Writing with a Breath of Life," *Video Manager* (October 1987): 12, 37.

5. Ibid.

CHAPTER 6

BUDGETING

Drawing up a budget — and sticking to it — is a primary responsibility of institutional video producers. Unfortunately, most production experts have little or no training in the process of budgeting, so to them it seems akin to an excursion into a foreign culture.

An institutional producer is well advised to learn the vocabulary and mechanics of budgeting. Bertolt Brecht offered a succinct justification:

> Ah, how very sorely they're mistaken
> Who think that money doesn't count.
> Fruitfulness turns to famine
> When the kindly stream runs out.

When that "kindly stream" of cash goes dry, the results can range from embarrassing to disastrous. At best you'll have to go hat in hand to the powers that be and ask for additional funding. At worst your project will self-destruct, and you won't be able to pay your outside contractors.

This chapter discusses the basics of drawing up a plan to prevent such a disaster. We will examine the vocabulary and layout of a budget, the ways in which budgets are estimated and constructed, and how costs are minimized and income, if any, is maximized.

A PRIMER ON BUDGETS

Although various sources can provide guidance on the "cookbook" approach to budgeting, it is worthwhile to briefly examine the underlying fundamentals of the process. *In the most basic terms, the business of business is predicting the future.* An odd notion, perhaps, but anyone who has dealt with corporate culture realizes that financial experts — the people who dole out the money to departments within an organization — live in a world of *projections*. This orientation stems in part from a basic assumption that business must expand to remain competitive. In a typical situation budget managers set yearly goals for increased profits and work their budgets out from there.

When an institution sets its budgetary policy, an action taken by the board of directors and handed down through the hierarchy, expansion is typically pegged to production. A profitable widget manufacturing division, for example, might have a net income of $400,000 on an investment of $2 million: a 20 percent *return on investment*. In five years, then, the initial investment will pay for itself.

But things aren't always that simple. In order to stay competitive, that widget division must look far into the future and project some numbers that reflect how the business will be expanded each year. Targets — long range, yearly, and monthly — must be set and met.

That in itself is a complicated task, but business managers must then cope with an enormous number of variables, including but not limited to the seasonal demand for widgets, the variable rates at which clients pay their bills, the rate of inflation, the tax rates, and the prices of raw materials.

But how does this calculation relate to the production of institutional video? In the most basic terms the factors cited above constitute business's need for projection of expenditures. Virtually all businesses are conducted on the basis of such projections, even colleges and universities, which regularly project returns from expected enrollments.

Audiovisual managers must, therefore, live in this land of projections. Unfortunately, they are typically not used to the corporate culture of cost projection. A creative person may be tempted to view budgeting and projection as a combination of busywork, makework, and guesswork. ("How do I *know* what a video production will cost? It's different every time. What's the point of pushing all this paper?") But financial officers view budgets as the primary tool of doing business. They are accustomed to interacting with managers who can assign reasonably precise estimates of costs and the return on those costs.

It is obvious that video producers cannot project expenses with the same accuracy as most manufacturing divisions. There is no precise way to figure, for example, exactly how much a tape will cost per minute. We can guess, based on experience with tapes of the same genre, that a production will cost, let's say, about $600 a minute.

After some experience we may also find that we're pretty good at hitting that target. We will typically come close by looking for expected and unexpected costs and, if we're approaching the anticipated ceiling, shaving a few corners in the final stages of production.

And that, for all intents and purposes, is a budget, with much of the mysticism removed.

THE BUILDING BLOCKS
OF A BUDGET

Although an intuitive approach can work well, more formal and reasonably extensive planning is necessary to allocate available resources and please the executives who control the budget. Yes, it is undeniably true that some experienced producers literally never put pencil to paper when budgeting a project, but most of them would admit to some horrendous mistakes in the process of developing their "intuitive" grasp of budgeting.

Gaining an understanding of the formal budgeting process is a worthwhile investment of time and effort. You can use pencil and paper to plan and anticipate as well as to interact positively with the executives who control allocations.

The head of the video department will greatly appreciate a written quantification of a producer's expectations, because he or she deals with department operating budgets imposed by the next supervisory level. The department head needs to provide that executive with projections and estimations of the operating budget.

Operating budgets may include what is known as *overhead*. Overhead refers to the cost of "keeping a roof over one's head." Some budgets, for example, must directly indicate anticipated costs of telephone service, secretarial backup, and other factors we generally take for granted. Somewhere, someone must include rent or mortgage payments in budget projections; this is a major consideration of independent production houses but is usually handled at a higher level in corporate environments. In other words, a company's video manager usually won't include heat and rent in his or her operating budget.

BUDGETARY VOCABULARY

For the sake of discussion let's assume that two types of budgets affect a video producer's work: a department *operating budget* and a *project budget*.

Departmental Operating Budget   The operating budget is simply an allocation to the entire department, whether it be corporate communications as a whole, public relations, or the audiovisual or video department. It is the total money a department head has to spend within a set period, usually a fiscal year. (The fiscal year may not coincide with the calendar year.)

The departmental operating budget includes such items as equipment, travel, telephone, office supplies, subscriptions, outside consultants, special events, miscellaneous supplies, and so forth. Sometimes, the salaries of staff members are included in the budget; often, they are broken out in a separate document.

The operating budget usually imposes an overall limit on yearly expenditures, and it is calculated on past expenses. For example, one department's budget for next year might be 3 percent higher than the allocation for this year. At the time of this writing that would be a reasonable figure, since those increases are usually linked to rates of inflation.

The department head often has great flexibility in the allocation of expenditures *as long as he or she does not exceed the maximum total allowance for that year*. In other words should the department head choose to move $2,000 from the category of "outside vendors" to "purchase of equipment," fine, as long as the overall ceiling is not exceeded. This type of flexibility is commonplace in business (less so in nonprofit institutions), even though financial managers frequently discourage it because it gives rise to spending patterns negatively characterized as "slush funds."

Two common methods keep department heads well aware of their ongoing budgeting status. First, many typical departmental budget-allocation forms show expenditures over a three-year period: the actual expense for the previous full year, the estimated expense for the current year (which usually is identical — in an ideal world — to the projection made last year), and a projection for the following year. To demonstrate, the category for outside vendors may look like this:

Expenses for 1990	1991 (actual totals for first nine months and projections for remaining three months of fiscal year)	1992
$13,011	$13,401.33	$13,803.69

Note that the figure for 1992 is totally projected, whereas that for 1991 is partially projected. Because budgets have to be made up before the following fiscal year begins, some of the current year's expenditures must be estimated. In many cases about three months will remain in the current year when budgets for the following year are projected. Basing future budgets on historical data is a common practice. In some cases "zero-based budgeting," meaning building each year's budget from the ground up, is used, but such budgets must still rely to an extent on historical data.

The second method used to keep department heads aware of their budgetary status is the *monthly report*. The accounting department takes all individual expenses and (usually) divides them equally into monthly increments. The 1991 category for outside vendors, for example, translates into $1,117 per month. If in the second month of the fiscal year the department has spent $3,122, its head will receive an indication that under the category of outside vendors he or she is over budget by $888. That deficit might be made up by lowering spending within that category or taking funds away from other categories in the operating budget.

Two realistic observations can be made about departmental operating budgets. First, many departments regularly exceed their budgets. If the department is a valued one in the organization, perhaps nothing will be said. If the department holds less prestige, the department head may be required to file amended reports justifying the cost overruns. If the department is in low esteem, the cash stream may simply dry up.

FIGURE 6.1

A work sheet for estimating the costs of a project, along with an attachment specifying each party's responsibilities, is a useful tool for the institutional producer. This example is used by an in-house production unit of the IDS Marketing Corporation, in Minnesota.

Form designed by Jeff Nielsen, Studio 55.

Second, the operating budget system based on historical data encourages spending. Department heads are often horrified by the prospect of *underspending* for one year, because that year's total will lower what is allocated for the next year. This fear encourages assigning money to vaguely named categories such as "miscellaneous expenses," because that money can be spent with great discretion — say, on a useful but not immediately necessary video tape recorder — if it appears that all the money in the budget won't be spent. This is "slush fund" spending; it is not necessarily dishonest or disreputable, but the finance department usually frowns on such practices if spending patterns are too loose.

This, then, is a thumbnail sketch of the departmental operating budget. Although you may never be responsible for such a budget, it is vitally important that you understand something of the process, because your individual project budgets are the bricks and the mortar that make up the operating budget.

Project Budget   Project budgets estimate expenditures for an individual production; a department head uses them to determine (1) if there is enough money to fund the production and (2) if the project is worth whatever percentage of the yearly operating budget it will use up.

LAYOUT OF A PROJECT BUDGET

A project budget is what the name implies: a listing of all expected expenditures. Various organizations have work sheets, based on the fill-in-the-blank system, that also spell out the responsibilities of each party in the venture (Figure 6.1).

Some organizations have complex budget forms. This practice is common when the organization typically mounts major productions. Note that a video budget is not a true accounting document. Accounting has its own format, much of it geared to anticipating tax consequences. Although an understanding of typical accounting practices is helpful to anyone in business, do be aware that the budgets you draw up as a project manager are not the same thing as an accountant's balance sheet.[1]

PRODUCTION COST ESTIMATE

Prepared for				Date	

Address			Project Title		
			End User		

Contact		Phone	Requested Production Dates	Confirmed ☐ YES ☐ NO

Project Description

FACILITIES

DATE	ITEM	RATE	HOURS or DAYS	COST

CREW

DATE	POSITION	RATE	HOURS or DAYS	COST

TAPE STOCK

AMOUNT	ITEM	PRICE	COST

PRODUCTION SERVICES

ITEM	EST. COST

COST SUMMARY

Facilities _____	Credit Approved ☐ Yes ☐ No
Crew _____	
Tape Stock _____	
Services _____	Deposit Due _____ by _____
TOTAL ESTIMATE _____	(See General Terms on Back)

Approved by _____ Date _____

(Studio 55)

The above estimates are based on information supplied by you concerning your communications needs. The actual charges that appear on your contract will be adjusted up or down at the time of production to reflect your actual usage of Studio 55 facilities and services.

GENERAL TERMS

HOURS

Normal production and post-production business hours are from 8:30 A.M. to 5 P.M., with one 45-minute lunch break.

Evening and weekend use of production facilities is charged at the straight hourly rate. Evening and weekend crew costs are charged at time and a half. All production charges are made in one hour segments.

If using the facilities beyond the allotted time results in overtime costs for crew members, time and a half charges will start automatically.

CANCELLATION

If cancellation of the use of Studio 55 facilities is not made at least 24 hours prior to the starting production time, you will be billed 50% of the estimated production costs as stated on the Studio 55 Production Estimate form.

DOWNTIME

Studio 55 agrees that if there is a delay in production due to malfunctions or equipment failure outside your ability to control, you will not be charged for facilities or crew during the down time. Studio 55 shall not be responsible for any additional expense you may incur, or business opportunity you may lose, resulting from such a delay.

DAMAGE

You agree to indemnify Studio 55 for all loss and damage to the equipment or premises (other than normal wear and tear) or injury to persons other than personnel which Studio 55 furnishes.

CLIENT'S RISK

Studio 55 makes no representations as to the facility's suitability or appropriateness for your use. You hereby acknowledge that the facilities are suitable for your purposes. You assume all risk that the end result of your use of Studio 55 facilities and services will not meet your expectations.

Studio 55 is not responsible for the loss, damage, destruction, or erasure of tapes and tape content originated or stored within Studio 55's facility. Replacement of tape stock in the event of loss, damage, or destruction is the only obligation of Studio 55.

Studio 55 is not responsible for the loss, damage, or destruction of any props, sets, scripts, costumes, or other materials that you may leave on the premises, unless prior arrangement is made in writing for the storage of such materials at Studio 55.

FORCE MAJEURE

If because of fire, weather, riot, public emergency, labor dispute, governmental order, or any other act of God, Studio 55 is unable to furnish any of the facilities and services listed here, such a failure shall not be considered a breach of this agreement.

ASSIGNMENTS

You may not assign the rights of this agreement to any other person or party.

FIGURE 6.1, continued.

BILLING

With approved credit, payment for all services and materials will be made net 15 days from date of invoice. If not paid by due date, the unpaid balance will be subject to a service charge of 1¹/2% per month from the date of invoice.

Without approved credit, or prior agreement, a deposit of 50% of the estimated production costs is due 3 days prior to the scheduled start of production. The balance will be paid and subject to the service charge described above.

You will receive an invoice from, and make your payment to:

IDS Marketing Corp.
Unit 26/287
IDS Tower
Minneapolis, MN 55402

HOW BUDGETS ARE DRAWN UP

Do not be intimidated by the seeming intricacy of a video budget, and bear in mind that there is nothing particularly mysterious about the process. It is largely a matter of experience, particularly when it comes to estimating the amount of time needed to perform particular tasks.

The way you will construct this estimate depends on the overall financial structure of your department. There are three primary financial structures, as introduced briefly in Chapter 2: (1) partial charge-back, (2) total charge-back, and (3) flat budget. According to a survey for fiscal year 1987 conducted by *Video Manager* magazine, 56.7 percent of the 275 video managers in business and industry who responded were using some sort of charge-back; 22.4 percent of all respondents used a total charge-back system, and 34.3 percent used a partial charge-back system, in which the departments were reimbursed for such costs as out-of-pocket expenses.[2] Here are how these arrangements usually work: *Partial charge-back* is probably the most common arrangement in organizational video. An individual department—let's use the medical products division as an example—contracts with the video department for a 10-minute product-demonstration tape; the division agrees to pay for *certain* expenses incurred in the production, usually the "extras."

Exactly what is considered an extra varies, but many video departments charge the client for such items as videotape, outside narration, externally produced graphic effects, out-of-house writers, and music—essentially, anything that the video department itself has to pay for out of pocket.

Total charge-back can entail billing the client for literally everything involved in the production, including hourly salaries of all employees and an hourly fee covering amortized depreciation of equipment, meaning a charge predicated on an estimate of how much the value of the equipment declines per year. This is much the same method that a profit-making organization would use to calculate its hourly fee. A profit-making organization would build in an extra measure of pure profit; but most in-house audiovisual departments are not constituted to turn an actual profit.

However, profit is often built into the calculations when renting in-house facilities to outside users. Some organizations do this in order to maximize return from expensive equipment that sits idle for a good portion of the working day. Although this is an intriguing strategy, some organizations have experienced difficulties, because it is troublesome to bump paying clients when someone at the top of the corporate hierarchy wants an immediate production job. In-house clients are remarkably understanding when they are told that their project must be delayed because the CEO wants a special project moved up; outside clients are not so sympathetic.

Flat budget arrangements mean that the department in charge of video production is given a set budget for the year and is expected to field any reasonable requests. Note that with flat budget and partial charge-back arrangements it is common for video producers to have to refuse certain requests. If the head of the medical products division wants a two-hour documentary on the company's European and Asian production facilities, the video producer must explain that the idea would quickly use up the budget and that unless the division can arrange to contribute substantial funding, the idea is impractical. Even a partial charge-back system that covered all video expenses except personnel would probably bankrupt the video department in these cases.

Surprisingly, such explanations hardly ever ruffle organizational feathers. I was once in charge of a flat-budget production setup and turned down (or drastically scaled down) production requests almost daily. Because it was apparent to most of those who inquired that the services offered were limited and were more or less free to them, there was no sense of entitlement and, therefore, no real feeling of rejection. Producers who work on partial charge-back arrangements usually report the same attitude on the part of their in-house clients.

How would an organization choose one system over another? Often, the decision is made purely by happenstance; the executive in charge of developing a video department simply picks the system with which he or she is most familiar. Sometimes, such systems evolve after one method fails. One organization with which I worked, for example, originally offered its services free to all comers; but this system led to overwork and underfunding, and a partial charge-back system was instituted.

PLANNING FOR EXPENSES

Success in production is often predicated on the ability to draw up an initial budget. Once the facts and figures are laid out in front of someone who has requested production services, he or she can appreciate *your* position or, if the system in place is a charge-back or partial charge-back, appreciate the investment that's going to be necessary.

In any event an approximation of expected expenses is always necessary, both for your purposes and for the client's. The approximation, which for all intents and purposes becomes the amount you have "budgeted" for the production, must include *every* foreseeable expense. Just a few unplanned expenses can put you drastically over budget. For example, here are some possible costs of typical extras in the Boston area:

An outside narrator working at union scale for three hours:	$1,020
Two or three video effects contracted out of house:	$900
Licensing fees for music:	$220
Grand total of surprise expenses:	$2,140

It is apparent that the budgeting mistakes can put you on the losing end of a rather high-stakes game. Someone must absorb unanticipated expenses, and that is an unpleasant situation to resolve.

Therefore, the first step in budgeting is to make an initial assessment of *what* must be paid for and *who* will pay for it. So when first evaluating a video production idea or proposal, ask the following questions of your client and of yourself:

≡ Based on the general scope of the project, can it be done with in-house personnel, or will we have to contract for independent crew members and writers?

≡ Will travel be involved? How much?

≡ Will an outside writer be required? Can the department making the request supply you with scripting help?

≡ About how long will the program be? Can the subject be adequately covered in this period? Alternately, are we overkilling the idea?

≡ What is the sophistication level of the production? Does the client expect high-tech video effects and, if so, are those effects really necessary to the overall thrust of the program? (Indeed, they might be, if this is a sales piece in direct competition with high-budget sales productions from other corporations.)

≡ What is the desired format? For obvious reasons, a half-hour documentary will involve more shooting and editing time than a half-hour interview show.

≡ What is the desired end product? Is this a one-time-only showing, or do we anticipate the need for tape duplication and syndication?

≡ Who will perform on camera? If the client suggests someone from in house, now is the time to make a realistic assessment of whether in-house talent can handle the job.

≡ What else can the client contribute to cut costs? Does he or she have research already done? Can the client contribute the part-time services of one or more staff members?

METHODS OF ESTIMATION

Now that you have some initial data, it is possible to begin the preliminary budget estimation. You can elect to "fill in the blanks" of your individual department's budget form or simply use your judgment to project expenses and build the budget from scratch.

Incidentally, your manager may find it quite useful if you can predict not only expenses but also the timing of those expenses. Department managers often allocate their resources on a monthly, quarterly, or semiannual basis, and the expectation of when various expenses will come due makes projections easier all the way up and down the chain of command.[3]

In any event you are now in a position (having asked some probing questions about the scope of the program) to make some generalizations about personnel and equipment. At this point you may be asked to estimate your above-the-line and below-the-line costs. *Above-the-line* costs include those of the executive and "idea" personnel (writer, producer, and director), as well as performers. *Below-the-line* costs include wages for members of the technical production staff as well as expenses associated with the facility.

Clearly identify those above-the-line and below-the-line costs for which you must budget. Is the script to be done out of house? You may want to seek bids from several writers with whom you've worked before. If you can briefly summarize the concept, a good writer can give you a realistic quote — say, $6,000 for a half-hour documentary of moderate complexity.

Define below-the-line costs, too. Does your client need a good deal of technical "glitz"? Perhaps you'll need out-of-house help with graphics displays. Graphics artists are usually quite adept at conceptualizing the idea and quoting a price.

Below-the-line costs can quickly get out of hand if the producer's poor time estimates result in production slowdowns. For instance, if you contract with an outside camera operator for a day's worth of shooting and the job really needs two days to complete, the delay can cause a "domino effect": Plans for Tuesday are hastily revamped for Wednesday, Wednesday's crew members are rescheduled for Thursday, and so forth, with each day's schedule disruptions increasing the total time needed for the project.

The moral is to estimate high. Build contingencies into your budget. Don't assume that you can grab some "quick cover shots" in five or ten minutes. You'll need to reset lighting, rearrange props, and set up camera angles for even the simplest cover. Allow at least an hour for setup time *anytime* you have to move cameras and lights. Build in an extra hour whenever you have to coach talent, especially nonprofessional talent, with whom you are unfamiliar.

The same warning applies to editing. Even if you have all 30 edits logged and planned, the simple act of spooling the tape to the appropriate edit points will probably eat up an hour in the editing suite. One mislabeled tape can easily cost you a half an hour of searching time.

ARRANGEMENTS FOR CALCULATING BILLING AND PRODUCTION COSTS

There is another dimension to cost assessment. Although you can view the calculations from the bottom up, as illustrated so far, it is also possible to use historical and other data to calculate the budget backwards. Ken Jurek, the director of the video and communications department of the firm Management Recruitment International, uses what he calls "cost justification" to gain an overall picture of the money situation and explain costs to clients and senior management. His methods are cost per program, cost per minute, and cost per viewer.[4]

Cost per program is computed simply by dividing the budget for the video department by the number of programs produced during the relevant period; this gives an approximation of what a typical program costs. You can also use this approach to cost out individual above-the-line and below-the-line expenses.

Cost per minute is calculated simply by dividing the total price of a program by its total running time. If you do this calculation by program category, you can arrive at reasonable approximations (assuming you have enough historical data

Financial people and the creative staff often have differing perspectives on the budgeting process. Members of creative departments, for example, sometimes feel constrained by budgetary limitations and contend that the budgeting process is simply so much busywork.

But as video producers often learn the hard way, video is a business. And when that business exists *within* a business, it is especially important to operate in a businesslike manner in assembling budgets and projections.

What do financial people think of as "businesslike" approach to budgeting? Here are some suggestions made by William Lasher, a finance professor at Nichols College in Dudley, Massachusetts. Lasher, who has worked as a financial executive in a number of firms, notes that a typical problem with budgets is an overall lack of reality. Financial people expect creative people to submit a realistic budget—that is, one that does not take all the best possible scenarios, roll those numbers together, and produce an unrealistic goal. The way to overcome this problem is to challenge each assumption during the budgeting process. Is this a realistic figure for equipment costs? Will you really be able to make that much income on the project? Ask hard questions, and you'll get hard data.

William Lasher.
Courtesy of Nichols College.

A caveat is that you should not confuse "best possible case" with "most likely outcome" when drawing up your budget. You *can* feel free to prepare a budget which reflects the best possible outcome of each and every entry—and such a document might be a useful speculative tool—but be sure to label it as such. It is also a good idea to make up a worst possible case.

Remember that missed budgetary goals eventually carry consequences. If you miss one budget, you may not have a problem, but continued misses just might instigate a witch-hunt by corporate managers. They will want to know *who* is missing targets by such a wide margin and *why*.

FIGURE 6.2

What financial people expect from members of the creative staff.

from which to generalize) for documentaries, interview shows, and so on. Should you become proficient with this method of estimation, you will find it an easy way to communicate with financial executives, who typically are quite comfortable with cost-per-minute projections based on historical data.

Cost per viewer is calculated by dividing the number of people who will see and benefit from the program into the program cost. It's a way to gain another perspective on your budgeting efforts.

Regardless of your particular strategies of budgeting — and those methods are as different as the people who invent them — you will undoubtedly find that any effort to accurately put projections on paper will be appreciated by the finance people. Remember, business lives and dies by the balance sheet, and the financial specialists do have the right to expect reasonable cooperation from the creative staff (Figure 6.2).

BUDGETARY MANAGEMENT

The philosopher Seneca noted that economy is in itself a source of considerable income. That observation is particularly noteworthy for the television producer, who must first estimate expenses and then meet or better that estimate.

In addition to controlling costs, the institutional video producer, on occasion, actively seeks sources of income for productions. A third skill of budgetary management involves keeping your source of internal funding happy with your programs and with *the amount of money spent* on those programs.

CONTROLLING PERSONNEL AND EQUIPMENT COSTS

In addition to careful tracking of expenses (making sure that tasks are performed in a reasonable period), a producer can cut costs in various ways. Although heroic cost cutting is not always a good idea — be careful of giving management the impression you can do *everything* on a shoestring — you can sometimes turn cost cutting to your advantage by saving money on low-priority projects and diverting those funds to the projects where high production values are a must. Following are some suggestions on cutting costs.

First, consider using low-budget video for projects that do not require high production values. Video editing controllers for VHS machines can be purchased for less than $250, and they produce fairly accurate edits. With consumers enjoying an increasing understanding of video recording units and cameras, video departments can often train members of other departments to produce their own video (a particularly good option for some training applications), leaving the video department free to tackle higher-end tasks, such as company news programs.[5] The video unit, however, must be careful not to foster the idea that anyone can create high-quality video. The spread of consumer-grade camcorders seems to raise questions in the minds of some executives about the need for a professional video staff.

Second, use creative alternatives to high-cost production techniques. Need a quick shot of the Atlanta plant? Instead of sending a camera crew, give some thought to having an Atlanta photographer take a good-quality still photograph of the plant, a particularly effective shot if the photographer uses a fairly wide-angle lens, such as a 35mm or 28mm. Do a simple video zoom-in or pan across the still. Chances are, most viewers will not even notice that it is ersatz video, and you've saved hundreds of dollars via that artful deception.[6]

Learn to think in *task-oriented sequence*. This means that you plan your shots according to the convenience and economy of obtaining them, not according to their chronological order in the script. You can shave a great deal of time and money from the production budget by task-oriented planning. For example, assume that the program in question begins and ends at the same location. Shoot the opening and ending in the same session; shoot the ending first, if that is most expeditious. Instead of hiring an actor to show up for several short scenes over three days, have him do all his lines on one day.

A fourth suggestion is to take advantage of free talent. Some people love the opportunity to perform before television cameras, and with some appropriate coaching they can produce surprisingly good performances. Under certain circumstances, however, amateur talent can hold up production and cost more in the long run than an expensive but competent professional.

SOURCES OF FUNDING

Nonprofit organizations have the opportunity to solicit outside money, funding available from a variety of sources. Although they are not particularly dependable forms of income, grants, subsidies, and awards can allow for production of programs that would normally not be feasible.

Grants are available from state, federal, and local agencies. Private foundations with special interests, such as a foundation established to promote the work of female artists, may also be sources of production capital.

State councils on humanities are good sources of funding for private television. (The most common federal humanities grants are usually for broadcast television.) Ideas that offer specific insight into state affairs seem to be most welcome at state humanities councils.

Although there is no formula for obtaining grants, experienced appliers do offer some guidelines:

≡ *Do your homework*, and enlist the aid of people who have done theirs. Your organization is likely to have on its staff someone who knows the ins and outs of grantsmanship. There are books on grants and awards in any major library.

≡ *Start small*. Granting agencies appear to react quite favorably to organizations that request small planning grants at first and use them to prepare a major proposal. Overly large initial proposals do not typically enjoy good prospects.

≡ *Stay focused*. Remember, your idea will be in competition with other proposals, and it will work to your advantage if the proposal is clearly defined. If you can't sum up the proposal concisely ("a half-hour documentary on how ethics is taught in major universities"), you'll be at a disadvantage during the conferences at which proposals are evaluated.

HOW TO EXPLAIN COSTS TO MANAGEMENT

One of the most difficult aspects of institutional video involves explaining to a nonvideo executive just why everything is so expensive. Earlier, I discussed some methods of quantifying costs, such as breaking down expenses on a cost-per-minute basis. But simply quantifying costs does not always settle the problem of showing tangible benefits from money expended. Executives unfamiliar with television production, for example, may simply be stunned by the fact that a documentary can cost $1,200 per minute. They may also have little understanding of why you need several thousand dollars for an arcane-sounding piece of equipment like a time-base corrector, which stabilizes the playback of a videotape. (I once requested funds for rental of a TBC and was asked why I needed such an expensive *clock*.)

There are no easy answers to this problem, but two strategies might help you close the gap between your department and nonvideo executives. First, try to have your corporate or institutional boss observe the process of production, especially editing. Just make sure that you let him or her know that things take so long because that is the nature of the art, not because you are a hopelessly slow incompetent. But don't worry excessively about your image; the tedious detail and real volume of work required for a short segment of video usually do become genuinely apparent to an intelligent observer.

A second strategy is to keep records of your success stories. One institutional producer, who asked to remain anonymous, says that he makes a diligent effort to collect sales figures about products for which he has produced promotional tapes. Although such before-and-after comparisons usually don't offer foolproof statistical validity, they can be persuasive if the effectiveness of the video effort is called into question.

There are, of course, many cases that cannot be quantified. You cannot place a monetary value on the goodwill created by preparing a tape for a United Way campaign or the increase in company morale generated by production of an in-house news program. But enlightened managers are, with increasing regularity, coming to understand the value of video. And armed with the right arsenal of figures, plans, and expectations, you can produce good video *and* please the folks who control the purse strings.

SUMMARY

≡ Any business runs on the basis of budgets and budget projections, even if it is a nonprofit entity. As a video producer you must learn to interact within that corporate culture and provide the financial planners with appropriate documentation.

≡ There are two types of budgets with which you will be concerned: the departmental operating budget and the budget for an individual project.

≡ There are many possible financial structures for video or audiovisual departments, but the most common are a partial charge-back system, a total charge-back system, and flat budgeting.

≡ The most onerous aspect of putting together a budget is anticipating every expense. Just a few surprises can result in cost overruns of thousands of dollars.

≡ Costs for programs are calculated by adding up as many expenses as can be anticipated. Aim high, because it is easier to have a surplus than to go looking for additional funds. You can also arrive at approximations of program costs based on historical data. The most common way of doing this is to determine the cost per minute based on what previous tapes of a similar format have cost to produce.

≡ It is generally not a good idea to consistently take heroic measures to cut costs, because you will wind up doing everything on a shoestring. It is sometimes necessary to cut costs, however, especially when trying to save allocated funds for a major program whose expense is necessary and unavoidable. One popular cost-cutting method is to use consumer-type VHS equipment for production of low-budget and low-priority programs.

EXERCISE

1. Here's a major project that can occupy a good deal of personal and class time. Prepare a budget for the video program whose script was shown in Figure 5.1. (Your instructor may provide you with a different script.)

    First, be sure that you anticipate every expense. As a hint, remember that there is a police officer's role in the opening. Be aware that if you intend to stop traffic and do a shot on a public road, which was indeed done, you will need a real police officer. For how long? Make your best estimate.

    Also note that there is an aerial shot in the closing. It was done from a cherry picker (a traveling crane designed to place a worker high in the air, similar to the ones used by telephone and power companies). The author-producer was lucky in that the firm happened to have one available, but for the sake of this exercise assume that you will have to rent one. Where do you get it? How much do you think it will cost?

    You will need a private plane or helicopter to take the aerial shots of the plant. Work that into your calculations, too.

    There is always an overhead cost involved. Estimate salaries, facility rents, and other hidden costs.

    Present your individual budgets to the class or working group and compare your estimates of cost and time. Can you compromise? Do members of the group have any special knowledge of certain aspects of the budgetary process? (Is there a private pilot in the group?)

    See if you can revise the budget, do some additional research, and come to a consensus.

NOTES

1. For a readable explanation of the budgets typically drawn up by a department manager and how those budgets relate to the formal accounting function, see Allen Sweeny and John N. Wisner, *Budgeting Fundamentals for Nonfinancial Executives* (New York: AMACOM, 1975).

2. "Salary Survey, Part II: Operating Budgets Lower for '87," *Video Manager* (September 1987): 1, 25.

3. For additional information on ways to project budgeting time lines see Douglas Garbut, *How to Control and Manage Cash* (Aldershot, England: Gower, 1985): 56–81.

4. Ken Jurek, "Justifying Production Costs," *Video Manager* (September 1987): 15.

5. Raymond Johnson, "Low/No Budget Video," *Video Manager* (June 1987): 12, 23, 25.

6. See Ken Cirelli, "Creativity on a Low Budget," *Video Systems* (September 1986): 60–64.

CHAPTER 7

EVALUATION AND

MEASUREMENT

At first glance the placement of this chapter at the end of Part 2, "Planning the Video Program," and before Part 3, "Executing the Video Program," may seem inappropriate. After all, isn't evaluation usually done after the dust has settled?

Actually, it is. And that's too bad, because a system of evaluation and measurement can help fine-tune the effectiveness of a program at all stages of development, from the conception of the idea to the day when the outdated program is consigned to the file cabinet. This chapter focuses on just that process: how a reasonably accurate system of evaluation and measurement can help give birth to a workable program concept and carry that concept through the production process.

WHY MEASURE AND EVALUATE?

Time, money, and personnel are being invested in institutional video. The people who do the work and pay the bills want to know *whether a program works*. Implicit in the evaluation of whether it works is the primary assumption of whether it was needed in the first place. And with budgets for institutional productions often running into the tens of thousands of dollars, producers have an obvious stake in heading off program failures.

Kristin Hall, vice president of the St. Pierre Group, a management consulting firm, points out that greater opportunities in institutional video go hand in hand with "greater chances for failure if the programming is faulty. Consequently, the need will become even greater for a system of evaluation and measurement that is comprehensive, controllable, and founded on valid techniques — a system that is an integral part of the entire communications process."[1]

Before we examine this process, it is worthwhile to clarify the vocabulary. An educational evaluation specialist, Robert F. Mager, offers these definitions:

> *Measurement* is the process of determining the extent of some charac-
> teristic. . . . For example, when we determine the length of a room, or
> weight of an object, we are measuring.

> *Evaluation* is the act of comparing a measurement with a standard and
> passing judgment on the comparison. We are making evaluations when
> we say things like — "it's too long, it's too hot, he's not motivated, he's
> too slow."[2]

EVALUATION AND MEASUREMENT IN COMMUNICATIONS

In practice we often use the terms *measurement* and *evaluation* interchangeably when discussing the methods of determining the effectiveness of a presentation. In general, though, *measurement* indicates a quantifiable study. As an example, we might measure the performance of workers on a piece of machinery before they have seen a tape and after having viewed it. *Evaluation* is often taken to be a more qualitative study. For instance, we could evaluate a videotape by showing it to a group of people and simply asking them for their opinions. *Evaluation* is the more comprehensive term, however, and as a matter of convenience and convention I will usually employ it in this chapter as an inclusive term for the entire process.

Evaluation is increasingly important in the realm of institutional video. Although "program evaluation" can conjure up visions of makework in the minds of action-oriented production personnel, it is, in the real world, an exceedingly vital function.

Major advertisers, as a case in point, have used evaluation techniques virtually since consumer-oriented mass-media advertising made its debut approximately 100 years ago. The pioneering advertisers began the process informally, *putting themselves in the position of the customer* and gearing their campaigns toward that person's needs. George Eastman, the founder of Eastman Kodak, was among the first to recognize the need for simplified consumer technology. He listened to what potential customers said and coined the grandfather of all advertising slogans: "You Press the Button — We Do the Rest."[3]

Today, an advertising agency would not consider mounting a major campaign without testing the appeal of the initial idea, retesting the concept as it is refined, and then testing the final production on a sample audience. As more time and money ride on the success of institutional productions, the producers of those programs are gradually recognizing the same imperative.

An important consideration must be stressed at this point: Research processes in measurement and evaluation can be extremely complex. Thus, this chapter must not be construed as a definitive guide to undertaking such research. For example, it is unlikely that you will have to prove your measurements to the point of statistical reliability; to maintain that position would be to overstate the rigor required of institutional video research. It is useful to *understand* reliability factors, however, because they point the way toward understanding research in general and will help in making empirical, intuitive judgments.

At the same time, some portions of the chapter are necessarily oversimplified. Questionnaire design is a science in itself, so I take only a broad-brush approach. Where appropriate, though, further resources are listed.

A PROBLEM WITH EVALUATION

Unfortunately, evaluation takes a back seat to production when deadlines are looming. A writer halfway through a script, for example, will not be inclined to take time away from the frantic rush to meet with a focus group, even though that is one of the best times for the intervention of a group evaluation.

We'll look at the case for early evaluation in the final section of this chapter, as well as some standard ways in which institutional producers use the tools of measurement and evaluation. First, though, it is worthwhile to examine the instruments themselves.

INSTRUMENTS FOR MEASUREMENT AND EVALUATION

We customarily refer to questionnaires and other methods of collecting data for research purposes as *instruments*. Note that the use of research instruments is a sophisticated business, and it is far beyond the scope of this book to demonstrate methods of producing statistically valid measurements. Although we can't embark on a crash course in research, we can look at two of the basic problems and examine resources for further investigation.

CAUTIONARY NOTES

The first problem with instruments for evaluation is that it is difficult to claim infallible or even reliable statistical validity for almost any study, even one done by a professional researcher in the social or physical sciences. You are probably aware that most before-and-after studies hinge on whether the results are likely to be reproduced by chance. For many researchers this means that statistical analysis shows an insignificant chance that the results were produced by pure luck.

Although the math involved is reasonably straightforward, the raw data are not. For example, you may be assigned to produce a training tape demonstrating the use of a particular machine. You develop a test for the workers that measures their productivity before they view the tape (let's assume you measure the numbers of items produced by the machines, taking the figure from standard output reports). You then show the tape, remeasure the workers' output, and decide whether the increase is statistically significant.

For the sake of argument let's assume that there is a major increase in output. Let's further assume that you compute, using standard statistical formulas and a table of probabilities, that it is extremely unlikely that the differences could have been produced by random chance.

Great! Your tape is a success.

Or is it? The skeptics in your department might ask the following questions:

> Hold on, now. . . . There was a month between the first measurement and the second measurement. How do you know these people didn't just get better at their jobs all by themselves? Some of these workers were new to the job when you first tested them. They certainly would have improved with or without your help.

> Just a second, here. When you made your second set of measurements, you *told* the people you were testing to see if watching the tape had improved their performance. Don't you think that might have changed the outcome?

Those two objections reflect the more typical difficulties encountered in measuring pretest and posttest performance.

The second problem with research instruments is that qualitative data can be unreliable, too, if they are not gathered and interpreted with some precision. *Qualitative* is usually taken to mean research in which opinions and verbal analysis come into play. Qualitative researchers are concerned with learning the perspectives of participants and "illuminating the inner dynamics of situations — dynamics that are often invisible to the outsider."[4]

Well and good, but when we ask for qualitative data ("Do you think this program does a good job of motivating employees?") we inject ourselves into the scheme of things. In other words people may tell us what they think we want to hear. Alternately, they may be unreasonably critical because that is their way of exercising their institutional power.

These two factors may persuade you that evaluation is an impossibly difficult task. That, of course, is not the intent. What *is* intended is to show that measurement instruments all have limitations, and it is important to realize that the results of a study rarely, if ever, *prove* anything. The best that can be hoped for in most situations is to gather data, examine them critically, and, to the best of the researcher's ability, *use them as information and not as a spurious "proof."*

RESOURCES

Many resources are available to help the institutional researcher develop tools for measurement and evaluation. If you work in a commercial business, your firm may be top-heavy with specialists in marketing analysis who can help you design valid methods for evaluation. Personnel departments of large institutions, both profit and nonprofit, may also have professionals familiar with measurement techniques, especially for evaluating training methods. Educational institutions have no shortage of people engaged in quantitative or qualitative research, and you may be able to arrange for some informal help.

A personal research library can help you design simple measurement and evaluation instruments. An overall perspective can be gained from such works as *Beyond Method: Strategies for Social Research*, edited by Gareth Morgan (Beverly Hills, CA: Sage Publications, 1983), and *Understanding Research Methods*, by Gerald R. Adams and Jay D. Schvaneveldt (White Plains, NY: Longman, 1985). Simple explanations of statistical concepts can be provided by *Statistics for Social Change*, by Lucy Horwitz and Lou Ferleger (Boston: South End Press, 1980), and *General Statistics*, by Warren Chase and Fred Bown (New York: John Wiley, 1986). Guidance on special applications of research techniques to communications is available in *Mass Media Research: An Introduction*, 2nd ed., by Roger D. Wimmer and Joseph R. Dominick (Belmont, CA: Wadsworth, 1987). Because the questionnaire is such a popular and convenient method of evaluation, some readers may find William Sims Bainbridge's *Survey Research: A Computer-Assisted Introduction* (Belmont, CA: Wadsworth, 1989) exceptionally useful. All the works cited are of such a basic and durable nature that they are unlikely to become dated within the next several years.

Should you be in a position to take course work in research techniques, by all means do so. We live in an information age, and those with specialized training in evaluating that information typically find their services in great demand. A solid academic foundation in marketing research would be a definite plus for an applicant for an institutional video position in either large or small organizations.

TYPES OF INSTRUMENTS

Among the more common instruments used in video evaluation are *informal or semistructured interviews*, *focus groups*, *questionnaires*, and, on occasion, *experimental testing*.

Interview   Informal or semistructured interviews provide basic information gathering. At its most informal, an interview may amount to making a phone call and asking someone for advice or information. Interviews may also be more highly structured, with a prepared list of questions and, sometimes, a special document that the interviewer fills out.

Focus Group   Focus groups are standard tools of ad agencies. Usually, they involve a gathering of people to discuss a specific issue under the guidance of a group leader, who is eliciting greater understanding of the subject as well as an insight into the group's perceptions.[5]

For in-house projects focus groups are frequently valuable in defining the need for a program and then outlining the basic approach. A collection of participants from differing disciplines and departments can help pin down the root cause of the problem that prompted the initial call for an instructional or motivational videotape.

For example, you may be approached by the head of the engineering department, who says there is a need for a training and motivational tape to encourage members of the clerical staff to file reports more promptly. But your focus group with this department head, the director of personnel, and the department manager for the clerical staff may uncover the fact that the employees have no problem with motivation. They simply cannot understand the jargon used by the engineers and have had no luck in convincing the engineers to use words like *front* and *back* instead of *anterior* and *posterior*.

In this case your focus group has accomplished three things:

1. It has clearly defined the problem.

2. It has brought people together to focus the problem directly without catching *you* in the middle of the dispute. (You're only a moderator.)

3. It has uncovered a new avenue that may lead to a solution of the problem: Perhaps the *engineers* need some training material on communicating with nontechnical employees.

Questionnaire   Sets of questions are frequently developed after some initial qualitative research, including interviews and focus groups. You may use a questionnaire, for example, to determine whether the point of view expressed in a focus group is really reflected by the organization at large.

Questionnaires sometimes allow for free responses (Figure 7.1). Such questions can be valuable if you're looking for a new approach to a problem. But free responses are difficult to categorize and quantify. (Actually, it can be done; you might, for example, count the number of times the word *jargon* is used in the free responses.) Should you want a quantified document as a research tool, you might elect to use the familiar Likert scale, a method of forcing a respondent to place a

QUESTIONNAIRE

The media services department is considering producing an instructional videotape about the new computer system. We would like your advice about the project. If you need extra room, please feel free to write on separate sheets. You can return this form in the attached envelope.

1. What is your job category?

2. Do you use the computer system often?

3. If so, what do you use the system for?

4. Have you experienced problems with the computer system? What kind of problems?

5. What steps did you take to resolve those problems?

6. If you had a private meeting with a computer expert, what would you like to ask about the system?

7. What advice would you offer a new employee who is trying to learn the computer system?

8. Some people maintain that the biggest problem with the computer system is the complexity of using the new local area network. Do you agree? If so, why? If not, what is the biggest problem?

FIGURE 7.1

A sample questionnaire used to gather information about a proposed video production.

numerical value on answers to a series of questions. A possible use of a Likert scale in evaluating a videotape is illustrated in Figure 7.2.

Be wary of using too many degrees of judgment on these scales. (Don't use 10 categories and include judgments such as "possibly too much some of the time.") And if your format permits, avoid having an odd number of choices. Five choices — "strongly agree," "agree," "don't really care," "disagree," and "strongly disagree" — provide a neutral refuge and may deny you the valuable data you would have obtained if you had used the scale to *force* the respondent to come down on one side or the other.[6]

There are other attitude scales, such as the semantic differential scale, in which pairs of antonyms are presented and respondents are asked to choose where their judgment falls. For example, "I find the field of institutional video . . ." (check appropriate line):

Exciting _____ _____ _____ _____ _____ _____ Boring

Semantic differential scales are often a bit tricky, though, because they rely on word meanings, and such meanings may be slightly different for respondents.

Experimental Test   Experimental testing in the realm of institutional video can involve statistical research into whether a program achieved its stated goal: selling more of a product, training workers to do a job more efficiently, or the like. Sometimes, we test for a change in attitude: "Did seeing this tape make you feel more confident about the company's insurance plan?" In any event experimental testing is usually an evaluation of pretest and posttest conditions.

Some pitfalls of testing were discussed earlier; there are many others. Included in our concerns are the ethical problems involved in having a *control group*, a number of people not exposed to the presentation and, therefore, the yardstick by which we measure the progress of those who did see the tape. In many instances that would not be a concern, but what about the fate of a control group in testing a safety tape? Do we withhold the tape from one group and see how many more accidents befall that group? That may be an extreme example, but we might also consider the ethical implications of withholding training from a specific group of employees. Does that unfairly put them at a disadvantage in terms of pay, promotions, and incentives?

There are many practical problems associated with experimental testing, too. The most basic type of study involves testing a group, intervening, and then testing again. But the test administrators need somehow to account for all the other variables, such as the natural inclination of people to get better at their work with experience, with or without the test.

PROGRAM EVALUATION

Name: ⎯⎯⎯⎯⎯⎯⎯⎯⎯⎯⎯⎯⎯⎯⎯⎯⎯⎯⎯⎯⎯⎯⎯⎯⎯⎯⎯

Department: ⎯⎯⎯⎯⎯⎯⎯⎯⎯⎯⎯⎯⎯⎯⎯⎯⎯⎯⎯⎯⎯⎯⎯

Your responses will help us in our effort to provide meaningful video programming to our organization. Please check the appropriate box below. At the bottom of this form you can enter additional remarks.

	Strongly Agree	Agree	Disagree	Strongly Disagree
1. I found the program interesting.				
2. The program met a need.				
3. The information was presented clearly.				
4. The technical quality of the program was acceptable.				
5. I will be able to use the information presented in my job.				
6. The program was too long.				
7. The program was too short.				
8. The people with whom I viewed the program felt it was worthwhile.				
9. The support materials provided were useful.				

Please make any other comments you feel would help us in producing future programming:

FIGURE 7.2

125

A sample evaluation form of the type circulated to viewers after they have seen a videotape. Note that there are informal "control questions" built in—items 6 and 7—to check whether people are really paying attention to the form. If, for example, a respondent answers "strongly agree" to both questions, he or she isn't reading the questions, and the responses probably aren't particularly helpful.

Using a control group is an attempt to eliminate this variable, but it injects a whole new set of problems. How do we know that the groups were statistically identical in the first place? Suppose one group had a much higher proportion of newly hired workers? or much older workers? or a larger percentage of non-English-speaking workers?

Such problems are exacerbated if the tester is working with a small group; 2 *new* workers in a group of 10 can significantly alter the outcome of the comparison with a group that has no new workers. Also, it is difficult to produce statistically significant results with small groups.

USING EVALUATION TOOLS IN INSTITUTIONAL VIDEO

Although there are undeniable difficulties in evaluation, the process is not daunting, especially when it involves qualitative research such as focus groups or interviews. Your research may not produce foolproof data, but it can give you, at the very least, an insight into how co-workers feel about a particular situation or video program. We'll briefly explore the role and process of evaluation *before*, *during*, and *after* production.

PREPRODUCTION EVALUATION

Organizations that undertake evaluation often make an audit of general or specific needs before production.[7] In assessing general needs, the video department can determine the source of current information, the desires of employees for video programming, and their assessment of the present success of the video effort.

Specific assessment for a program can be done at this time, too. Is there a need for the program? What is the correct format? (For example, will the employees respond well to a comic format, or will they view the approach as condescending?) Exactly who is the audience for the program? (Additional information on this aspect of preproduction evaluation is contained in Chapter 3, "Analysis and Design.")

Some experts recommend starting such evaluation by conducting interviews and then using the qualitative data to construct a questionnaire. This is a good idea, because a questionnaire constructed in a vacuum can produce realistic-looking data with very little basis in reality. The questions may be virtually irrelevant to the situation at hand if you have not assessed the categories of questions to submit to respondents.

Types of general questions worth asking before production, first in an interview and then, possibly, in the form of a questionnaire, include:

≡ Where do you get information about the organization? From the company newsletter? the rumor mill? Do you feel underinformed about our organization?

≡ What would you like to see on video? Would you, for example, want to view a program dealing with the latest company news? Why or why not?

≡ Can you think of any subjects that would be worthwhile video productions for your department?

Some sample questions for evaluating a specific idea in the preproduction phase are:

≡ Do you feel that this program, as it has been described to you, will be successful? Why or why not? What is your personal definition of a successful program?

≡ Does the message of this proposed program come through clearly? How would you sum up the message?

MIDPRODUCTION EVALUATION

The middle of scripting or production seems like an awkward time to conduct an evaluation, and it probably is. But it is also a valuable point at which to head off incipient problems. You may wish to show storyboards, portions of the script, or — ideally — test shots of some video to a test audience and to other evaluators while production is still in progress. Questions you might ask, either through interviews or a questionnaire, include:

≡ Is this tape telling you things you already know? Do you like the approach? Do you like the actors?

≡ From your experience in doing the task demonstrated on the tape, do you feel that the demonstration is worthwhile? Can someone new to the job learn from the demonstration? Can you learn from it?

≡ Are we getting the message to the right people? Should others be shown this script (storyboard, tape segment)?

POSTPRODUCTION EVALUATION

If you have targeted your audience and carefully produced a tape that meets its needs, you may have a perfectly pitched tape. Then again, you may not. Even the most experienced producers in all levels of media production produce a few failures now and then; notice how many advertising campaigns backfire and how many television series die after a few weeks. So there is no disgrace in producing an occasional dud. The real problem surfaces when you or your department never makes an attempt to separate the bull's-eyes from the misses.

At this point you must deal with a tricky problem in evaluation: People are often less likely to be critical (at least to your face) of a *finished* program, because they realize that it is the culminating effort of your work and is at a point where it can't be changed. A questionnaire is useful now because it eliminates some of the onus of face-to-face criticism. But anonymous questionnaires pose another problem: If people are not accountable for their opinions, that in itself can skew the response. Some respondents may resent the video or training effort and may give irrelevantly negative responses as a form of retribution.

Another difficulty with the anonymous questionnaire is that you may have difficulty monitoring compliance with its completion. It is generally not a good idea to let response be optional, because that skews your sample: You are not sampling people who saw the tape but, rather, people who saw the tape and took the time to fill in an optional questionnaire. Those groups are not identical.

A good compromise is to ask respondents to sign their questionnaires but promise them that their individual responses will be kept confidential. A bad compromise is to give the impression that the questionnaire is anonymous but to code it secretly. There's really little point in this tactic: If you find that the questionnaire was not completely filled out, for example, you cannot very well go back to the respondent, because you will tacitly be admitting your deception.

In postproduction evaluation you can sample attitudes ("Do you feel that the firm is making a good-faith effort to resolve the seniority issue?") before and after employees view the tape and quantify the results. You may, in the same way, sample knowledge ("What is the very first action you must take if chemicals are spilled on the production floor?"). Should you be adept at measurement, you can also test performance before and after viewing, but the problems inherent in this type of study have already been well documented.

THE OVERALL EVALUATION STRATEGY

It is apparent that evaluation is not a one-shot affair. Rather, it is the common thread that runs through initial program design, program use, and the long-range goals of the video or audiovisual department. A corporate communications consultant, Marlys Thompson, points out that in order for a program to be effective, a producer must first establish (1) an objective that matches some portion of the department's overall plan, (2) program objectives stated in observable terms, and (3) a method to measure the program's results based on the original objective.[8] The last point merits particular attention. Expressed in one way, it is important to remember that although evaluation is certainly a valuable tool in determining the effectiveness of your programs, in the long run it can be a measure of the effectiveness of your overall video effort. Expressed more directly: Be sure you know the rules of the game before you sit down at the table and ante up.

SUMMARY

≡ Evaluation and measurement have a place at all stages of production: before, during, and after.

≡ The term *evaluation* is often used to express qualitative estimates; *measurement* usually refers to quantitative analysis, although these are connotations and not strict definitions.

≡ Instruments used in evaluation and measurement include interviews, focus groups, questionnaires, and experimental testing. Sometimes, testing is done before and after a program is viewed.

≡ Although evaluation and measurement are not extraordinarily difficult, they do present challenges. Statistics do not always speak for themselves, and accurate numbers can produce misleading results if they are not gathered and interpreted correctly.

≡ You can usually find people within an organization who are familiar with methods of evaluation and can help you design instruments. There are also many good books on the subject.

≡ It is important to keep in mind how the program will be evaluated at the time you are conceiving the program itself. This, in part, is done to make sure that your results are measured fairly.

EXERCISES

1. Conduct or participate in a focus group with your class or co-workers. The point you wish to explore and narrow down: How can we evaluate textbooks used to teach institutional video?

2. Using the results of that focus group, *individually* prepare a questionnaire that you would administer to students who are taking a course in institutional video. Compare your questionnaire with those produced by other members of the group. Are there significant differences? Do any questions seem hazy or unfocused? Does your questionnaire — or someone else's — seem to have a built-in bias, positive or negative? If feasible, administer the questionnaire.

3. Write a brief paper (two or three pages) describing a proposed video production you feel would be valuable in teaching institutional video. Be sure to include as much detail as possible on how that videotape will be evaluated. Be specific. Propose the questions and methods you feel are appropriate.

NOTES

1. Kristin Hall, "Program Evaluation and Measurement," *Video Manager* (February 1987): 8, 33, 34.

2. Robert F. Mager, *Measuring Instructional Intent* (Belmont, CA: Lear Siegler, Inc., Fearon Publishers, 1973): 8.

3. Carl Hausman, "Eastman: 100 Years of a Marketable Camera," *Media History Digest* (Fall–Winter 1988): 8–16, 39.

4. R. D. Bogdan and S. K. Biklen, *Qualitative Research for Education* (New York: Allyn & Bacon, 1982): 30.

5. "Using Focus Groups: Put the Audience to Work," *Video Manager* (April 1987): 9, 10.

6. For additional information on this aspect of scale composition see Fred Percival and Henry Ellington, *A Handbook of Educational Technology* (New York: Nichols, 1984): 136–137.

7. Hall, "Program Evaluation and Measurement," 33–35.

8. Marlys Thompson, "Surviving the Critical Zone," *Video Manager* (October 1987): 32, 41.

PART 3

EXECUTING

THE VIDEO

PROGRAM

1

CHAPTER 8

CHOOSING

AND DIRECTING

TALENT

The word *talent*, as used in the video industry, is applied to any on-air performer regardless of how "talented" that performer really is. Unfortunately, many people who are to appear in a video presentation are badly lacking in acting skills, and it is often the producer's role to coach them into an acceptable performance.

In certain cases the goal is explicit: Your job is to make the chief executive officer look good. Sometimes, the task is more subtle. You may, for example, be called on to produce a program featuring interviews with members of your organization or instructional tapes involving a lecture and demonstration by members of your firm's research staff. Here, your objective is to help the performers deliver a credible and understandable message.

In any event a poor performance by the person occupying the screen can ruin the production. At best, an incompetent performance can make the entire program seem stiff, awkward, and amateurish. At worst, the show can be downright laughable.

Talent is frequently the weakest link in the chain of events leading from conception of an in-house video program to its completion. A case could be made that talent is the least understood problem facing the in-house producer and, because many producers do not themselves have on-camera experience, one of the most difficult to correct. We'll examine several methods for dealing with this critical aspect of program planning and production, focusing primarily on working with nonprofessional talent. Nonprofessionals are more common in the in-house environment, and they certainly present the majority of performance problems.

Effective techniques for directing talent are often important to your job performance as viewed by supervisory personnel. As alluded to earlier, making the CEO look good may be the most important part of the in-house producer's job and may, indeed, be the reason the video specialist was hired in the first place.

This chapter, then, presents a discussion of (1) when to use in-house or outside talent and how to choose performers, with the specific goal of matching them to the purpose of the presentation; (2) how advance planning can help you get the best possible on-camera work from your performers; and (3) how to direct talent during a taping.

CHOOSING TALENT

Do you have a choice between hiring professional talent and working with in-house performers? If so, give careful consideration to the professional performer, because in the time-intensive world of video economics your initial efforts at cost saving may backfire.

"Choosing [in-house] talent because it costs less can be a false economy," notes Kim Titus, creative supervisor for Texas Utilities Services, Inc., in Dallas. "Studio time is expensive. Novice talent will take more rehearsal time. The final product will usually not look as professional. If budget is the only or primary reason for using nonprofessional talent, look at all expense factors before making this choice."[1]

One important point is that it is difficult to have a member of the production staff (writer, producer) in a talent position. In addition to the blurring of lines of responsibility, the performer's performance may be compromised because he or she is thinking about production problems.

Many other factors do affect the decision, of course. Both options — expensive professional and inexpensive nonprofessional talent — present pluses and minuses in the production process, and definitive formulas simply don't exist. However, the following discussion does offer some general guidelines.

PROFESSIONAL TALENT

Professionals include people who make their living entirely from on-camera performance or skilled and experienced performers who work part time as on-camera announcers or actors. Often, performers come from the ranks of moonlighting broadcast professionals or from the faculties of college broadcasting departments.

Incidentally, there is an important distinction to be made between announcers and actors. In the most common usage we usually take *announcer* to mean someone who is experienced in reading broadcast copy over the air or cable but who does not, for all intents and purposes, attempt to project another identity when performing. *Actors* are role players; that is, they assume the personality of another person and act out what that person would do in a particular circumstance.

A good announcer is not necessarily a competent actor, and vice versa. Someone adept at reading a narration may be hopelessly inept at playing the part of a salesman. Indeed, announcers in such a situation often project the aura of an announcer reading a salesman's lines. Actors — people used to adopting the mannerisms, speech patterns, and even accents of various characters — can adapt much better to role playing. On the other hand, actors, especially stage-trained actors, frequently do not understand the mechanics of video and do not have the proper delivery for presenting news copy or conducting interviews. Stage actors sometimes have great difficulty playing to a television camera. They are used to speaking and gesturing in ways that will carry to the last row of theater seats, a quality that can seem positively ludicrous on video.

In general, you will be on steadier ground by selecting actors for acting jobs and announcers for announcing jobs (as defined above), but the rule is not iron-clad. In particular, experience has shown that actors often do a better job than announcers when reading long narrations.

How do you contact professionals? That problem is often obviated by the fact that they will contact you. Energetic and ambitious performers, ostensibly the most desirable type, routinely send résumés, glossy portraits (called head shots), and audiotapes or videotapes to in-house production facilities in their area. Word of mouth is also a reliable method. Colleagues in your professional organizations will generally be glad to share their experiences with performers in the area.

Should you require talent and not know how to locate performers, your first step might be to monitor television or radio for a performer who projects the quality you desire. Broadcast performers in all but the largest markets are surprisingly poorly paid, and moonlighting in industrial or institutional productions is a welcome source of additional income for many of them.

Some problems may arise when hiring broadcasters: News reporters are generally, but not always, prohibited from appearing in industrial productions. Occasionally, they are allowed to do voice-only work. Staff announcers, disc jockeys, and other types of TV and radio program hosts do not usually have such stringent restrictions on their moonlighting activities.

Many communities have professional or semiprofessional theater groups that you can contact. Request actors with television experience if they are available. Despite the problems typically associated with stage actors who appear on television, there is a definite advantage in casting from among a pool of actors, as opposed to announcers: Actors come in a variety of "types." Should you need a "distinguished doctor type" or a "Bronx cab driver type," your contact at the theater group will immediately understand your needs.

In very large markets where the producer of an institutional program has significant discretionary funds and a need for talent of the highest quality, talent agents may be the best contact. (Look in the Yellow Pages under "talent agencies," or, better yet, ask a contact at an advertising agency for a referral to a reliable agent.) Agents will supply you with prospects from a variety of clients in their "stables" and can usually provide a photo and videotape or audiotape. Advertising agencies also typically receive tapes from performers, and they may be willing to share these with you.

Performers represented by agents are almost always members of unions, notably the American Federation of Television and Radio Artists (AFTRA) or the Screen Actors Guild (SAG). The guild is primarily concerned with productions shot on film. Union scale can be high, and you must comply with union regulations concerning audition procedures and on-site working conditions. Local AFTRA and SAG offices will usually be quite helpful in explaining those procedures. Note that expenses for talent vary from market to market and according to the type of job to be performed.

As alluded to earlier, as a producer you often get what you pay for, and an initially higher talent cost may translate into a payback in the long run. However, there are diverse advantages and disadvantages associated with professional talent.

Advantages of Professional Talent   For one thing, obviously, professionals are more competent. They are less anxious about the experience of performing on television and have a much better understanding of the technical requirements. For example, teaching an amateur how to handle a prop so as not to have it glare into the camera can involve many expensive minutes of studio time and several retakes.

A second advantage of professionals is their credibility. Although it is a mistake to assume that effective in-house video must always emulate popular broadcast television,[2] it is often an advantage to use a performer who can give a polished appearance to the show.

Finally, professional performers work for you. You pay their salary, and as a result you can expect that your directions will be followed and that they will be on the set and ready to work at the appointed time. Such is most assuredly not the case when dealing with executives of your firm, who may be uncooperative or may cancel appearances to accommodate an appointment they deem more important.

Disadvantages of Professional Talent Professional performers are naturally more expensive. In addition to the hourly or daily rate you must pay, most performers will have a guaranteed minimum amount of time during a day for which they must be paid. This is, on examination, a fair arrangement: A performer simply cannot afford to dress in the required clothing, put on makeup, and travel across town for half an hour of work.

Availability can also be a problem. Performers have other jobs, and should you run over your shooting schedule, there is no guarantee that the performer you featured will be available tomorrow, next week, or next month. Moreover, if a section of the presentation needs to be reshot in a year, it is quite possible that the performer will no longer be available. In-house talent may tend to stay with the company for quite a while and be available for retakes months or years down the road.

A third disadvantage is that even the most experienced performer may not be able to convince the viewer that he or she is an expert in thermonuclear physics. If that's what is mandated by circumstances, the physicist may be the only viable choice for on-camera work.

NONPROFESSIONAL TALENT

Most in-house productions are constructed around the available on-camera performers. They may be the chief executive officer, a training expert, or someone who simply possesses a unique insight into the topic at hand.

What follows are some of the advantages and disadvantages of working with nonprofessionals. The remainder of this chapter will focus on ways to improve their performance (the most immediately visible element of your production). Of course, any and all points on planning and execution presented in the chapter will certainly apply (in a more limited scope) to working with professional talent as well.

Advantages of Nonprofessional Talent   Because the people in the production work for your organization, they are likely to be on hand for extended periods. They will usually be on the site. When assigned by their supervisor to work on your production, they have some inherent motivation to perform responsibly and well.

You won't have to pay talent fees or travel expenses to nonprofessional talent. It is rare for departments that contribute personnel as performers to insist on any intramural payback arrangement.

Lastly, nonprofessional performers usually have more interest and knowledge. As an example, consider the common in-house video scenario involving an experienced sales representative demonstrating a piece of equipment. He or she has an inherent desire to make the production as effective as possible; at the most basic level this desire arises from the idea that the show could translate into increased personal income. In addition, the sales rep understands the workings of the product and can frequently offer invaluable advice on better ways to structure the presentation. It is worth noting, though, that this understanding can turn into a disadvantage if the person insists on numerous script changes.

Certain cases demand the presence of the real thing: If the CEO must respond to a serious allegation, the CEO is the only man or woman for the job.

Disadvantages of Nonprofessional Talent   Performance anxiety can be a problem for nonprofessionals. Possibly the most notable difference between professional and nonprofessional talent is the fact that television represents a threatening situation to the amateur. To put this problem in perspective, bear in mind that studies have shown fear of public speaking to be the most pervasive phobia among those surveyed, in some cases even surpassing the fear of serious disease. For many, speaking on television is even more terrifying than appearing before groups. Nervous performers, at least those paralyzed by their nerves, can be very difficult people with whom to work.

Awkwardness with the technical constraints of the medium is a second disadvantage. Executives often have great difficulty reading a prompting device, looking directly into the camera lens, or handling props. It is difficult and, in some cases, impossible to correct such problems without extensive coaching. Busy, high-powered executives (and those who envision themselves as busy and high-powered) frequently cannot or will not take the time to practice in the studio environment and critically assess their performance.

A related disadvantage involves problems with the power structure. It can be difficult to offer criticism, even the most constructive criticism, to a major executive. Quite frankly, executives are often defensive about advice from those whom they do not regard as their peers. (If such criticism must be made, it should be done in private.) But the most vexing problem often has to do with scheduling. Major executives cancel appointments often, and they may have no conception of or concern with the drastic impact that a cancellation has on your shooting schedule.

Furthermore, an executive who fares poorly on a television production may blame you. Truly, this is a classic damned-if-you-do and damned-if-you-don't situation.

These problems are not insurmountable. Several methods alleviate or eliminate many of the drawbacks associated with nonprofessional talent. Proper planning is the first step in the process; innovative on-set directing and coaching techniques can further polish the performance of your talent.

PLANNING FOR ON–AIR PRESENTATIONS

Video producers, who are generally task- and action-oriented, like to keep planning time to a minimum. There is nothing inherently wrong with this preference. Veteran producers can often plan with great efficiency, because their experience has shown them the proper way to order priorities and allocate time. But poor planning can cost time and money, and nowhere does time more directly translate into money than in the television studio or on the remote set, where costs per hour can run into the hundreds or possibly thousands of dollars. Methods of planning the production itself were detailed extensively in Part 2, but here we will take up the oft-neglected concept of preparing talent. This job may be handled by the producer or delegated to a subordinate.

GOALS OF TALENT PREPARATION

In addition to the expense involved in wasting studio time, logistical matters mandate the most efficient use of time possible when producing institutional video. Training tapes, for example, must often be produced on deadline, usually to correspond to the installation of new equipment or procedures, such as a changeover to a new computer system. There is little if any time to be spared in the studio for preparation of the speaker, announcer, or presenter. Such preparation could have and should have been done out of studio.

The same caveat applies to a message from the chief executive officer. Such messages are often prepared in response to a specific timely situation, and the time pressure is intense. There is simply no time to send out for a change of clothes if the executive appears on the set inappropriately attired for a TV appearance. Schedules just cannot accommodate an extended tutorial on how to use the prompter. There is no cushion in most corporate or institutional video situations for endless retakes of flubbed lines.

As an in-house producer, you have as one of your primary responsibilities the preparation of talent for what may be a traumatic and difficult situation. Such preparation could be general (on-camera training for executives) or specific (an office conference to go over what will be included in tomorrow's presentation). In many cases such training can involve introducing an executive to proper television demeanor, an increasingly important task because television is a common fact of corporate life today. George Glazer, senior vice president of Hill and Knowlton, one of the nation's most prominent public relations firms, maintains that "it's unthinkable that a CEO of even a medium-sized corporation won't be on TV at least twice a year in some form, whether it's a teleconference, a videotape, or a guest of a network business program."[3]

Advance planning for CEOs is not the only aspect of an institutional producer's talent preparation. Other planning responsibilities may revolve around preparing a training director to give a video demonstration of a piece of equipment or preparing a sales manager's video presentation on the key sales points for a new product line. Many acted scenes, such as demonstrations of the proper method to carry out a performance review, can be extensively planned and rehearsed off camera. Even executives' appearances on teleconferences, which are difficult situations to rehearse, can be immeasurably improved by knowledge of the medium's requirements. Sometimes, institutional directors are required to work with child actors. This can prove extraordinarily difficult; children may panic or simply refuse to cooperate. Be sure to "screen-test" any child scheduled to appear in your production.

In each case *you* will profit immeasurably from meeting with nonprofessional performers and informing them what will be expected. Optimally, you will have the opportunity to rehearse some of the lines and possibly videotape the talent and critique one or more playbacks. Videotaping can be done in an office setting with portable equipment or in studio without a full crew during nonpeak times. (Sometimes, this process can backfire. Performers may become upset by their appearance and become more flustered.) Following are the most basic categories to be considered during your planning session with prospective talent.

Clothing   Video producers sometimes approach the matter of clothing from a mechanical, rather than an aesthetic, viewpoint. When executives ask you, "What should I wear?" (a very common question), think first in terms of image rather than appearance. For example, a corporate executive explaining the necessity for budget cutbacks in the firm would not be well-advised to appear in his taped message wearing a $600 suit and a white-on-white shirt with diamond cuff links. The impression, for obvious reasons, will be all wrong. Rolled-up shirt sleeves would be a much better option.

The engineering director of a plant who is appearing on a training tape stressing the safety of chemical-handling procedures might make a better impression in a white lab coat. A teacher delivering a videotaped lecture is certainly allowed to look like a teacher. Tweed jackets and sweaters are not out of line in such a case. These guidelines generally prove adequate in planning what on-air talent will wear:

≡ Solid-color suits for men and women are generally the best choice. Patterns can be distracting and, in some cases, will not register well on camera. Herringbone patterns, in particular, can cause video problems. Dark or medium blue is always a good choice for a solid-color suit. In addition to being non-distracting, they tend to make the wearer look thinner, almost always desirable on television.

≡ Women who wear dresses should avoid patterns, if possible. Many dresses are manufactured in patterns that simply do not appear well on video. Jewelry, for men and women, should be minimized. Women's earrings, for example, can be very distracting if they are too large. Sometimes, reflection from jewelry can cause problems with glare. Also, warn women not to wear necklaces, as they can touch a lavaliere microphone and create unwanted noise.

≡ Socks must cover a man's calf. Pant legs can and do ride up during interviews.

≡ White shirts are perfectly acceptable for most television appearances today. There was a time when color cameras could not handle the contrast between a white shirt and a dark suit, but most equipment is not bothered by white shirts. Some older and less expensive gear will be affected, though, and in that case a blue shirt is a better option. It is advisable to warn talent not to wear black suits. A black suit and a white shirt can cause contrast problems, even on good equipment, and in any event black suits carry a funereal association that is rarely appropriate for television.

≡ Usually, tighter clothing will appear better on television. A fairly tight, dark-blue suit of a lightweight fabric will make its wearer look better than a bulky, heavy suit. Lightweight suits are also useful because TV studios often get hot.

Demeanor   The very qualities that may combine to produce a successful businessperson may undermine her appearance on television. Executives, in general, value a sedate appearance and a businesslike, understated verbal delivery. Those qualities can be deadly on television, and there is usually no way to do a "quick fix" on your talent's delivery. Plan the delivery in advance by advising your talent of three factors.

First, television requires a higher energy level than does ordinary conversation. The natural inclination of most people is to assume that because their entire being will be compressed into a little box, their activity and intensity must be scaled down. But just the opposite is true.

Although it is advisable to limit physical movements, it is essential for the talent to project a high energy level. As a medium television is enervating; that is, it tends to dissipate the apparent energy level of a performer.[4] Probably the most common complaint lodged against poor performers is that they failed to project enough energy. Warn your talent about this property of video.

A second factor is that gestures and posture must be appropriate. Warn performers in advance that stiff or exaggerated gestures do not play well on television. Advise them that when they are standing, the best place for their hands is held loosely at the sides. Standing hand positions are always a problem with nonprofessional talent. One way to help is to tell performers to keep their fingers loosely apart and to keep one hand in a slightly different position from the other, to avoid "soldier hands." When seated, performers usually hold their hands loosely on the lap. Seated men will look better on camera with their legs crossed at the knee or ankles. If a man feels comfortable in such a position, he can also sit with both feet flat on the floor. He must never, though, spread his knees. Women should cross their legs at the ankles.

Finally, it is important for talent to sit up straight. Slouching postures are negatively exaggerated by properties of the lens, clothes do not hang well when performers slouch, and breathing is made more difficult when they slump.

The best time to inform the talent of these considerations is, of course, long before the cameras roll. If you are directing, or acting as on-site producer supervising the director and crew, you will have enough trouble on your hands during taping without having to do remedial work with your talent. Guidelines for clothing and demeanor, similar to those listed above, are often written down and sent in advance to those who will appear on camera. At the very least you should discuss these fundamentals of on-camera appearance with talent well in advance of production.

Releases   Be sure to have all performing talent sign a release giving you the right to use them in your production. It is advisable to have releases signed before you do any taping, in case someone very necessary to the production has a change of heart after seeing his or her performance.

It would be worthwhile to consult with senior executives in your department on the exact contents of your talent release; situations do differ, and your legal department may have specific requirements. (Note that it is especially important to have a release signed by a parent or guardian when using minors.)

Try to make release-signing a matter of routine. If you ask all performers to sign a release as soon as they step on the set, the process will appear to be standard operating procedure, which it is. The choice of whether to ask your CEO to sign a release is yours and depends on the situation.

PLANNING FOR APPROPRIATE DELIVERY OF THE SCRIPT

Meeting with talent early in planning a production will allow you to adapt the script to the speaker. E. Carlton Winckler, the senior production consultant and director of the education division of Imero Florentino Associates in New York, advises an early meeting "to become familiar with the subject's mannerisms and speech patterns so the script can be adjusted to fit them. A commentary may be well written, clear in its wording, but at the same time it may not speak well, or it can be foreign to the presenter's manner."[5]

Can the performer handle the script (or other performance task) as planned? If not, how can it be adjusted to fit the talent? Those questions are not always easy ones, but several strategies are available to the producer of industrial television.

Most importantly, be sure that the script itself is speakable. As professional announcers know from painful experience, there is a huge difference between a script that reads well eye-to-mind and one that works eye-to-mouth-to-mind. For example, try reading the following line out loud:

> It is imperative that we do not allow our organization to fall behind the competition, and therefore we must cut costs or increase sales, and the former is the only viable option.

While (barely) acceptable as a printed statement in an annual report, the statement is very difficult to read and to understand once it has been read. What is "the former"? The listener cannot go back and refer to the sentence to deduce the former or the latter option. Notice also how the line has an awkward, unnatural rhythm.

Unfortunately, many lines such as this do wind up in corporate scripts. The only cure is early excision, before the words wind up in the mouths of your performers. Suppose, for example, that the performer speaking this line is a hard-driving, vibrant executive. You certainly would not want to hamstring him or her with such flat, lifeless copy. Instead, consider having the executive point a finger to the camera, and say:

> Competition in this business is brutal — you people in the field know that better than I do. We've only got two choices: Cut costs, or increase sales. But the market right now is limited. I think cost cutting is our only option.

Be sure to read any script out loud as you write it.

A second strategy is to avoid "committee-speak." One reason such terrible lines are fed to talent is that the various people involved in constructing the script introduce unspeakable language and sentence structure. An engineering executive, for example, may insist on including a technical disclaimer that could not have been delivered convincingly by Laurence Olivier.

A cure for this problem is to read your proposed script aloud to the committees involved. Avoid, if at all possible, letting members read and change a printed script. (You can satisfy their desires for input by circulating a written memo describing the content and asking for suggestions.) Read the script out loud; when the person with whom you are meeting suggests an alteration, ask him or her to suggest an alternative. Write down what he or she says, and read the new line back.

Finally, realistically assess the ability of the on-camera players. Although you usually cannot hold auditions for in-house personnel, you can frequently get an idea of their capabilities during the formation of the program. Whenever possible, shift the majority of the presentation to the people in whom you feel some confidence.

How can you evaluate prospective performers? Experience with people on previous productions is, obviously, the most reliable predictor. But you can learn a great deal during an initial meeting with the talent. You might, for example, ask a sales manager "what you think of this line in the script" and induce her to read it out loud. She will, thus, be auditioned while thinking she is advising you on script structure.

Look to assign the majority of on-camera work to people who express interest and animation off camera. The low-energy executive who displays a blasé attitude during a preproduction meeting is likely to perform terribly on camera. Do not, however, be excessively worried about prospective performers who profess trepidation about appearing on television. People who are worried about appearing well on camera are often worried about doing a good job, precisely the type of person you want working on your project. Nerves can usually be calmed in preproduction meetings and again on set.

WORKING ON THE SET

Nonprofessional performers need a great deal of assistance and support during tapings, and the director or producer must bear much of the ultimate responsibility for their appearance and performance. Many editing sessions result in a bout of collective hair pulling as production people reflect on how the guests, hosts, or roundtable participants turned in such awful, awkward, and inept performances.

Such problems cannot be fixed after production, of course. You must head off talent-related disasters before or during the production. This responsibility primarily centers on three tasks: overcoming performers' stage fright, coaching them to work appropriately within the confines of the studio or remote shooting site, and helping them deliver their lines well.

OVERCOMING STAGE FRIGHT

Television equipment can make people nervous, but in strict terms it is the performers who make themselves nervous. There is no real, physical threat posed by the camera; it is the performer's anxiety that causes problems. A good floor director (the chief crew member in the studio) can alleviate much of this fear by informing the talent of two factors.

The first suggestion is to tell performers: "Even if you are very frightened, no one will notice." An exaggeration, really, but it is quite true that audiences are very poor at perceiving stage fright, a finding borne out by a large body of research. Audiences simply cannot tell when a speaker is nervous unless the speaker totally falls to pieces, which happens with extreme rarity and only when fear of the fear takes over. The "fear of fear itself" is a feedback reaction, in which fright causes physical symptoms, which cause, in turn, more fear. Break the fear cycle by informing the performer that his or her nervousness is likely not to be detected by the camera.

Secondly, "Being nervous helps your performance." Even the most experienced performers feel stage fright. Barbra Streisand, for example, generally becomes physically ill before a concert. But she, and all other competent performers, uses her nervous energy to galvanize her performance. Some people feel no emotional qualms about most aspects of life, and those people are by and large terrible performers. They appear flat, lifeless, and uninterested. Up to the point of panic, where the performer cannot function, tension will always help, rather than hurt, on-camera performance.

Familiarity with the equipment and process is another factor in calming anxiety. It is advisable to give the talent a complete explanation of what is going to happen: for example, that the cameras may move during production and that the lights may soon feel very hot. Tell performers that the floor director is their link to the director and that the floor director will be the one who provides talent with cues. Also, note that it may be advisable to have the director disable or mask the tally lights (the red lights on the camera that indicate when it is on the air); tallies sometimes confuse and distract talent.

It is usually not advisable to tell performers that the segment can be taped over and over until it's right. This can result in a perfectionist attitude on the part of your talent and can additionally cause you, the producer, to have to deal with 40 takes in which the performer yells, "Cut!" In most cases tell performers that you are trying to make the next take the one you use, even if you are not. Remember, too, that the talent's conception of perfection may not be good video. (However, it is useful to inform performers that more than one take may be necessary because of unforeseen or uncontrollable circumstances.)

Experienced announcers learn early in their careers that doing 20 takes of a spot does not produce a significantly better selection from which to choose than doing only 3 takes. Sometimes, the prospect of many takes is detrimental, because the performer feels exhausted and overwhelmed even before the project begins. In sum, keep expected takes to a minimum.

You can frequently help nervous performers overcome anxiety and reduce the number of takes by doing one or two rehearsal takes. Clearly indicate that the takes are for rehearsal, and tell the performers that they are "helping you out" by delivering their lines (so you can check your camera angles, see if the lighting works, and the like). This takes much of the performance onus off of the talent. A playback of the take will allow performers to observe themselves in a nonjudgmental way

FIGURE 8.1

A prompting device is basically a one-way mirror located in front of the TV camera lens. The mirror reflects script shown on a monitor located below the unit.

Courtesy Philip Benoit, *Announcing: Broadcast Communicating Today* (Belmont, CA: Wadsworth, 1987).

(after all, they weren't really trying to look good, but only helping you) and adjust their performance for the real take.

WORKING WITH EQUIPMENT

Whatever performance anxiety is encountered on set is often directly related to the presence of the TV equipment and the generally unnatural setting caused by that equipment. Although experienced performers can perform quite naturally in a cramped set with blazing lights, such an environment is foreign and hostile to the newcomer.

Explaining the equipment and process, as mentioned above, will help. However, some specific areas cause frequent problems and need available remedies. Prompting devices (Figure 8.1), for example, sometimes cause concern to nonprofessional talent. But there is often no other option. So-called idiot cards are rarely effective with nonprofessional talent, because the performer's gaze is so obviously diverted from the camera.

If you do elect to use cards (which are sometimes useful when they serve as an outline of points to be ad-libbed), hold them below the lens, not to the side. It is very natural for people to look down when collecting their thoughts. It is unnatural — and "shifty" looking — for performers to look to the side. Make sure to check for nearsighted or farsighted performers when determining how far away to place the camera and cards.

The most common difficulty caused by prompting devices is that the performer is afraid that he or she will not be able to keep pace with the machine.

FIGURE 8.2

People who have trouble adjusting to someone else's rate of running text on a prompting device can use this small, inconspicuous control to control their own rate of text scrolling while reading into the camera.

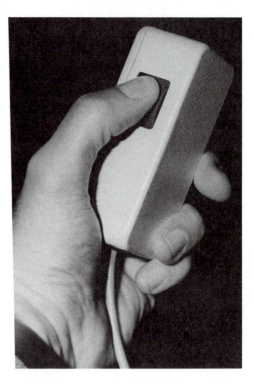

Although a real fear to the talent, prompter phobia is unrealistic from a technical standpoint. Depending on the size of the script, a prompting device can easily display seven lines of copy. A competent prompter operator will usually have no trouble keeping the scroll rolling at a pace that can accommodate the talent.

Another option is to allow performers to run their own prompters with a hand-held control (Figure 8.2). This is sometimes not the best option, because it gives an already preoccupied performer one more physical action to worry about, and it can negatively affect the timing of the delivery.

A proven technique to overcome prompter problems is to instruct talent to read the third line from the top of the screen during the performance. This leaves enough cushion at the top so that performers are not worried about having their lines cut off, and it allows a generous amount of copy displayed on the bottom to reassure them that they will not be kept waiting for new lines. Realistically, performers will eventually be reading copy from all areas of the screen, but focusing on the third line bolsters confidence and gives the prompter operator a target for controlling the pace of the machine.

Incidentally, the discussion of performers' reactions to prompting devices primarily centers on their *initial* reactions. Once the director helps them overcome primary trepidations about the prompter, they often begin to very much enjoy using the device.

A second piece of equipment that needs special attention is lights, which cause severe problems for many performers, both psychologically and physically. Psychologically, bright lights isolate them from their surroundings (they simply cannot see past the circle of lights) and have unsavory mental connotations — interrogation and the dentist's office, to name only two. Physically, harsh lights cause performers to squint and, in some cases, perspire.

These psychological and physical problems can often be overcome by a more careful lighting job. There is a strong temptation among some producers to throw up more light until the scene looks bright enough. But the appropriate option is to use better-placed light, not more light. Whenever possible, eliminate a shadow by repositioning the key and fill instead of simply plugging in another floodlight. As you remember from basic production, the key light is the instrument that provides the direct, primary light on the subject. The fill light does exactly what it says: It fills in the harsh shadows created by the key light.

Higher positioning of lights can eliminate some of the squinting problem. Very good lighting can be achieved with instruments hung or mounted on stands quite high and quite far away from performers. Resist the temptation to use low lights very close to the performers. They are easier to position, but the drawbacks outweigh the initial benefits.

You can alleviate some of the lighting problems encountered by performers who feel uncomfortable because of the resemblance of a TV studio to a police lineup by leaving the room lights in the set on during the take, although some directors don't like to do this, with good reason. For one thing, having room lights on affects color temperatures, the mix of "cool" red lights and "hot" bluish lights. Secondly, if there is a great deal of activity in the studio, it can distract performers and prove counterproductive.

Be particularly sensitive to the problems encountered by performers who wear contact lenses. Bright lights can be irritating and sometimes painful to them. Try turning the lights off during long breaks between takes; this will cool the room and make performers more comfortable.

Eyes are also involved in what is probably the most common problem among TV neophytes: where to look during a performance. Give performers very clear instructions:

≡ "If you are interviewing a guest, look into the camera for the opening and closing of the segment[s], but look at your guest at other times."

≡ "If you are a guest on an interview program, ignore the camera. Look directly at the host."

≡ "When you speak to the camera, look directly into the center of the lens. Even a tiny diversion is obvious."

≡ "It is not necessary or desirable to maintain eye contact during each and every second of on-camera performance, even if a prompter is used. Do not be reluctant to look down to gather your thoughts or even to examine notes. But don't look to the side. Do not be afraid to blink, either. Blinking is far less distracting than a fishy-eyed stare."

DELIVERING LINES

The quality of the final production can, as mentioned, depend to an enormous extent on the quality of the performer's delivery. It is on set during the performance that you can play what may be the most critical role in the success or failure of your production. You must prod, exhort, challenge, and motivate your talent to give the best performance possible. There are three good ways to accomplish those tasks.

First, coach talent to read for meaning. This sounds obvious, but it is not. Inexperienced performers (and some experienced ones, too) read words and not thoughts. For example, a performer merely reciting words can put completely inaccurate stresses on the thoughts contained in the sentence:

> A job *review* is a *good* opportunity to let *employees* express their thoughts, and to *make* them feel as though they are an important part of the *company*.

This example — a real one, by the way — shows how a poor delivery alters meaning and hinders communication. Often, inexperienced performers seek to "punch up" their delivery by adding stress to various words, but the stress is frequently added to the wrong words. Read the above example aloud. Now read the following example:

> A *job review* is a good opportunity to let employees express *their thoughts*, and to make them feel as though they are *an important part* of the company.

Note that the second example even makes some sense when the key words — those that receive stress — are spoken in isolation: "job review . . . their thoughts . . . an important part."

Writers, artists, and other creative people often use a similar technique to clarify their ideas. Theater set designers, for example, must make simple structures to convey complex messages. They sometimes play a mental game that involves distilling a play into a paragraph, then into a sentence, and then into one word. The approach is obviously oversimplified, but it does force them to think about the most essential points that must be communicated.

Use the idea of reading for communication when working with your talent. If circumstances allow, underline or capitalize key words in the script. The key words are those that express the distilled thrust of the sentences and paragraphs.

In some cases you may be able to simply ask the performer to stress the appropriate words. Done in a nonthreatening way, such suggestions can significantly improve the final product.

A second guideline is to coach performers to focus on the line they are delivering. Poor deliveries often result from their preoccupation with whether they will remember all the copy to follow, and the line being delivered suffers.

It is very productive to develop strategies so that performers will not feel as though they are confronted by an impossibly large task (memorizing huge blocks of copy or reading five minutes of copy error-free from a prompter). One way to cope with this problem is to shoot the scene from multiple camera positions, single-camera video style, and edit the takes together. You can, for example, have the performer speak two sentences to the camera in a straight-ahead medium shot. Then the camera position can be changed, and another two sentences can be delivered (with a head turn) to a close-up at a different angle. Taping can be stopped and two more sentences delivered to the same camera, same angle, with the expectation that cover video will be used to obscure the jump cut.

What you've done is to break the performer's task into bite-sized pieces; he or she has to memorize only two lines at a time. The results will almost always be a vast improvement over the effort of an inexperienced performer obviously struggling to remember the copy. The time to plan such inserts, of course, is before the performance. You may create more work for yourself in the editing room, but in the long run you may save takes and actually conserve your time.

You can use this technique to virtually eliminate the need for memorization and also inspire better performances by feeding the lines to talent. Read the line aloud and ask the performer to repeat it. In this way you can convey the inflection you want ("Please look right into the lens and say, 'You can save *money* because this equipment uses *much less power*'") and take some of the onus off the performer. You can also produce several takes very quickly.

A third overall suggestion is to coach performers to be themselves. There is no point in having a performer attempt to impersonate the delivery of a network anchor. He or she is a chemist, an engineer, or a financial manager but not an anchor. Imitation, conscious or unconscious, can make the performer look ridiculous. Coach your performers not to artificially lower the pitch of their voices and not to break into unnatural disc-jockey cadences.

By the same token you will extract much better performances by convincing your performers to honestly display their true emotions. If a corporate training manager is excited about a new computer system, convince him or her to show that excitement. There is no need to blunt such emotions.

These three techniques are commonly used by directors in all media, and they represent a synthesis of many of the methods used to extract good performances. In sum, it might be best to remember that *characterization* is the ultimate goal of all performers, whether they are playing themselves or someone else.

Although it is not traditionally thought of as a part of institutional television directing, the interdisciplinary marriage of directing techniques is playing an increasing role. Many directors strive for that all-important characterization, and any observer of the medium can note that performances are, by and large, improving.

Remember the advice from the acting teacher Konstantin Stanislavsky: It is the sum of many small physical actions, and the audience's belief in those actions, that helps produce a character.[6] This means that all elements — gestures, clothing, rate of speech, facial expression, voice pattern — are the threads from which the fabric of believability is woven.

And finally, don't forget that your role as a director involves translating those qualities to video. Experts such as the Broadway director Aaron Frankel point out that actors' *personal qualities* do not always translate to their stage or television identity.[7] It is up to you to make sure that the intelligent and urbane executive appears intelligent and urbane on camera. That will not always happen by itself; you must make it happen by translating reality to video via your knowledge of the medium.

SUMMARY

≡ Talent is the most visible production element in an institutional television program. Performances can make or break your program. In some cases the producer's job is to make people associated with an organization, particularly the CEO, perform well on TV.

≡ Professional talent costs more initially, but it may be worth it in the long run because experienced performers require fewer takes and less studio time.

≡ It is important to do as much talent preparation as possible before going into the studio. Studio time is too expensive and production time too limited for extended tutorials.

≡ The script must be fit to the available talent. Meet with performers; adjust the words to their abilities and mannerisms.

≡ Make performers comfortable. Do not blind them with lights; show them the proper use of the prompter.

≡ Instruct performers to be themselves. They should not attempt to ape the deliveries of professional announcers.

EXERCISES

1. Pair off with a classmate or co-worker. Each of you will write a two-paragraph section of copy explaining the workings of some device with which you are familiar and that can be shown on camera. If you are a photographer, for example, write a script describing how to change lenses. If you are an avid tennis player, write a script explaining the advantages (or disadvantages) of wood racquets over metal ones. You must coach your partner in delivering the lines and handling the props. If equipment is available, produce the demonstration. Do not be reluctant to ask for precisely the delivery that expresses the idea you want to communicate. (Your partner will eventually do the same process involved in this exercise and exercise 2.)

2. If time and facilities allow, repeat the process, but this time you will perform your own script and demonstration, acting as your own expert commentator. You can do this on camera, if available, or simply before the class. Evaluate both demonstrations, and see if you can detect a difference between your partner's performance and yours. Which was more convincing? Which flowed more easily? The results may surprise you; if so, discuss the reasons why.

3. Assume that you must cast actors for three productions.
   a. An actor will deliver a videotaped message that will defuse a potential labor action.
   b. An actor will demonstrate a piece of scientific equipment. As part of the demonstration, the actor must express a great deal of wonderment and enthusiasm for the equipment.

c.   An actor must inject some life into a rather long and boring presentation on company financial plans.

Hypothetically cast a well-known actor, male or female, for each role. In a brief paper explain your reasons for each choice.

NOTES

1.   Kim Titus, "Directing Professional Talent," *International Television* (September 1984): 80–83.

2.   "Video through the Eyes of the Trainee," *Training: The Magazine of Human Source Development* (July 1987): 57–59.

3.   Quoted in "Making the CEO Look like a Million," *Business TV* (Fall 1987): 36–37.

4.   For a discussion of energy level and ways to increase it see Lewis B. O'Donnell, Carl Hausman, and Philip Benoit, *Announcing: Broadcast Communicating Today* (Belmont, CA: Wadsworth, 1987): 62–63, 74.

5.   "When the Director Calls," *Video Systems* (September 1986): 22–26. For another discussion of working with amateur talent see "Nat Eisenberg: Directing Non-Professionals," *Educational and Industrial Television* (March 1987): 43–45.

6.   See Konstantin Stanislavsky, *Building a Character* (New York: Theater Arts Books, 1977).

7.   Advice given to the author during instruction taken at the HB Academy in New York.

CHAPTER 9

STUDIO PRODUCTION

TECHNIQUES

Modern television studios and control rooms are high-tech environments; an unknowledgeable observer might be hard pressed to distinguish a video switcher panel from the controls of a jetliner. But the advancing technology can be both a blessing and a curse to the in-house producer. First of all, the type of equipment that can produce the most sophisticated effects is, even though prices are declining relative to technology, stunningly expensive. Secondly, sophisticated facilities require sophisticated personnel to use and maintain them.

This chapter, however, does not present a catalog of hardware and lavish production facilities. For one thing, equipment changes so rapidly that any attempt to survey the "latest" developments would be futile. Above and beyond that, television production is television production, whether it is done with old or new equipment. *If you know the fundamentals of any piece of television production equipment, you can pick up the particulars of a new model in a few days.* The principles of good video are always the same. Producers enamored of gimmickry can produce glitzy but artistically poor video. It is far too common to observe producers and directors spending valuable time setting up elaborate technical effects for a production that features bad camera work, poor lighting, and illogical editing sequences. If you have invested your time in learning the *fundamentals of production*, you will be able to adapt quickly to new equipment. But if you have concentrated on learning the rote mechanics that produce the fanciest gimmicks, you will have a difficult road ahead.

This book assumes that you have already taken one or more classes in production or directing. However, if you are a manager in charge of production — and have, yourself, little hands-on experience — the list of suggested readings at the end of this book provides sources for acquiring a working knowledge of the basics.

This chapter presents the fundamentals of studio production as they specifically relate to institutional video. It also surveys methods of directing an institutional production as well as editing techniques specific to this form of video.

BASICS OF STUDIO PRODUCTION

This chapter focuses on the fundamental needs of an institutional producer in his or her studio environment. Note that the next chapter gives the same perspective on *field* production.

LIGHTS, CAMERAS, AND ACTION

First, be aware that the operations of an institutional video studio are often quite different from those of a commercial television station. Also keep in mind that much of the training given in college classes is still geared toward commercial video work. There are two major contrasts.

First, the institutional studio is likely to be smaller than the commercial studio, and the staff is not as large or as specialized. Engineering help is typically in short supply in institutional video. This factor is quite clearly reflected by the type of equipment popular in institutional settings. Modern cameras, for example, are much easier to use than their ancestors (Figure 9.1). The solid-state-chip camera is rapidly becoming the technology of choice in many institutional environments because it needs little repair and does not require the complex engineering support and adjustment frequently necessary for tube cameras.[1] Some broadcasters, though, are willing to put up with the complexities of tube cameras because they feel the tube devices produce a richer, less harsh picture. That is a perfectly

(a)

(b)

FIGURE 9.1

A three-chip video camera (*a*) uses chips instead of tubes, making it lighter and not so vulnerable to damage. Another easy-to-use camera (*b*) features extensive self-diagnostic indicators and an auto-setup function.

Courtesy (*a*) Sony Communications Products Company and (*b*) Ikegami Electronics (U.S.A.), Inc.

reasonable choice for a broadcast station with a large engineering staff; it is less realistic for the majority of in-house departments.

The second major contrast with commercial video is that, in *general*, an institutional producer will not have a highly specialized crew. This usually does not present a problem until disaster strikes. For example, a broadcast audio crew member with 20 years of experience doing nothing but audio can usually track down a microphone phasing problem and fix it before the rest of us have figured out which button to press for the initial check.

FLOW OF A TYPICAL PROGRAM

There is another important difference between institutional and broadcast studio operations: In a broadcast operation the producer and director are dealing with professionals who understand the complex process of putting a show on the air. That is assuredly not the case in institutional video. Studio guests may be much higher in the corporate hierarchy than the production staff and completely intolerant of what they regard as time-wasting inefficiency. This situation is not to be taken lightly. In large organizations the *only* way people know about your department may be the second-hand report of a bald executive who was kept waiting for 15 minutes while you diplomatically tried to make some emergency lighting changes. If that's the case, your department can lose respect ("They sure are disorganized — it took 'em 15 minutes to turn the lights on") in the short run and resources in the long run.

Every circumstance is different, of course, and many of the problems associated with working with amateur talent were covered in the previous chapter. But some additional points relating to the flow of a program may help get things started and keep them moving during an in-studio production.

Before the studio session run a test *tape* of the program setup. It is intuitively obvious that the producer or director should warm up the cameras and check the microphones well in advance of the arrival of studio guests, and that is usually done. But a dismaying share of production problems arises from the video tape recorders or the link between the board and the recorders. Recording and replaying the tape (usually made with crew members in the guests' places) will allow you *and your crew* to objectively view the setup and ensure that you do not, for example, have the VCR patched out of the system.

A second suggestion is to take no chances with microphone setups. The time to figure out where the host's mic comes up on the audio console is not when he or she sits down in the chair. Microphones are responsible for an enormous amount of production delay; check them out well in advance.

Have a crew member, usually the floor director, be "talent coordinator." Guests and talent can be much more cooperative if they know what is going on. Ask the coordinator to keep guests informed. "We're taking a moment to adjust the lights to highlight your dark suit" will always be more welcome than letting the guests sit in stony silence while crew members "fiddle" with the lighting instruments.

Finally, during a taped program keep a careful record of any mistakes that can be fixed immediately following production. Note, by frame number or running time (depending on your equipment), any flubs made by you or the performers. That way, you can immediately check the tape and evaluate the situation. You may be able to fix a problem that would be insoluble if the guests had left. For example, suppose your announcer has made an obvious mistake, once calling a guest "Mr. Kirkpatrick" when the guest's name is Mr. Kilpatrick. You can fix this error by asking the announcer to repeat the sentence and editing the shot in later. But you will need to know what the situation was (who was on camera, what was the shot) in order to make a usable piece of cover video before the host and guests leave the studio. Conversely, assume that *you* ruined the shot, accidentally punching up color bars instead of a camera. You might recue the tape to that point and cover the flub with a staged reaction shot from a cooperative guest. This can even be edited in on the spot by making a video-only insert.

THE CREW

Crew availabilities vary greatly in institutional video. Some studio installations feature fixed-focused cameras locked in place, for example, whereas other studio arrangements call for a full camera crew making complex dollies and zooms.

If you enjoy the luxury of a full-time, highly trained crew, you can simply employ the basics of good TV production and shotmaking. However, many institutional studio productions, usually special, short-notice projects, involve crew members who are interns, newly acquired production assistants, or conscripts from other departments. Following are some basic principles for working with an inexperienced studio production crew.

To begin with, appoint your most experienced crew member as floor director. (He or she may have to run a camera as well, of course.) Be sure that the entire studio crew knows that the floor director is their link upward in the chain of command.

Second, if you have three cameras, consider keeping one locked on a cover shot. This camera is a good one on which to station your floor director, who can check from time to time to make sure that it has not been nudged off frame. If you are working with inexperienced camera operators, you will probably need this shot at some point — as an emergency cover — and you will need it in a hurry.

Those who are experienced in television all know that what appears on the studio camera's monitor may not be the same as what appears on the program monitor. Inexperienced or novice camera operators, though, often simply cannot be convinced. Despite your initial instructions on how to frame the shot, they will instinctively return to framing by what they see on their camera monitor. One solution is to have a program monitor visible to the camera operators, but that can distract them. Perhaps a better solution is to mark the *real* frame in grease pencil or masking tape on the camera viewfinder.

A fourth principle is that novice camera operators have difficulty with the concepts of headroom and "noseroom" (looking space). In general, they tend to leave too little headroom; and if they do allow headroom, they often maintain it even on a tight close-up, where it is clearly inappropriate. The need for looking space is generally more easily grasped, but not always. As you direct the program, you can adjust for these shots *before taking them* by giving instructions to the individual camera operators. However, it is better to give such instructions before the show starts (as opposed to making last-minute adjustments over the headphones while the show is running). If you have difficulty communicating the idea, try asking camera operators to keep the eyes of the performers about a third of the way down from the top of the viewfinder. If they have consistent trouble with noseroom, instruct them to mentally divide the viewfinder screen in half from top to bottom and keep the *tip* of the talent's nose aligned with an imaginary line drawn down the middle of the screen. This really does not produce accurate looking room under all circumstances, but it does prod camera operators into making some allowances for the performers' head position and need for looking space.

Finally, be sure to slate all your shots. You can slate either verbally or visually or — preferably — use both methods. A slate simply means an identification of the take number and any other relevant information.

DIRECTING THE PRESENTATION

Dealing with a mix of inexperienced crew members and sometimes self-important performers can be an unenviable job. Such, though, is the task of a director. Teaching directing is obviously beyond the scope of this book, but some considerations can considerably simplify matters for the institutional producer or director.

FUNDAMENTALS

When a show is produced in studio, it is generally an interview show, a company newscast-type program, a message from the VIP, or a demonstration.

Interview Shows   From a director's standpoint, interview programs require accurate and timely cuts between speakers. For directors not experienced in the talk-show genre, things can become a bit confusing. It is not unusual for a director to get entirely "out of sync" with the rapid flow of questions and answers. Three special techniques can be used in directing an interview show.

The first principle is that good directors watch their camera monitors closely in order to determine when someone will speak. Don't become "hooked" on watching the air (program) monitor; you'll be consistently late in picking up responses or interjections. Another hint: *Listen* for the intake of breath when someone is about to speak. This will help you prepare for the camera change.

Secondly, don't be afraid to use your cover shot. Often, the cover (establishing) shot is used only for the opening and closing. It doesn't hurt to go back to it from time to time. The viewer will become accustomed to seeing the cover shot, which will be useful in the event that you need it to recover from a mistake made by you, the technical director, or a camera operator.

Lastly, when interview shows fall apart, they usually do so at the beginning or the end. You can help avoid such disasters by ensuring that the host has a *scripted* opening and closing. Try to ensure that the host has the guests' names written down on a notepad or in some way visible. Be sure that the host knows precisely what to say in the opening and closing. "Winging" intros and outros is far more difficult than the uninitiated may expect. Probably the most treacherous portion of the talk show is the closing, especially when the program must end at an exact time. Not only must the host catch the floor director's cues and *wrap* up; he or she must also convince the guest to *shut* up. A director can considerably ease this problem by using theme music for the beginning and end, and playing the music via the studio foldback system when the show should be wrapped up. (A foldback system feeds audio back into the studio but at such a level that it does not cause feedback.) Everyone instinctively knows what the music means, and the show will wrap up naturally.

News Programs   Directors can better cope with the news format by remembering two points.

Newscasts are talent-intensive. Inexperienced performers can look very bad on camera. To make matters worse, we're all used to watching commercial newscasts, which, even in the smallest markets, feature professionals with certain talents, abilities, and experience. For this reason it is often wise for the director not to place heavy burdens on an inexperienced newscaster. As an example, consider editing in sound bites rather than attempting to coach the newscaster into hitting the sound bites cold. (This assumes, of course, that the newscast is not live.) You may be making additional work for yourself in the editing room, because it mechanically takes longer to edit together a show than to do it live, but you may be saving yourself time in the long run.

A second tip is to keep production elements simple. Newscasts are probably (after sporting events) the most difficult of all TV programs to direct. It is hard enough to handle the basics without complicating matters with elaborate effects. A simple graphic placed over the newscaster's shoulder can convey the proper effect without appearing too glitzy.

Messages from the VIP   Message programs require skill and discretion on the part of the director. You want the message to come across, and, of course, you want the VIP to make a good appearance. There are two basic principles.

First, avoid putting your VIP in the guise of a television performer. Do not, as an illustration, put him or her behind an anchor desk. Your VIP will suffer by comparison (and so might you, indirectly). If you choose to shoot the message from the VIP in the studio, rather than in his or her office, try a soft chair (living-room-style rather than office-style) and a potted plant, and perhaps add a soft lighting effect to the background.

Second, don't be afraid to make camera moves. A typical objection lodged against some types of institutional video is that the programs consist of "talking heads." This, really, is a misunderstanding; perhaps more to the point is the viewer's innate dislike of *immobile* talking heads. Notice that we change our visual point of focus during a normal human encounter. We do not stay fixed on one point of view. You can avoid some of the talking-head syndrome simply by mimicking what human eyes would see when entering a room: Start wide, perhaps do a dolly or zoom in, and then cut to a close-up as the VIP turns his or her head to the side (as might really happen if you sat down beside the VIP).

Demonstrations   Showing a product or process can be much more difficult than you might suspect. Three points may help simplify the task.

Always have a good monitor on hand to view your taped replay of test runs of the demonstration. The camera eyepiece simply won't show enough detail to let you know if your framing and lighting are accurate.

A second point is to think about continuity, and think about it constantly. Nothing is more unsettling to the viewer than a sudden movement forward in time. If a covering on an electronic device that is being demonstrated must be replaced, for example, be sure to show that replacement or at least to make reference to it. Otherwise, you'll confuse the viewer.

Finally, keep the perspective as consistent as possible. Don't keep alternating shots taken from the front and the back, or the viewer won't have a clue to what's going on. Try to shoot from eye level if possible. When a shot is not at normal eye level, be sure that narration explains the point of view. ("So that you can see the inside of this device, we're looking straight down into the unit, using a magnified view.")

THINKING AHEAD

Directors need to think several shots in advance to keep them from getting caught without a shot or unprepared to air the appropriate piece of material. In this regard an institutional production is no different from a broadcast show. Some cautions do relate more closely to the institutional director, though.

As discussed earlier, your camera operators may not always have extensive experience. Thus, it is incumbent on the director to carefully check shots before putting them on the air. Focus is almost always a problem; be careful to check for fuzziness before punching up a camera.

Be sure to show your camera operators how to set focus in advance of the production. The best procedure is usually to focus the camera on the important object farthest from the camera. If you're lucky, the operator will not have to adjust focus again. If focus adjustment is necessary, though, it is wise to do it off the air. Should you take a shot and find it fuzzy, go to the cover shot. Then, and only then, work with the camera focus.

By the same token, give careful thought to any on-air move or unusual camera shot. Rehearse dollies, zooms, and trucks several times before the performance. If there is a prop involved, leave absolutely nothing to chance when setting up the shot. Be sure that the performer understands the complexities involved, and make it clear that he or she is responsible for holding the prop in *precisely* the rehearsed position.

TECHNIQUES OF ORGANIZATION

The moment of truth, when you roll and record, need not be traumatic if you have made the proper preparations. When problems occur, they often arise because of a failure of organization that occurred hours or days before the program's beginning.

Some methods of organization have been mentioned earlier in this chapter. Among the most important, and worth repeating, is the warning to run a taped test session before your performers arrive. Following are other techniques to ensure that the program starts on time and proceeds without incident.

First, be sure that you have copies of the script and all other written material. Yes, this sounds ludicrously obvious, but it is simply astounding how many productions have been scuttled because somebody forgot the script, the sheets listing the shots, the prompter scroll, and so forth.

When you arrive at the studio, call together the members of the crew, and clearly give them their assignments. TV crews that are unsure of their responsibilities have a tendency to look busy while doing nothing. This is a reflection of their nervousness with unfamiliar surroundings, and they will generally welcome explicit assignments. Also, be clear on the time schedule, including planned time for breaks. Keep crew members busy. To be blunt, it does not reflect well on you to have important officials see your crew lounging.

Next, fire up all the equipment to make sure it is working. Don't wait a second longer than necessary to do this. If you catch a technical problem early, you may be able to fix it before air (or tape) time.

The two biggest causes of production delays are lights and microphones. Work on these elements right from the start. Point, balance, and measure the output of lighting instruments immediately; you may have to spend considerable time in adjusting them. If possible, use similarly complected stand-ins for light adjustment. Plug in the mics, find their pots (the knobs or vertical sliders that control the mic levels on the audio board), and do a preliminary level check as soon as possible. Never be caught scurrying to find a connector when your VIPs are on set. That last-minute panic appears — and actually is — rather unprofessional.

A final technique is to instruct your crew members to be at their posts at least 15 minutes before tape rolls (or the program goes live). You are likely to hear some grumbling from camera operators who resent standing like statues with nothing to do, but the alternative often involves chasing them down seconds before airtime. You can overcome some of their reluctance by using the time to rehearse zooms and other shots. You might not actually *use* these shots, but you'll hurt no one by practicing them.

EDITING

Although not something done "in studio," per se, editing is considered here as a function performed at the production facility rather than in the field. A full course in editing is, again, beyond the scope of this book, and a basic knowledge of editing procedure is assumed.

Advance planning is the key to good editing, whether you do the work in house or take it to a postproduction facility. Although that seems self-evident, Bette Jenneman, senior editor at Unicorn Video Productions in Braintree, Massachusetts, noted that editors all have horror stories about disorganized clients. Some of hers:

> Example: Client "A" arrives at 2 P.M. for a "quick, one-hour edit." No script, no real idea of how this production is going to look. Ideas are shuffled, redesigned. With the meter still running at 2 A.M., the edit is finally finished.

> Example: Client "B" arrives for the edit with one source tape. And 25 stills, a half-dozen slides, a couple of overheads. Are there projectors and a camera available?

> Example: Client "C" is in the middle of his session. Shot 40, he says is on tape four; he doesn't know where. Tape four is scanned — no shot 40. It's not on tape five, either. Or tape three . . . Or tape ten.[2]

Such disasters can unfold whether you are working in your own suite or renting out someone else's. Note that as the producer in charge of budgetary control you can run up enormous bills by renting a postproduction facility and then committing the types of fumbles described above.

REVIEW OF THE EDITING PROCESS

Although you may have had extensive experience in editing at this point, a quick review can, if nothing else, clarify the vocabulary and add some perspective to the in-house producer's role in assembling the final product.

Editing is the process by which the raw tape is converted into the finished program. The word can be used to indicate both the mechanical act of doing the choosing and assembling and the act of building an artistic effect and theme by the methods used in constructing the program.

An editor's physical equipment generally consists of two or more video tape units controlled by a device variously called an edit interface, edit deck, or editing control unit. That device is a remote control unit for the tape decks and also allows the two decks to be synchronized. Synchronization is important for many reasons, the most immediate being that in order for the material from the left-hand tape deck to be transferred to the right-hand tape deck, both decks must be backed up a bit and prerolled in order for the motors to get the tape up to speed.

In addition, the editing control unit allows you *precise control* over both decks. You can search frame by frame for the exact edit point and also fast-forward through the tapes, watching the speeded-up picture to find the correct takes.

Of course, the whole point of editing is to copy material from one tape deck onto another; you may have ten cassettes of raw footage, for instance, and you will use this raw footage to compose your final program. In general usage you will play back the raw tape on the source cassette unit (which is usually, but not always, on the left-hand side) and record the finished program on the record deck.

To further define the terminology, remember that there are two types of editing methods, *assemble editing* and *insert editing*. Assemble editing is used to join segments together sequentially. As an example, should you wish to make a tape with only two elements — a three-minute shot of an announcer speaking to the camera and a one-minute address from the CEO — you could use an assemble edit to lay down the announcer shot and then add the CEO shot directly after it.

Insert editing is pretty much what the name implies: You insert video, audio, or both at any point on the tape. Perhaps you want a shot of a new machine placed over some of the announcer's opening spiel. You would establish the announcer for a minute or so, and then do a video-only insert edit of the machinery in operation.

The only real difference between assemble and insert modes — and this causes some confusion even among relatively experienced TV students — is that assemble editing lays down what is called a sync track, whereas insert editing does not. Insert edits are laid down over an *existing* sync track. A *sync track* is exactly what the name suggests: a series of impulses placed on the tape so that the video tape units can keep track of the speed of the tape and location of the electronic frames placed on the tape and synchronize them with other video equipment. Sometimes these impulses are called *sync spikes*. The sync track is something akin to the sprockets on film, except that on video those "sprockets" are laid down electronically. When we refer specifically to the pattern of the sync track on a videotape, we often call that pattern the *control track*. The terms are basically synonymous.

The most common form of editing is to lay down a control track on the entire slave tape (the tape that will eventually hold the final program) or at least on the amount of tape you anticipate will be needed for the program. Then, insert editing can be used to lay down audio, video, or both in any combination. How do you lay down a control track? Simply by recording black or color bars on the record tape. Although you can construct a program in sequence on a blank tape without a control track, the edits are usually not as precise and have a tendency to "break up."

In keeping with the purpose of this discussion — to review the basics and clarify sometimes murky terminology — remember that insert editing is not necessarily the same thing as control-track editing. *Control-track editing* means using editing hardware that reads the sync pulses and uses those pulses to coordinate the tape machines.

There is another type of editing, known as *time-code editing*, or *SMPTE time-code editing*, which is different from control-track editing. The time code is not the same as the pattern of sync spikes. Instead, a time code is a signal recorded directly onto a portion of the videotape not normally seen on standard playback; that signal is a readout in hours, minutes, seconds, and frame numbers, which provides an extremely precise *address* for the tape. The SMPTE time code does not replace the control track; the control track is still necessary to synchronize the tape with the other equipment. (By the way, SMPTE, pronounced "simpty," is an acronym for Society of Motion Picture and Television Engineers, the organization that sets standards for equipment used in the two media.)

SMPTE time-code editing equipment is more expensive than control-track-editing hardware, but it allows considerably higher precision. The biggest advantage, though, is that the editor can use the time-code addresses (sometimes called "birthmarks") to computer-program an entire series of edits. In theory the editor can program and preview all the cuts, throw a switch, and come back in an hour to remove the final product. I say "in theory" because it is rarely this easy; for one thing the operator still occasionally needs to change tapes.

To return to the original distinction, you can see that insert editing can be done on control-track equipment and SMPTE time-code equipment.

Two other frequently confused terms are on-line and off-line editing. *On-line editing* generally refers to SMPTE time-code editing done through a video switcher, the same device used in studio directing. On-line editing allows for the use of dissolves, introduction of special effects, and sophisticated A-B rolling with dissolves. (A-B rolling means combining shots from two tapes. The term derives from the practice whereby filmmakers manufactured dissolves by placing one scene on a roll of film marked A, while the corresponding portion of film on the reel marked B was black leader. When scenes were to be changed, the relationship of reel A to B was changed accordingly, with the next scene placed on B and black leader on A. Both reels were run at the same time, and the output was printed onto a third reel.)

On-line editing allows great flexibility, but at a price. In order to combine all these sources, you need not only a switcher but also a device to coordinate all the sources: either a time-base corrector or a genlock system. Genlock is a method of linking synchronization generators together in lockstep; a time-base corrector stabilizes the output of a VCR, making it synchronize with other equipment and producing a more stable picture. Both devices use different technologies to solve the same problem: keeping the various pieces of video equipment in sync with one another.

Off-line editing is done on a basic system of two VCRs and an interface. The term *off-line* is typically used to indicate the practice of using simple editing equipment to provide a rough cut (without such elements as complex graphic effects or dissolves) that will be used as a guide for the final cut. Rough-cutting off line might seem like doing the same job twice, but it can actually save money in the long run.

On-line editing is quite expensive, whether you rent an on-line suite or purchase the equipment for an in-house facility. But such hardware offers many significant advantages in the long run. Computer control allows for great precision and flexibility. (Computer control refers to a microprocessor within the editing unit, as shown in Figure 9.2.) Such a setup can list all edits and, depending on the level of complexity and interactivity of the program, integrate the actions of various pieces of studio equipment.

THE ART OF EDITING

The use of sophisticated editing equipment is, of course, not an end in itself. The art and craft of editing involve creating a program and using effects that reinforce the idea behind the show. Good editors devote years of study to developing their skill through observation and practice.

Although it is not the point of institutional television to ape commercial TV, certain conventions are nevertheless followed. Well-composed camera shots, cutting on action (making the cut when something is happening in the shot), and

FIGURE 9.2

The latest generation of software can turn a personal computer into an editing controller. More accurately, SMPTE time-code lists can be stored and fed into the controller without tying up the editing gear, vastly reducing the time demands on the main controller in the editing suite. The personal computer also offers huge storage capacity for editing-decision lists.

logical sequencing of shots are important for *any* video production. Many good references are available to guide you in the fine points of visual expression. Among them is *Sight-Sound-Motion: Applied Media Aesthetics*, by Herbert Zettl (Belmont, CA: Wadsworth, 1990). Conventions specifically related to television news production are clearly explained in *ENG: Television News and the New Technology*, by Richard D. Yoakam and Charles F. Creamer (New York: Random House, 1985).

A point at which the commercial and institutional media clearly diverge is the level of attention required by the viewer. An episode of a network police show can be quite exciting, but viewers' attention can wander for several minutes without their losing the thread of the plot. But we certainly don't want viewers "tuning out" during, for example, a tape demonstrating safety procedures. How can an institutional producer maintain a level of excitement higher than that of a cop show? Obviously, he or she cannot. The best available option, then, is to keep the presentation as short as feasible and to make the information readily accessible. Some very basic learning theory was outlined in Chapter 4, but in terms of *editing*, remember that any presentation designed to inform must have peaks and valleys. No one, viewer or producer, can sustain 100 percent interest throughout a presentation. You can emphasize important information with high-impact editing, such as quick, exciting cuts and inspiring music. But don't think that you can make the whole presentation mesmerizing by quick cuts and high-powered music, because that just cannot be accomplished. The viewer needs a mental and visual rest on occasion.

A related point is to use editing to create variety. Grant Williams, a writer and institutional TV expert, notes that clever, varied editing can make dull scenes interesting. For example, an extended scene of a business meeting (now doesn't that sound hypnotic?) can be made electrifying by using reaction shots; cut to them an instant *before* the reaction takes place.[3] Are you skeptical that meetings can be made dramatic and exciting by this technique? Then watch an episode of *L.A. Law* and see how this exact strategy is put to work.

Always remember that unless you are taping purely for archival purposes, you are creating an integrated, complete program in the editing suite. No matter what the format — newscast, message from the VIP, documentary — your show must have a beginning, middle, and end. It should have a common thread woven throughout, some element that maintains continuity.

Finally, *audio* quality is affected by the editing process, and good audio is an essential component of the production. It is helpful for institutional producers to have a reasonably sophisticated audio production console, such as the unit pictured in Figure 9.3. It is handy — and sometimes vital — to have sound-shaping and special-effects controls available for audio editing.

The video studio and other in-house facilities, including the editing suite, are centers of creativity but also places of business. Working in a businesslike manner controls expenses and establishes your professionalism within the organization. Nowhere is the expression "time is money" more apparent than in the studio or editing suite. Advance planning and strategic organization, though, can save studio time as well as ulcers. The same caveat applies to operations in the field, the subject of the next chapter.

FIGURE 9.3

Good audio-processing equipment is extremely useful for the institutional producer. Consoles with sound-shaping controls, such as filters and equalizers, can "clean up" audio tracks and lend the video program high production values.

SUMMARY

≡ The goal of good studio production — indeed, the goal of any type of production — is a high-quality product. Although sophisticated pieces of equipment are useful tools, running hardware is not an end in itself.

≡ Usually, but not always, institutional video studios are smaller and less well equipped than studios in broadcast stations. Institutional personnel often take on many more roles than their broadcast counterparts.

≡ As a producer or director you may be responsible for helping crew members learn specifics of equipment operation. In particular, you must be prepared to help camera operators produce good-quality shots.

≡ Some of the more common in-studio institutional productions are interview shows, company newscasts, or messages from a VIP.

≡ Good directors must think several shots ahead. They must have the next shot planned, because it might have to be taken immediately, and must be thinking about the shot *after* the next shot.

≡ Editing is the process of taking raw tape and converting it into a finished program. Some terms to remember are *control-track editing*, *time-code editing*, *insert editing*, *assemble editing*, *on-line editing*, and *off-line editing*.

≡ Editing is part science and part art. Remember that a finished program must have a flow, peaks of intensity, "rest periods," and a distinct beginning, middle, and end.

EXERCISES

1. Write and illustrate (to the best of your artistic ability) a two-page handout explaining studio camera operations *to a novice*. Remember that you cannot simply recite what you know about camera operations. You must compose the material in such a way that an *uninitiated* operator can understand your handout and find it useful. Make revisions suggested by your instructor, and keep this handout; experience shows that it will come in handy sooner than you might expect.

2. Write a sample scene (using the two-column script format shown in Chapter 5) dramatizing a meeting. Make the scene approximately three script pages long. In your script make an effort to use reaction shots and any other reasonable device you can invent to make the meeting interesting. Be sure, though, that each shot or other device has meaning within the overall context. (In other words it must logically follow past developments and be within reason; although it might maintain viewer interest for one participant to gun down the chairman of the board, that is not contextually reasonable.)

3. Watch an institutional videotape supplied by your instructor. If one is not available, this exercise can be accomplished by viewing a commercial television program. While watching the tape, plot or graph the high points and

the sections that seem to drag. (The format of the plot or graph is up to you; it is part of the exercise, and comparing visual representations with your colleagues will be of interest.) Make notes on what was happening during the peaks and valleys, and also keep notes on why you felt the action was picking up or slowing down. Try to do this all in one take. Rewinding and re-viewing the tape will throw off your perspective.

NOTES

1. Michael A. Rivlin, "Studio Production: New Technologies, New Options," *Educational/Institutional Television* (March 1988): 24–27.

2. Bette Jenneman, "An Editor's Guide to Anxiety-Free Editing," *Post* (April 1988): 74, 73.

3. Grant Williams, "Editing and Pacing," *Video Manager* (June 1987): 10.

CHAPTER 10

━━━━━━━━━━━━━━━━━━━━━━

FIELD PRODUCTION

━━━━━━━━━━━━━━━━━━━━━━

TECHNIQUES

━━━━━━━━━━━━━━━━━━━━━━

One of the realities of institutional television is that the subject often promises to be somewhat less than compelling, possibly downright boring. A producer assigned the task of demonstrating the disassembly of a piece of equipment or taping a lengthy sales presentation may wonder how anything of visual interest can be made. Yet the producer must make it interesting. From the aesthetic standpoint there should be no essential difference between the approach used in commercial television and institutional television. The assumption that an institutional tape should receive short shrift in production values because it is a "training film" is exactly the reason why the term *training film* carries the connotation of "nightmarishly boring piece of junk."

This chapter discusses methods by which the institutional producer can inject strong production values into field operations. In addition, the chapter serves as a guide to the specific techniques to make those operations run smoothly and efficiently. (If you are reading chapters out of order, note that the previous chapter dealt with similar approaches to the use of studio production and editing facilities.)

A knowledge of basic production techniques is assumed. If you need to brush up on rudimentary operations and terminology, several excellent books on television production are listed in the suggested readings.

SHOOTING IN THE FIELD

It is true, as just mentioned, that the aesthetics of institutional television and broadcast television should not differ. It is unfortunately also true that those in charge of allocating resources to institutional video often make a fundamental error in their expectations of the needs of a remote field crew. That misconception centers on the fact that a novice's idea of a shooting crew is sometimes that of a television news crew, which often consists only of one reporter, a photographer, and, occasionally, a field producer. But the typical institutional piece is not news coverage; it often borders on being a full-fledged documentary, with swatches of staged drama to emphasize important points.

So what we conceive of as a fully staffed "film crew" would be more in order. The field producer for institutional video ideally needs a director, gaffers, lighting specialists, audio experts, continuity people, a camera operator and assistant operator, script assistants, prop managers, and a host of other personnel.

Obviously, that can be an unrealistic scenario — but so is the expectation that good-quality location shooting can be accomplished by a two-person camera-and-mic operation. As a result, this chapter will attempt to tread a middle ground by outlining how to obtain the best results with the resources typically available. The goal of this approach is positively not to reinforce the notion that a few tricks of the trade can produce high-quality video on the cheap. But we will explore ways to maximize resources given practical limits on equipment, funds, and personnel.

Under ideal circumstances the field production crew would operate with the same artistic and creative autonomy as its counterpart in commercial television and film. In many instances that is indeed the case. Sometimes, though, the realities of corporate life dictate the relinquishing of some control to the powers that be; those powers, of course, are often the very people you are taping. The arts of politics and compromise, then, are as essential to the producer's job as technique and resourcefulness.

THE BASICS OF INSTITUTIONAL FIELD SHOOTING

Being "on location" can mean anything from taping in the office next door to jetting to a country across the globe, but the principles are the same regardless of the logistics. Essentially, the field producer needs to return to the editing suite with the following:

≡ A complete range of video from which to edit the final product. Returning for additional takes is always inconvenient and sometimes impossible.

≡ Video that is inventive and visually intriguing.

≡ Video that is easily accessible; that is, it has been logged accurately and can be located easily during editing.

≡ Video that accomplishes the purposes of the script. Sometimes the pictures are shot with a shot sheet, an incomplete script, or (rarely) no script at all, but the essence of what has been put on tape must reinforce the thrust of whatever initial planning document was constructed.

≡ Flexible video, meaning footage with enough takes and angles so that unexpected difficulties can be circumvented in the editing suite.

≡ Technically good pictures and sound.

Many strategies are used to meet these goals, and although the format of a shoot can vary, most field production is done as *electronic field production, multicamera production*, or *single-camera video*.

Electronic Field Production   Commonly known as EFP, electronic field production is a rather imprecise term that refers, variously, to recording on tape that will later be edited or the recording in one take of a complete show, using several cameras and a mobile switching unit. In some cases broadcast and cable news or public affairs units transmit the output of EFP back to the station for live broadcast. In such a situation EFP is similar to what we commonly think of as a "remote." To repeat, the term is used to cover a variety of functions. An institutional producer is wise to determine precisely what is expected when he or she is assigned some "EFP" work.

Multicamera Production   Generally, multicamera production is taken to mean recording the output of several cameras through a video switcher—in effect, directing the program on the scene. It is particularly useful when covering an event involving several things happening at once. Also, if it is anticipated that dissolves will be a necessary component of the presentation, it is often simpler to create them through the switcher than through A-B rolling back in the editing suite. (Note that multicamera production does not mean the same thing as electronic field production. Multicamera production is any production done with more than one camera; it can take place in a studio or in the field. Electronic field production refers specifically to programs produced in remote locations.)

Again, be wary of imprecise definitions. Multicamera production does not always mean doing an entire show in one take. Nor does the use of two or more cameras necessitate a switcher. Field production units commonly use "iso" cameras, feeding unconnected VTRs, to capture events that will be edited together later. One example would be the use of two cameras to cover a two-person interview; one camera would stay on the interviewer and the other would focus on the subject. Each would feed a separate VTR, and the takes would be edited together later. This approach may be particularly useful if the two persons are of equal stature and a relatively equal amount of airtime for each is expected. Editing in this manner is also appropriate if the producer of the segment has ethical qualms about shifting the camera after the interview and having the interviewer re-ask the questions. Some producers do believe that manufacturing cutaway shots is unethical, since it is a distortion of what actually happened during the interview. Also, some interviewees are reluctant to "pose" while the camera angle is shifted and the interviewer repeats the question, sometimes with an actual or perceived difference in inflection.

Single-Camera Video   SCV, sometimes known as shooting "film style," is an extremely popular mode of production. In the hands of the right producer and director, single-camera video offers tremendous flexibility at reasonable cost. Short of a linear event where one-time-only shots are needed, such as a live or shot-live-on-tape interview show or a sporting event, SCV can accomplish virtually any production task.

Although SCV is certainly the most popular and practical method of producing field-location programs, it is one of the most complex production techniques. SCV requires an excellent eye for continuity and the ability to think in terms of the usefulness of the shot for the *eventual edited product*. Many of the techniques in this chapter will be geared toward that strategy.

Note that SCV also has significant advantages over the overlapping genres of EFP and multicamera (when multicamera is taken to mean cameras fed to a switcher). The first is freedom. Crew setups are generally less elaborate than in other production modes; one man or woman with a shoulder-mounted camera and perhaps a camera-mounted light can get shots virtually impossible for a tripod-mounted studio camera.

The second advantage of SCV is variety. Does the shot of the machine being demonstrated adequately convey the essential information? If not, you can quickly try a closer shot, or a wider shot, or a low-angle shot, or a high-angle one. In short, the field producer can take as many shots as time and energy will allow and sort out the good from the bad back at the editing suite. Remember, though, that the time to sort through multiple takes is when you have leisurely access to a single VCR, not when you are tying up an entire editing console and a technician.

When shooting SCV, be sure to keep editing in mind. This is easier said than done and is largely a learned skill, but it should be foremost in your mind. Make certain that you'll have enough footage — and proper footage — to compose the piece once you arrive back in the editing room.

RUNDOWN OF EQUIPMENT NEEDED

Each situation will vary, of course, but field production for institutional television has its own particular demands. Here is a generalized list of the pieces of equipment that prove useful to producers venturing into the field. It is essentially geared toward producers of SCV.

Camera Options   Choose a sturdy and light camera. Many cameras are portable, in the sense that they can be moved from place to place and, if need be, shoulder-mounted. But not all cameras perform equally well under field conditions. Some cameras, for example, have controls mounted awkwardly for an operator who must point and shoot and then run to the next location.

Choosing a camera is obviously a matter of personal choice and budget, but many experienced field shooters prefer the latest generation of easy-to-operate chip cameras. Simplicity can prove important in the quite common event that inexperienced crew members inherit camera duty when the regular operator is reassigned, ill, or otherwise engaged.

VCRs, Tape, and Batteries   The most fundamental advice deals not with the equipment itself but with the supplies needed. In short, whatever VCR you use, take along approximately three times the supply of tapes and batteries you expect to use.

First, a note on VCR selection: The choice of the particular VCR format will probably be made for you, because compatibility with other VCRs and editing equipment is important, and purchase of videotape systems is typically a decision made on a very high corporate level. In many cases the choice of a single camera does not have to be blessed at such a high level and may, indeed, be made by the user. Standard 3/4-inch U-Matic tape remains quite popular for institutional use, and professional 1/2-inch (as opposed to consumer 1/2-inch) produces excellent quality. Many major users of institutional video, such as Prudential Insurance and Pizza Hut, are moving toward the exquisitely light and high-quality 8mm video format.

Electrical power and videotape present recurring problems in institutional video. Aside from the inconvenience involved, the fact that "the people from the TV department ran out of tape" is not the impression you want to leave with an executive of your organization. Institutional TV producers are particularly vulnerable to battery and tape problems, because their shoots sometimes have no predictable time limit. Factors beyond their control can drag out a session.

Never place a great deal of faith in batteries. In addition to the occasional problems of defective batteries and personnel who forget to recharge them, inhouse producers with a variety of duties may relegate a relatively small amount of time to portable operation. As a result the batteries get irregular, infrequent use. This causes a problem with what is known as "battery memory"; that is, when the type of battery often used in TV equipment is repeatedly partially discharged before being recharged, it begins to go dead at the point where the draining process was last completed. Because of this phenomenon, two completely recharged batteries with memory problems may go dead faster than one that has been completely drained and recharged regularly.

In addition to bringing an adequate supply of properly charged batteries, be sure to bring enough videotape. Not only will a stock of many tapes prevent the embarrassment of running out; you will find your editing process greatly simplified if you use many tapes with short segments. Use one tape for your 10 takes of the quick interview, another for the machinery demonstration, a separate tape for outside cover shots, and so on. This will allow easy location of the right tape during editing and will also prevent wasting valuable editing time spooling through a long reel of various, unrelated shots.

Lighting Instruments Use a professional-quality lighting kit (Figure 10.1). The need for television light is obvious (the camera has to see), but for the on-location industrial producer there is another, not-so-apparent problem: Shooting

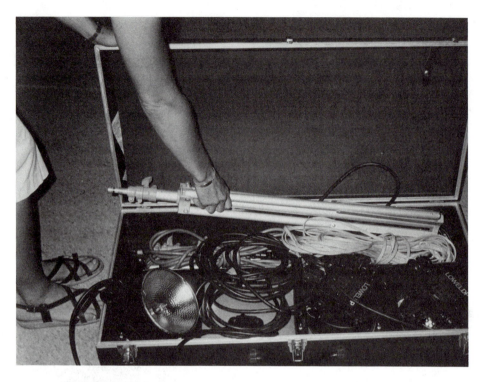

FIGURE 10.1

A professional-quality lighting kit is an excellent investment.

sites change from week to week, day to day, and sometimes hour to hour. The site that was so carefully scouted last week may have a new furniture arrangement or coat of paint. Should an outdoor shoot run long, the direction and *color* of the sunlight will be quite different. That is why it is essential to be prepared for many alternatives. Your lighting kit should include units that throw narrow beams and broad beams. The ability to quickly set up and aim a small instrument to highlight a dark area can save a shoot (Figure 10.2). Also, your kit must have some flexibility in terms of the color temperatures that can be produced.

Good lighting instruments can be expensive, but high-quality equipment from a reputable firm is worth the investment. David Clark, who has received six Emmy nominations for lighting and scenic design, points out that, in some cases:

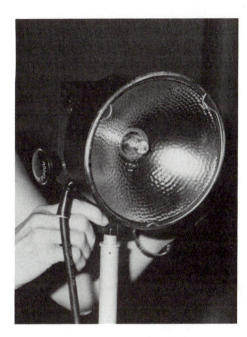

FIGURE 10.2

A small, accurate, and versatile lighting instrument can save the day when you encounter unpredictable conditions. Institutional producers often suggest buying the best lighting equipment you can afford and taking as much of it with you as you can carry.

You can get twelve of the same lights for the same price as only six of some other lights. Take the six! There is good reason why some equipment is expensive: It works better. The light output may be similar, but the durability and flexibility in handling is worth the extra cost.[1]

Audio Equipment Audio does not "take care of itself." In fact, poor-quality, get-it-any-way-you-can sound is the hallmark of a cheaply done program. Even if the viewer does not perceive an audio deficit, poor sound quality definitely contributes to an overall negative effect. If you have any doubt, flip through the menu of options on your cable box, and take note of the first impression you receive from the perfunctorily produced local-access program. The chances are that your impression will be of a hollow, flat audio signal.

Producing good audio is a special concern of the institutional producer, because it is sometimes difficult to obtain the personnel or equipment to do an adequate job. It is not unusual for the camera operator to be asked to "keep an eye on the VU" (the volume-unit meter, which registers audio levels on the VCR) and act as the sole arbiter of sound fidelity during taping.

If possible, have a designated crew member handle nothing but audio monitoring and microphone setup. Be sure that he or she is armed with a good arsenal of mics, including several lavalieres, some sturdy moving-coil hand-helds, and a variety of booms or fishpoles. A shotgun mic, if you can afford it, is a fine option. (It should be emphasized that this is an *ideal* situation. You may not have, in an academic or a professional setting, a comprehensive array of audio equipment.)

Be certain that the audio director is equipped with a pair of good-quality headphones that not only allow for high-fidelity reproduction of the sound but also exclude background noise to whatever extent is possible. Noisy environments are common in industrial shooting, and the audio director has a difficult enough job trying to determine whether ambient sound has ruined a recording without having to contend with additional ambient sound while he or she is listening to a playback. Earphones with large, flexible plastic muffs are a good choice for an institutional field producer.

Cables, Connectors, and Other Paraphernalia   The lack of a connector can quite literally scuttle a morning's work. Be sure that an adequate supply is included. (Male-to-male and female-to-female XLRs seem to be among the most common missing links.) Double the amount of power cable and audio cable you think you will need. Incidentally, be certain that you'll be able to plug in all the equipment without overtaxing the building's electrical supply. (That determination should be part of the site survey, which is discussed in a subsequent section, "Avoiding Typical Problems.")

It is not possible to make a definitive list of other equipment for all occasions, but in any case it is imperative to carry a good-quality color monitor. Some producers rely exclusively on the camera viewfinder for viewing setup and even playback, but such a small monitor cannot be depended on to give an accurate representation of perspective and, obviously, color composition.

WORKING WITH THE REMOTE CREW

There is a perceptible trend toward relying on free-lancers to round out the institutional producer's crew. Although there are good and bad points to any aspect of crew composition, one plus for the free-lance crew is that a wide variety of talent and experience can be harvested. A surprisingly competent work force is seeking free-lance employment.

Note, too, that in some cases institutional video producers hire an entire crew from an outside production house to shoot the tape and then use that house or another specialized postproduction facility to edit the tape.

It is incumbent on the in-house video manager to make crew selections wisely, and this means *on the basis of proven ability*. Ask to see a demonstration tape, or "reel," of the free-lancer's work. Check applicants' references. The credits at the end of a program do not always indicate that the person presenting the reel was indeed the director or writer or videographer; the credits may simply mean that he or she knew how to operate a character generator and how to edit in the appropriate name during the dub.

Many free-lancers market themselves on the basis of the equipment they own. Although a camera operator equipped with the latest high-quality model can be a definite asset, good equipment does not necessarily represent the ability to use it well. And on the subject of equipment and free-lancers, don't focus on choosing a camera operator and neglect the fact that you need extremely competent audio and lighting people, too.

One of the unique challenges frequently encountered in institutional video production is the ad hoc nature of the crew composition. As producer or director you have the responsibility to knit this group together and provide for fast, efficient production. Some suggestions follow.

First, keep the crew informed. As the producer Fred Ginsburg notes, one of the most important tasks is to tell the crew what's going to happen next. "The crew must be told what the upcoming shot is supposed to be," he contends. "Not the history and planned future of the entire six-day shoot, but merely the next shot. It sounds simplistic, I know, but describing just the single shot for the crew usually stumps a lot of the new directors."[2]

Another point is to take shots in the most convenient sequence for shooting, not necessarily in the order they occur in the script. Do the beginning and end of the program take place in the same location? Shoot them back to back, if possible. Use the editing process to structure the sequence.

Use stand-ins to set up shots for your VIPs. Have a crew member of similar physical stature and complexion (and, if you know what the VIP will wear, wardrobe) do the sitting around while lights are set and camera angles worked out. You'll have to do some fine-tuning when the real article shows up, but the process will be greatly simplified. Also, use this opportunity to set preliminary mic levels, or at least just make sure that the mic is working and that the sound mixer knows on which pot to find the VIP's mic. It is an unfortunate fact of life in the corporate world that although high-ranking executives are often willing to keep others waiting, they bristle when their time is wasted "by that disorganized TV crew." Give the impression of clockwork organization; protect your corporate reputation.

Finally, use waiting-around time to maximum advantage. By the very nature of institutional television you *will* spend a portion of your on-location time waiting for latecomers. Don't let your crew stand around drinking coffee. It reflects poorly on your organization and wastes time. There are always things to be done. While waiting for a late-arriving interviewee, shoot cover video, wrap cables from the previous shot, check lighting levels at the next scene, get signatures on releases, or discuss the next scene with the crew.

AVOIDING TYPICAL PROBLEMS

It is apparent that the corporate producer faces some unique challenges during the location shoot. Although an adaptable and imaginative producer can usually work out solutions, it's important to remember that problems are best solved in advance.

A site survey should be undertaken if at all possible. When checking out the location for the shoot, pay particular attention to:

≡ *Clearances to shoot.* Be positive that you have obtained written permission to tie up the location. Be sure that you send a letter (and keep a copy) to the person in charge of the office or other site explaining exactly what you will do, the space you will need, and how long you will need it. Try never to rely on informal clearances. The manager of an office who gives you verbal, off-the-cuff permission to shoot may change his or her mind when it becomes apparent that your crew is (as is almost always the case) a major disruption to workaday business.

≡ *Availability of talent.* It is essential that the supervisors of people assigned to appear in your tape free those performers for an adequate period of time. Supervisors must know that a five-minute appearance in a video program does *not* translate into a five-minute time commitment sandwiched into the employee's normal workday. Finally, be sure that you can get photo releases signed. It is a good idea to have talent sign them in advance.

≡ *Power supplies.* Have an experienced technician calculate the wattages of your equipment and determine whether the circuits at the site can handle the demand. (Cameras and VTRs are generally no problem, but lighting instruments create a large power drain.) Often, the solution is as simple as determining which electrical outlets are on different circuits and plugging in lights accordingly.

≡ *Unusual lighting conditions.* Must you take a shot that includes an entire factory wall? If so, bring plenty of lighting instruments. Check all your planned shots for such predicaments.

THE OFFICE ENVIRONMENT

Institutional producers spend an inordinate amount of time in offices, environments that present a particular set of shooting problems. One need typically encountered is to create pleasing *atmospherics* out of what might be a sterile environment. Another challenge involves proper *lighting*. Offices can be devilishly difficult to illuminate.

ATMOSPHERICS AND PROPS

To those trained in journalism, media, and communications an office is typically just a place to store equipment, talk on the phone, and occasionally grab lunch. Most visitors are surprised to find that the offices of major-market television news directors are small cubicles rather than executive suites; that's simply the nature of the business.

But it is important for an institutional video producer to realize that in the business world office environments often assume an exaggerated importance. The cliché of executives jockeying for the best corner office and flaunting their environmental perks has, like many clichés, a grain of truth in it. The point is that many executives are quite sensitive to their office surroundings, in general, and their executive demeanor, in particular. Although this concern may seem rather fatuous, experienced corporate media producers will confirm that real problems ensue from executives' preoccupation with their office environment.

Many executives want to sit behind a large desk during taping. Although this is not inherently a bad location shot, it becomes a bad shot when it is repeated to the point of triviality. Also, the deskbound executive produces the ultimate "talking head" scene. Another consideration is that an executive who wants to communicate to employees that he or she is friendly, concerned, and "one of the boys" is best advised not to do so from behind an aircraft carrier–sized slab of mahogany. The solution? Coax the executive to walk around during taping. This will eliminate the barrier of the desk and also liven up the video. Perhaps he or she could walk into a scene. Or instead of starting with a standard wide shot to a zoom-in, you could have the executive move from behind the desk and walk *into* a close-up. Some executives may balk. If that happens, take the advice of the corporate production expert Grant Williams: Tell them that "this technique is what makes Lee Iacocca look so good."[3]

Office scenes are, by nature, rather static. If you have the opportunity and a cooperative executive, try to introduce some props to break up the monotony. For example, if your CEO is talking about the latest financial projections, have him or her turn to the computer terminal and punch up the screen displaying the figures. Does the shot concern the manufacture of a new component? If the component is small enough to hold, encourage the CEO to do so. It will liven up the shot and add interest.

LIGHTING THE EXECUTIVE

Many desks are located in awkward lighting positions, especially when they are placed in front of windows. However, most problems can (usually) be overcome by the following techniques.

First, if there is a large window in back of the desk — a very common layout — shoot from the *side* of the desk and have the executive turn so that the window strikes him or her from the side. If you can persuade the executive to turn far enough, the window can actually provide the key light. You'll need to balance color temperatures, though, so be prepared to use an instrument that burns at daylight temperatures, such as a halogen-metal-iodide lamp, to serve as fill.

Barring that (if the subject insists on facing forward with the window in back or if there is no practical way to shoot from the side), you can attempt to adjust your iris to the light level falling on the executive. This often results in an overexposed background. That effect can be minimized by throwing a good deal of artificial light on the executive (which, if he or she is a blinker, will admittedly cause other problems). Another option is staying tight on the executive. Whether your executive looks good in an extreme close-up, of course, is a decision to be left to you, the executive, and your conscience.

If you have no alternative but to shoot with a window in the background and you have some flexibility in your schedule, wait for a cloudy day, or shoot in late afternoon. The reduction in brightness can sometimes be just enough to make the shot acceptable.

If the window shot can't be avoided and all else fails, try taping tracing paper or sheets of plastic lighting filter material over the window.[4]

SHOOTING TECHNICAL VIDEO

Photographing *people* on location can be relatively simple compared with taking good video of *machinery and equipment*. Such videography requires a special "feel," a feel that is largely developed through experimentation and experience. The most widely experienced technical videographers, in fact, are generally quite reluctant to offer cookbook formulas, because each situation encountered in the field can present very different obstacles. Some general guidelines do exist, though, and may prove helpful for the producer charged with the responsibility of videotaping machinery, lighting a technical demonstration, planning and shooting a demonstration, and injecting some attractiveness into technical shots.

PROBLEMS ASSOCIATED WITH PHOTOGRAPHING MACHINERY

Whether you are attempting to demonstrate the operation of a pumping station or the repair of a computer, the primary challenges are the same: (1) to produce a recognizable image that conveys the intended information and (2) to keep the viewers' attention. Aside from the question of lighting (which is discussed next) some relevant suggestions include the following.

First, use shots that include people as well as machinery. Hands are an excellent way of providing perspective and scale. If it is necessary to use a pointer, show the hand holding the pointer.

Second, produce a *videotape*, not a slide show. A series of immobile shots won't really show the viewer how something is done. If you are demonstrating the method of assembling an electrical component, include shots of the actual action and motion of assembly, not simply snapshots of the various stages.

Use whatever method works for you to ensure that you know what's going on when the machinery is being demonstrated and photographed. If you intend to do voice-over and do not need the audio recorded on the scene, have the technician or demonstrator describe what is going on. If he or she does not provide an adequate narrative, ask questions. This way you will know in no uncertain terms whether the technician is demonstrating the flamjimmit installation or the widget sprocket disassembly.

Use as many angles as you need to illustrate the machinery, but do not use such extreme angle changes that perspective is lost. Too-large perspective changes, sometimes known as "crossing the axis," make it difficult for the viewer to tell the front from the back or the side. If you must show the back of a piece of machinery, make it very clear that the perspective is changing. If it is a small unit, show the human demonstrator physically picking up the unit and turning it around. On larger units, arc or truck the camera to the back, and make the motion apparent; let the viewer know the camera is moving.

Lastly, clean the machinery up as much as possible. Industrial operations can be grimy. We expect them to be so in reality, but on tape such machinery can simply look sloppy and neglected. To make matters worse, machines coated with a layer of grime will produce a less-than-distinct picture. Sometimes, if the technical supervisor permits it, you can spray a fresh coat of paint on a part you want to highlight. Quick-drying paints available in most hardware stores, such as Krylon paint, can be dry to the touch in an hour or so.

LIGHTING FOR THE TECHNICAL DEMONSTRATION

Machinery and other equipment are difficult to light, because they typically have many nooks and crannies. Also, various pieces of scientific apparatus are nothing more than black boxes; this makes it very difficult to achieve the effect of dimensionality on camera. Much experimentation is in order when lighting a technical on-location shoot. You may invent your own best solution, but try these general suggestions first.

Use a soft, highly diffused light from directly overhead as a baselight. It will usually give a good overall illumination that is especially flattering to machinery. Next, introduce some horizontal diffused lighting to reach into those crannies. After you've illuminated the machinery so that everything you need to see is visible, use horizontal focused lights to highlight the places where the action will take place. In tricky situations you can achieve a good effect by using a focused light from an angle lower than the horizontal. Some producers with particular expertise in lighting small products favor the use of several 200-watt minimoles with focusable snouts to get that light into the places that need special illumination.[5] Black boxes, such as some electronic component housings, are trouble. Try using a light-colored background, such as white seamless paper, and a strong backlight. This will help emphasize the three-dimensionality of the object.

DEMONSTRATION OF ACTIVITIES

The very definition of demonstrating an activity includes the concept of presenting action. The producer working on a field assignment must constantly devise ways of using *active visuals* to reinforce the presentation.

Visuals are an excellent shortcut, by the way. Alan Babbitt, a California video and film producer, once used a low-angle shot of feet and legs to illustrate the huge staff and busy atmosphere of a particular organization. His approach was much more evocative and much less time-consuming than listing or describing the duties of each employee.[6] Be inventive in your approaches toward demonstrating activities. By all means vary your camera angles and tightness of shots.

But also be wary of continuity. If a person is sitting on the edge of a desk while demonstrating a widget and you cut to a quick close-up of the widget, your demonstrator must be in the same position when the medium long shot returns. On a similar note, attempt to tape demonstrations involving a person in one continuous session, or at least during the same day. Continuity problems can arise if your demonstrator appears the next day with slightly different clothing, not wearing the wristwatch he wore during the previous day's close-up demonstrations, or sporting a fresh haircut.

If at all possible, assign a crew member to keep track of continuity. Maintaining continuity is a particularly serious problem in demonstration tapes. If you are showing a piece of equipment being reassembled into a larger piece of machinery, for example, be absolutely sure that you have footage of it being *dis*assembled in the first place. Otherwise, viewers will justifiably wonder from where, exactly, that new component came.

Here is a practice that has proved helpful to me: Use an instant camera to record the positions of scenes in which continuity might be a problem, such as when pieces of disassembled equipment are spread out on a table. If the session must be stopped for the day and the equipment reassembled, the Polaroid provides a much more convenient reference than does scanning the previous day's videotape to find out what piece goes where.

Another vital consideration when producing demonstrations: *Always* slate your shots. Use verbal slates or visual slates, but use some method. Sequences of hands inserting some sort of thing into some other sort of thing may make perfect sense to you the day you are taping, but in a week those scenes may be totally incomprehensible. So after the tape has come up to speed, try saying, loudly enough so that it can be heard on the talent mic, "This is the shot of Jim inserting the memory board into the first expansion shot. Take 2. It rolls in five, four, three, two . . ." and then cue talent. (Don't say the "one," because it will be too close to the start of the take to eliminate; allow a silent beat for the "one.")

ADDING CINEMATIC VALUES TO TECHNICAL SHOTS

Although it is not the job of an institutional video manager or producer to create art, per se, a little art doesn't hurt now and then. Your efforts will be much more effective if you use techniques of the videographer's and cinematographer's craft to enliven the effort.

Would a little Hitchcockian flavor spice up a demonstration tape about interviewing for a job? Then by all means try a "point-of-view" shot, with the camera seeing through the eyes of the job applicant. How about adding some Orson Welles-type perspective alterations? Because a job interviewer can be an intimidating figure, use the Welles technique: Shoot her from a very low angle, making her tower over the interviewee. Are you taping your hospital's annual simulation of a disaster scene, used as an exercise for emergency personnel? Mimic news coverage by using a hand-held camera; show the jerky movement as you run from place to place.

Finally, be sure to use plenty of close-ups. Observe how experienced filmmakers and television producers use the close-up to relieve visual monotony. Cover shots serve the same purpose and also make editing easier.

It is well within your purview to use the cinematic qualities of moment, color, and framing in your work. Don't forget that suspense and characterization play a part, too. (That subject was dealt with in Chapter 5.)

In sum, you must be concerned with producing good industrial, institutional, and technical television when sent on assignment. But these are secondary goals. The paramount goal is to produce good *video*, period.

SUMMARY

≡ The production values in institutional video need not necessarily be lower than those in any other type of television. Do not use the fact that you are doing an in-house production as an excuse to halfheartedly produce the stereotypical "training film."

≡ SCV (single-camera video) is among the more popular methods of producing institutional programs. It provides great flexibility to the producer.

≡ You may have an entirely in-house crew, or you may supplement your crew with free-lancers. Either way, it is incumbent on the video manager or producer to effectively lead the crew. Two major points: Always let them know what the next shot will be, and keep them busy. Waiting around with hands in pockets looks bad and wastes time.

≡ Executives are often concerned or even obsessed with their office environment, a factor that can cause problems for the producer. Try to coax the executive out from behind the desk. Encourage him or her to use props. Do whatever you can to avoid shooting the executive in front of a window. If it can't be helped, try to turn the subject so that the window acts as a key light.

≡ Machinery is difficult to photograph under the best of circumstances. Be sure to include people in the frame to give scale, and always provide some action. Don't make your demonstration look like a slide show.

≡ When lighting machinery, try first illuminating with a diffused light from directly overhead, filling in the nooks with a horizontal fill, and then using a focused horizontal key to highlight the most important elements.

≡ Don't be afraid to experiment. Use some cinematic techniques. Investigate the effects you can produce with different camera angles or dramatic strategies.

EXERCISES

1. If a camera and lighting instruments are available, experiment with lighting the interior of an office typewriter. Almost all typewriters have a removable cover. Take it off, and attempt to produce a clear picture and close-up of the ribbon-feed mechanism. Then try a computer with a keypad.

2. Regardless of whether you have video facilities, use the same typewriter to plan a demonstration of how to load the ribbon into the typewriter. Produce a short script (modeled after the ones presented in Chapter 5) to demonstrate the process. Try to use about six different scenes. The format, such as voice-over or live presenter, is up to you. By the way, the operator's manual for the typewriter will help with your preparations.

3. Write a brief precis — just a paragraph for each item — on what sort of prop you might use, and how you might use it, to augment an executive's explanation of:
   a. financial projections for the coming year
   b. a merger that will combine your company into a worldwide empire (hint: *world*wide)
   c. the announcement of a new corporate video department

NOTES

1. David Clark, "The Location Lighting Game," *International Television* (March 1984): 40, 42.

2. Fred Ginsburg, "What Your Crew Expects," *AV Video* (September 1986): 51.

3. Grant Williams, "Between Takes: . . . and Action!" *Video Manager* (December 1987): 5.

4. This recommendation comes from Herbert Zettl, who offers an excellent section on dealing with various lighting problems in his *Television Production Handbook*, 4th ed. (Belmont, CA: Wadsworth, 1984): 167–196.

5. This suggestion was provided by Hal Schneider, president of NEV Productions, Worcester, Massachusetts.

6. Alan Babbitt, "Sell the Concept and Enhance the Visuals," *Video Manager* (March 1987): 12.

PART 4

SPECIALIZED

APPLICATIONS

CHAPTER 11

COMPUTERS AND

INTERACTIVE VIDEO

After years of sputtering false starts interactive technology has come into its own. Today, interactive instruction is commonplace, and it is not limited to the halls of higher education. If you have ever used one of those informational video kiosks in a hotel lobby, you have — whether you knew it or not — engaged in learning via interactive technology.

Many firms and institutions use interactive technology at various levels. The U.S. Army has undertaken a huge training program involving interactive video. Schools and colleges program learning into interactive systems. At one major insurance company in Hartford, Connecticut, employees with questions about their W-4 federal tax withholding forms (forms that have recently become much more complex) can use an interactive television touchscreen to enter income information and receive answers to their questions. That system also provides information on company benefits.[1]

Although interactive video is a technology whose time has come, it is also a technology in the midst of great change. This chapter focuses on the basics of interactive technology, those principles that are likely to have a reasonable "shelf life." An unfortunate reality of book publishing is that any text attempting to convey the state of the art in an evolving technology is likely to be outdated almost as soon as it is printed. What follow, though, are basic premises unlikely to change quickly. In this chapter we consider the physical aspects of the technology first and then examine its application in production situations.

WHAT IS INTERACTIVE TECHNOLOGY?

At its most basic level interactive technology simply involves placing a student in front of a television screen and allowing him or her to stop, start, or rewind a videotape at will. This was, in fact, a popular strategy in the earliest generation of interactive programs. Stopping and starting allowed the student to absorb bite-sized lessons at his or her own pace and also allowed consultation with a workbook or other printed material. Such an approach is often termed Level 0 interactivity. When more sophisticated options are added, the interactivity is classified at higher levels, from Level 1 to Level 4.

LEVELS OF INTERACTIVITY

Classifications of interactivity are not universal. The levels cited in this chapter reflect current usage in popular trade publications, but differences in terminology abound.[2]

Level 1 Interactivity   It is apparent that Level 0 interactivity has severe limitations. It does not, for example, allow the student to make choices. Level 1 interactivity allows the viewer to make certain choices about how the program will proceed.

Level 1 interactivity can be accomplished with a video tape playback unit or with a video disc player. Video disc technology will be described later in this chapter. Computer technology also plays a role in interactive presentations. Essentially, a Level 1 program will play until it is stopped by the viewer or encounters a cue on the medium. Some "branching" is possible; that is, the viewer can select material and determine the "flow" of the program.

Level 2 Interactivity   But wouldn't it be more efficient if the device playing back the interactive program could in some way respond to the user? At Level 2 a computer program gives instructions to the viewer about how to play the program and responds to, and remembers, the viewer's input. A Level 2 program is also distinguished by the technical manner in which the control information is stored, a point not important here.

Level 3 Interactivity   Level 3 differs from Level 2 in that it allows for computer-generated graphics "overlays" to be placed on top of video. Typically, Level 3 interactivity relies heavily on computer graphics (as opposed to video-generated graphics) and allows for many more alternative selections than does Level 2. *When video producers speak of "interactive" programs, they are usually referring to Level 3 interactivity.*

Level 4 Interactivity   The difference between Level 4 and Level 3 is primarily the technical process by which a computer extracts data stored on the video medium. In addition, a Level 4 program can be distinguished from Level 3 when the program utilizes touchscreen or voice-activated commands from the viewer.

As the flexibility increases, so does the complexity of production. This leads to a logical question: Why would anyone produce an interactive program instead of a "linear" presentation, which simply runs from beginning to end? The remainder of this chapter will demonstrate how the flexibility of allowing a viewer to choose his or her own options provides effective training — effective in terms of cost and performance. First is an examination of interactivity from the standpoint of the apparatus utilized.

EQUIPMENT FOR INTERACTIVE INSTRUCTION

Videotape   The earliest interactive programs were designed to be run off videotape, a format that had a serious problem: If the viewer desired to move from one part of the tape to another, several minutes' worth of spooling might be involved. In addition, the mechanisms for finding precise locations on videotape were simply not up to the job.

Let's look at a simple interactive "program" to illustrate the problem with videotape. We are teaching elementary school students how to subtract. The tape begins by displaying this problem:

$$6 - 2 = ?$$

The narration says:

> This is a lesson in subtraction. If you have six apples, and subtract two, how many are left? Please press the appropriate number on your computer keyboard.

Our student enters "8." We have programmed our computer to react to this answer by finding the appropriate portion of the tape that says:

> No, that is not correct. Please try again.

But should the student answer "8" once more, we need to go to the portion of the tape that says:

> No, you *added* instead of *subtracting*. Do you want to try again?

And if the student is still befuddled, we want the interactive device to return to the basic lesson on subtraction. That basic lesson, though, is probably at the beginning of the tape, so our student has to wait for the tape to be rewound, restarted, and brought up to speed. As producers, we know how impatient *we* become when spooling through a cassette; imagine how a 7-year-old would react.

Video Disc   Television engineers solved that problem with the *video disc*. The video disc resembles a cross between a standard phonograph album and a compact disc (which, in a way, it is). Most discs used in interactive programming are 12 inches in diameter and about a 10th of an inch thick. But from the institutional video producer's standpoint the important thing about a disc is that it stores video information *that can be accessed virtually instantaneously*. (About two seconds is the longest wait you will encounter when randomly accessing material on disc.)

There is no mechanical stylus on a video disc player; instead, a laser beam reads the information on the disc, which is packed on the tracks with incredible density. About 50 "grooves" can be placed in an area the width of a human hair.[3]

In addition to fast access, a video disc can provide crystal-clear still frames. There is no degradation of the picture, as is caused by the cumbersome mechanical spinning of a head across a nonmoving videotape. (Note that no matter how good a VCR you use, freeze-frame and slow motion are never of very high quality.) Instead, the laser beam simply reads the grooves on each side (meaning left and right side, not front and back) of the disc that provide the two scanning frames; the laser can repeat this process over and over, with no wear on the disc.

(To jump ahead momentarily, additional technical information is necessary here to clarify this process. A television screen fills with information twice to produce a single "frame." There are 525 lines of information in an American television scanning pattern. The device that produces that picture produces the odd scanning lines and then goes back and produces the even scanning lines. The two sets of lines add up to one complete picture. Each field is produced 60 times a second; each frame — the additive product of the two fields — is reproduced 30 times a second. To accommodate this scanning pattern, the video disc is divided into two fields as well, so the laser will scan one field — for the sake of explanation we'll call it the left-hand field — and then the other, or right-hand, field. These two fields are added together to form one frame, which can be viewed as a still frame or as part of a normal motion sequence, one of the 30 frames per second that "blend," because of the eye's "persistence of vision," into a nonflickering, moving picture. This explanation may not seem particularly relevant now, but it does have an important application to the disc mastering process, which will be discussed later.)

A standard video disc has two sound tracks. In some cases technical information is placed on one track. Producers often use the second sound track for a bilingual translation of program material.

Video disc is a method of *optical storage* of information, as opposed to *magnetic storage*. When a video disc is "mastered," a laser beam burns tiny "pits" into the tracks, and those pits are read via laser light (optically) during playback.

A video*tape*, on the other hand, is a strip of material coated with iron oxide, which is a fancy name for rust. When a signal is encoded onto the iron oxide, it makes the particles line up *magnetically*, and the playback head of the VCR reads the magnetic signals and translates (the technically correct term is *transduces*) them back into audio and video.

A computer also uses magnetic storage. Computer discs, whether hard or soft, are essentially a circular form of recording tape. The advantage of magnetic storage is that it allows for easy recording and rerecording. All you have to do is rearrange the pattern of the oxide particles, which is exactly what happens when you rerecord a tape or write over a computer disc. The disadvantage of magnetic storage is that there still must be some mechanical contact between the storage medium and the playback device, which not only causes wear but also slows down the whole information-accessing process. Also, magnetic storage cannot approach the colossal density of information that can be packed onto an optical device, a factor not unnoticed by computer designers. For example, a CD-ROM disc — meaning a compact disc with read-only memory — can hold something like 500 megabytes of information on each side. If you are familiar with computers, you know that 30 megabytes is a healthy-sized memory for the hard disc drive on a high-quality personal computer.

Optical devices have their drawbacks, too. In most applications you cannot rerecord over an optically encoded signal. This is exactly the reason why video disc technology foundered on the consumer marketplace, whereas magnetic-storage devices — namely, videocassette recorders — are now the rule rather than the exception in most American households. At the time of this writing, however, significant developments were being made in hybrid technologies that combine the advantages of optical storage with the flexibility of magnetic rerecording. Disc technology, too, is in a state of flux. There are various methods for optical storage, and standards for disc technology may change in the near future.

The video disc is a powerful storage medium, but in itself it has no "brains." That is, the disc player cannot stop, start, recue, and respond. The computer is the controlling factor in interactive technology, and it will be considered in some depth in the next section. In fact, the computer is usurping much of the interactive function, even to the point of reproducing diagrams and simple animation. Computer technology has already advanced to the point at which many of the interactive graphics that were formerly produced on video-based instruments such as character generators and paintboxes are being created by computer.

Some have argued that in the field of training, video production people dropped the ball a few years back and allowed the computer specialists to take over the playing field. Maybe that is so, but in any event the adversarial relationship that developed is no longer necessary or, to a great extent, possible. In interactive training computers and video are now *inextricably linked*. So although I will follow the convention of referring to these programs as *interactive video*, remember that video, as we know it, is no longer the be-all and end-all of interactive programming.

COMPUTER TECHNOLOGY IN INTERACTIVE INSTRUCTION

Many highly successful interactive programs are entirely computer-based. Virtually all educational software is highly interactive and allows the user to follow various branches while playing the game or learning the lesson. But computers cannot yet replicate the type of personalized approach that makes video so compelling; that is, we cannot see totally realistic images of people and objects in a real-world context on a computer screen.

Today, video and computers exist in partnership. In most interactive programs the branching, or following of different paths of an interactive program, is planned and run by computer, and the video disc player serves up the appropriate pre-recorded scenes. In the most basic terms an interactive system consists of:

≡ The video disc player.

≡ The computer, usually (but not always) a standard personal computer or a modification thereof.

≡ An interface to link the outputs of the computer and the video disc player. That interface is commonly a card that is inserted directly into a personal computer.

Some interactive units allow either computer-alone interactive programming or, by adding an optional video disc unit, computer-video interactivity (Figure 11.1).

HOW COMPUTERS ''THINK''

Actually, computers themselves do not do any real thinking. In fact, all a computer can actually do is determine whether a signal is on or off. This is known as *binary* coding; the word's root, of course, is the same *bi* of bicycle or binocular: two.

But computers can do this on-and-off thinking with incredible speed, and technicians can code a bewildering array of problems into the computer's binary lexicon. This is done via a *program*, a method for using the computer's ability to do huge amounts of calculating at lightning speed. Programs that allow the user to perform a certain function are generally known as *applications software*. Common examples include word-processing packages, electronic financial spreadsheets, and entertainment programs — such as WordPerfect, Lotus, and Flight Simulator, respectively.

If you dissect applications software, you'll find that it is written in "programming language," the most basic method of communication between the machine and the user. For example, a simple word-processing program might ask you a question in plain English:

Are you sure you want to erase from here to the end of the page?

(a)

FIGURE   11.1

The IBM InfoWindow ™ system allows the user to interconnect a personal computer, touchscreen monitor (*a*), and video disc player to produce interactive presentations. By touching the screen (*b*), users can begin a presentation, select an option, or answer a question. This system is useful for classroom instruction or (*c*) for consumer-run presentations.

Photos courtesy International Business Machines Corporation.

(b)

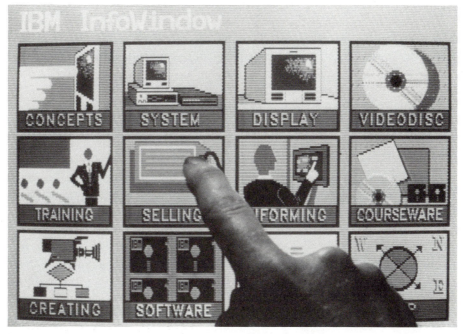

(c)

But what you are seeing has been generated by the programming language, a deeper method of ordering the processes of the computer's central processing unit. Programming language is a series of symbols and commands that make no sense whatsoever to the uninitiated. Some common programming languages include Basic, Microsoft C, and Pascal.

AUTHORING LANGUAGE

The same distinctions can be drawn for the software used in creating interactive programs. The applications software used in creating an interactive program is known in the trade as *authoring language*. Authoring language is simply an application program that allows you to interact with the computer — in plain English — to plan the interactive instructional message.

Remember, though, that the authoring language is the "veneer" hiding the *programming language*, the commands that actually make the computer do the work. The programming language might instruct the computer, for example, to go to a certain location ("address") on the video disc and play a certain number of frames, then call up a graphic that asks the viewer to respond, and then execute certain actions based on that response.

This is an important distinction, because some producers shy away from interactive video because they feel that they do not know how to "program a computer." Although authoring languages require a functional level of computer literacy, they do not require you to "program" a computer, any more than does word-processing software.

Authoring languages are continually becoming more user-friendly and available for specialized applications. A program called Laser Write, for example, uses very simple English commands to allow the user to invent educational programs. Laser Write offers ready-made structures for true-false tests, multiple-choice tests, and other lesson-planning structures. Other authoring languages allow users to structure programs that allow the viewer to interact with the computer via a touchscreen. Modern touchscreens fit over the standard computer screen and allow the user to touch the area of the screen indicating the correct answer.

Many producers of instructional video *do* use programming language, however, or at least hire someone to use it. Why? Because a programming language offers maximum flexibility. You are not required to limit yourself to the constraints of the authoring language. Also, many computer-savvy programmers feel that using program language allows an interactive program to run much faster than using authoring languages does. But programming in fundamental computer languages takes more initial time and effort on the part of the programmer than does using an authoring language.

One other point: You generally license an authoring language; you don't buy it outright. In addition to the initial fees you may incur further expenses when you want to make changes to the program.

PRODUCING AN INTERACTIVE PROGRAM

Interactive video programs are almost always a team affair, involving a producer, a programmer, and several outside technicians and consultants.

THE TECHNICAL REQUIREMENTS

You cannot stamp out your own video disc; this is a process done at a relatively small number of locations, and it is not cheap. The master disc, at the time this was written, typically cost about $2,500, with additional prints running $11 each.

Nor is it practical, in most cases, to make the master *tape* yourself. The master tape, from which the video disc will be cut, must be engineered to extremely precise specifications, and usually these specs can be met only by a production house equipped with highly sophisticated equipment. There are other technical considerations of which you should be aware.

First, the master tape is usually dubbed (from your edited tape) on a high-quality, one-inch, computerized postproduction system. One reason is that you must generally avoid *mixed field dominance*. To understand what this means, refer back to the discussion of how the video disc produces fields, frames, and scanning patterns. The intricacies are really not important other than to illustrate that in order to make a still frame the video disc player has to find the even-line portion of the scanning pattern and the odd-line portion of the frame where it expects them. The computer-controlled tape-mastering facility must make the master tape consistent with regard to the order of odd and even frames. (Having said that, note that you can overcome this problem by taking a large number of frames for your

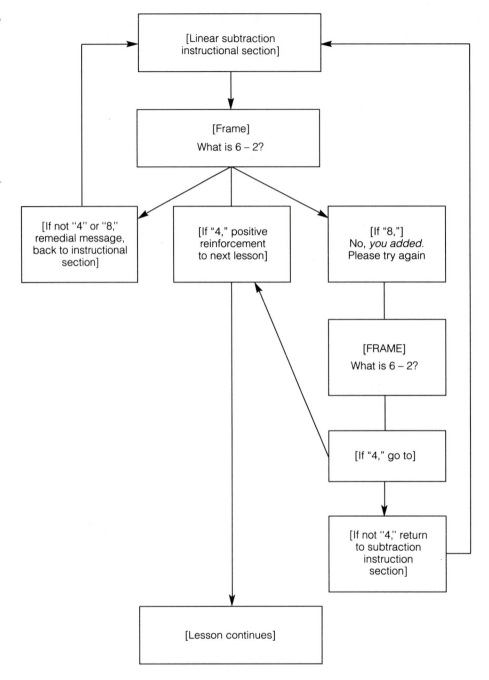

FIGURE 11.2

207

How a subtraction lesson might be visually represented in a flowchart.
The frames, or video that will be shown on the screen, would be
scripted, shot, and mastered on disc, and then the programmer would
use this general design to program disc addresses.

still-frame shot and then programming the computer to stop the video disc somewhere in the middle of those frames; this uses up more space on the disc but can
sometimes circumvent the need for a computer-controlled master to control field
dominance.[4])

You cannot have hot spots on the master tape, and since it is very difficult to
correct this problem, you should not provide your tape-mastering company with
hot-spotted tape. Hot spots are high video levels. Readings of 100 IRE are iffy, and
any over 110 are too high. The reason is that the laser beam that embeds the "pits"
in the master disc will burn right through the master if the levels are too high.
From the producer's standpoint this means that you must be very careful when
shooting. It is far easier to correct the hot spots at the scene (possibly by simply
moving the barn door on a lighting instrument) than attempting to technically
correct the levels later on.

Also from the producer's standpoint, remember that an interactive program is
designed to jump from place to place. If you have many short segments with action
starting as soon as the scene is cut to, you are going to produce a program that will
confuse and jar the viewer. When you shoot segments, be sure to leave a couple
of seconds' worth of "adjustment time" before action starts. Your viewer will
need it.[5]

DESIGN OF THE PREMISE

Now that the technicalities are largely out of the way, we can give some thought to
how an interactive program is actually put together. Let's return to the example of
the subtraction lesson. A flowchart of the beginning of the lesson might look like
Figure 11.2. And that is exactly how most interactive programs are conceived: by
flowchart. The flowchart is simply a representation of the different branches a
program might take. It is not a standardized form; it is simply a representation of
sequence. The sequence is the important concept, and following is a typical sequence for a program slightly more complex than the subtraction example.

First, the overall concept and theme are determined. As an example, an interactive program produced by a department in which I once taught was designed for students studying English as a second language. Its theme was: "There are many options for combining education with work. You need to work in order to have money to live, but you need to continue your education in order to get a better job. The two things are not mutually exclusive — you can do both. We will show some options."

With that theme in mind (and if you cannot sum up the theme in a few sentences, the program lacks focus and is already in trouble) the producer designed the opening. The main character, Luis, lost his job and was, at the same time, faced with certain family problems. The video was to show a scene of Luis and a companion going through the newspaper and picking various jobs for which he could apply.

Now, the branching would begin. Luis has a choice of several options. He reads them aloud from the newspaper. One option, for example, is a job at a printing plant. Another option is skills training at a local educational center. Now, at the first branch point, a graphic appears: "What do you think Luis should do?" A checklist is provided, and the viewer can choose an option from the screen. Suppose the viewer chooses the printing plant. That branch of the video disc is played: It turns out that the job is all right, but it is 50 miles away, and Luis does not have a good car. Another graphic appears, asking the viewer if taking this job is a good decision; if the viewer thinks it is, the presentation is programmed to move to the final scene, which shows Luis at home with his family announcing his decision. (Not entirely a logical conclusion to the branch, but illustrative of the fact that endings must be dealt with somehow; the viewer has already been prodded into exploring other choices, but if he or she chooses to stick with the printing plant, the story might as well have a reasonably happy ending.) Most viewers, though, would elect other choices, would see the problems involved with each, and would be routed back into some sequence that shows Luis combining work with education.

Further choices (paths among branches) would then be made. The viewer gets to choose and evaluate, for example, the problems associated with working full time and going to school part time, as well as the problems of working part time and going to school full time.

In the end all branches converge back to the "happy ending" with Luis and his family. Note that this is not a mandatory protocol. You can branch off into virtually as many endings as you want, and they don't have to be happy. This ending was chosen to communicate a nonjudgmental attitude, but producers designing a

tape simulating jetliner piloting have no trepidations about showing the wrong choice ("Do you put the flaps up or down?"), resulting in the plane crashing and burning.

EXECUTION OF THE PROGRAM

Here are some of the procedures used in producing a program such as the example cited above:

- Once the various branches were represented on a flowchart and the producers were sure that there were no dead ends in the presentation, the various scenes were scripted. Actually, many were so short that they were ad-libbed from the director's instructions.

- Next, the graphics were designed and recorded. This particular presentation used video graphics generated at a production studio.

- The master one-inch tape was then assembled. *The scenes and graphics that were to be most frequently used were placed near the middle of the tape.* This was the only concession to putting scenes in any particular order. Remember, a video disc is a random-access device, and the programming of scenes in sequence will be done later. The video disc is copied directly from the master tape. So why were the most frequently utilized scenes and graphics placed in the middle of the tape? *To shorten access time on the video disc.* The farther the electronically guided "stylus" has to move, the longer it takes to get from one scene or graphic to another.

- The master tape was sent to a facility in Wisconsin for mastering onto a disc.

- When the disc was returned, the programmer used an authoring language to identify the locations of scenes and graphics and plotted those locations into the computerized branching system provided by the assembly language.

SUGGESTIONS FOR EFFECTIVE
INTERACTIVE PRODUCTION

Although this chapter has certainly not been a complete course in interactive design — in fact, even a complete course would probably not qualify anyone to handle such a complex task alone, at least for the first time — the information presented above and below provides you with a foundation on which to build your future

investigations into this medium. To conclude, here are some very basic suggestions that may help in the conception and execution of interactive video.

First, keep current with computer programs, especially those designed for producing animation and graphics. At the time this chapter was written, most producers polled would probably have said that computer-generated graphics (which are discussed in the following chapter) were largely inferior to those generated by television production equipment. That may be true. However, facilities capable of generating high-tech video graphics can often run several hundred dollars an hour. There are other problems with computer graphics, by the way. They take up enormous blocks of memory, and it takes the computer some time to "call up" and assemble graphics from its memory.

Second, pay particular attention to continuity. Continuity problems are one of the major bugaboos of interactive video. Remember that scenes can be viewed by the user of the program in many different sequences. It is possible, for example, for a particular branching sequence to carry the viewer from a scene that was shot at a desk on Monday to a scene shot in the same locale on Friday. Changes in the scene — clothing of the woman behind the desk, location and amount of debris on the desk, and the like — would be insignificant if there were *supposed* to be a time lag between the scenes. But can the branching juxtapose the scenes? Be careful, because you don't want the woman's jacket to change from blue to red and back to blue again during a job-interview sequence. Graphics can pose similar continuity problems. Different fonts, letter sizes, and background may not be readily apparent when graphics are made over a period of days, but when juxtaposed, the differences can be awkward. Here is an aspect where the computer shines: A computer's memory can store graphic templates and recreate them endlessly. Most art-producing programs (usually called "paint programs" in computer technology) allow this function, and they provide written specifications of point sizes, fonts, and screen dimensions.

Keep current with trade journals as well. They offer frequent updates on new authoring languages and equipment.

Finally, for high-quality applications consider using film instead of tape for recording initial sequences. Many viewers, as well as purchasers of programs, enjoy the aesthetic appearance of film. Motion picture film is, of course, more difficult to edit than is videotape, but this does not matter in the interactive mode, because it won't be "edited" in the traditional way, anyhow; it will be sequenced and dubbed onto a master videotape. Film cameras are more easily portable than video cameras, so you may be able to obtain shots not easily gotten with television gear. However, film is more expensive, and the program may wind up costing you an additional 25 percent of a video budget.

SUMMARY

≡ Interactive video has become a widely used training tool. It is used by firms and institutions, the armed forces, and by many schools and colleges.

≡ There are various levels of interactive technology. The most common level encountered by the video producer is Level 3, which combines a video disc with a computer control. *Interactive* means that the viewer is allowed to participate in the flow of the program, making choices and, if necessary, being corrected.

≡ A video disc is an optical storage device. It is read by a laser beam. Discs are much more useful than videotape for interactivity, because the information can be accessed randomly, without having to spool through several seconds' or minutes' worth of tape.

≡ The computer is the brains of the video disc. A standard personal computer, equipped with an interface, can run an interactive program. Many specialized units do not run on a personal computer. In any event most interactive material is programmed by an authoring language, which is a computer's software for writing interactive programs.

≡ A video disc is dubbed from a high-quality master tape. You will usually need specialized, high-end equipment to produce the master tape. The disc itself is made in only a few locations.

≡ The pathways of an interactive program are shown by a flowchart, which is simply a diagram of the branches of the program. After the scenes are scripted, they are shot, mastered, and placed on the disc. Then the programmer enters the information (in authoring language or programming language) that allows the computer to automatically find the addresses on the disc and perform the functions of cutting, freeze-framing, and calling up graphics from the computer or disc.

≡ Continuity is often a problem when designing interactive programs. Remember that the viewer will move from place to place in the disc or tape, so be especially careful about details such as clothing of talent and placement of props. Graphics presentations must be coherent, too.

EXERCISES

1. This exercise is provided for those readers who have access to a personal computer and educational software. (If you do not personally own either, check at your college or university library.) Choose an interactive educational-software package. Remember, this is not interactive *video*, but most educational software follows a branching strategy. Attempt to trace the paths you encounter in the software. These paths are supposed to be "transparent" to the casual user, but with some thought you should be able to see where the program leads you, where it doubles back on itself for "remedial work," and where the branches converge. Write a brief paper, illustrated, describing and tracing the paths you perceive.

2. If you live in a metropolitan area or live near firms or organizations that use video for training, do exercise 1, but use an actual interactive video. (You may have to do some footwork, but if you call local organizations and ask for the training department, you will probably uncover an interactive program somewhere. Also try your college or university library.) Be sure to ask for the least complex video available. As a point of interest you might ask for a printout of the screen that shows the branch path. (In some programs this is less than completely comprehensible, but it may provide some illumination.)

3. Write a brief script for a portion of an interactive training tape. Write it on whatever subject you like, but follow this format: Propose a situation and offer three solutions:
   a. Solution 1 is clearly wrong. Explain why, and route the script back to the proposed situation.
   b. Solution 2 is clearly wrong. Explain why, and route the script back to the proposed situation.
   c. Solution 3 is correct. Explain why, and move on to the next situation. The next situation has two branches, one correct and one clearly wrong. (For example: "You have now removed the back of the television set without the use of explosives or a jackhammer. Now you have two choices: Do you discharge the capacitor by (1) grounding the charge with a screwdriver or (2) standing in a pail of water and reaching in with your hand? Please enter your choice.")

NOTES

1. "Interactive Expert Systems Video Helps Employees with W-4s," *Administrative Management* (August 1987): 10.

2. The definitions of Levels 1–4 are adapted from "Interactive — They're at the Post: The Pre-Mastering Step," *AV Video* (May 1987): 30–36.

3. Frank Price, "Disc Dynamics," *Audio-Visual Communications* (February 1986): 40–43.

4. There are ways for a technically skilled producer to circumvent the high-end master-tape route; some are described by Jan K. Glenn in "Video Pre-Mastering," *Audio-Visual Communications* (March 1984): 45–46.

5. This is a very common problem. A good discussion of how to deal with it was compiled by James A. Lippke, Focus Group Editor, in "Interactive Videodisc Productions: Short Segments Raise Continuity Problems," *Educational/Institutional Television* (May 1987): 30–34.

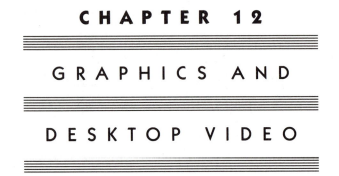

CHAPTER 12

GRAPHICS AND

DESKTOP VIDEO

Probably no area of video is as technically volatile as graphic design. With the advent of powerful hardware for image production and manipulation, the mind-set in video graphics seems to be "Can you top this?" Even fairly low-budget institutional presentations now feature rotating logos, "airbrushed" paintlike designs, and animated charts.

This chapter assumes that you have a basic knowledge of TV graphics and that instruction in the graphics techniques available to you at your facility is best left to your instructor. My primary purpose is to give you a quick introduction to the graphics revolution and the new wave of equipment that continues to change the medium: the increasingly powerful personal computer and the software designed to produce video graphics on your desk top. We'll take a look at the purpose of using graphics, the hardware for generating graphics, and the new generation of "desktop video."

THE PURPOSE OF GRAPHICS

Graphics images on the video screen seek to convey an idea or present information that is not easily spoken aloud or communicated through live action. They can make such ideas or information effective, convincing, attractive, and powerful.

DEVELOPMENT OF GRAPHICS AS A VIDEO COMMUNICATION TOOL

One of the earliest uses of video graphics was, as you might suspect, to create credits listing the production staff of television shows. Early TV reporters also found that maps were a necessity for newscasts and weather reports.

But during the first decade and a half of television graphics were quite crude. If you have viewed archival footage of newscasts from the 1950s and early 1960s (or are old enough to remember them), you'll recall that newscasters of the era frequently had no other option than to point directly at a hand-drawn map mounted on an easel. Printed graphics were also cumbersome. They were printed in the literal sense — on a graphics card — and then superimposed through various means over the video signal.

Things began to change in the early 1970s, when methods of electronically generating characters became practical and attractive. The late 1970s and early '80s saw tremendous advances in the development of special effects, such as those used to dress up weather segments of newscasts. In the mid-1980s the development of "painting" systems — devices to electronically produce and manipulate art — further changed the shape of the television image.

It can be argued that election coverage was the mother of invention, so to speak, of advanced TV graphics. Elections have always been something of a dilemma for video directors: How do you keep viewers' attention when the subjects about which you are broadcasting are primarily sets of numbers? Well, the networks and local affiliates attacked the problem with vigor, and each election brought forth a new parade of animated swooping numbers, colorful state-by-state vote totals, and 3-D graphs of electorate counts. Today, computer-driven election displays are the norm, and the technology has trickled down to local markets.[1]

HOW GRAPHICS COMMUNICATE

Election coverage is a perfect example of the logical use of graphics: Although some might argue that there is too much emphasis on glitz, it is apparent that *some* mechanism must be in place to communicate ideas that are primarily visual in nature. For example, a U.S. map showing which states have been won by each presidential candidate is a far more efficient and evocative journalistic device than simply having an announcer face the camera and toll off the vote counts.

Institutional video has also found that graphics displays can communicate complex ideas simply. Here is how Tanya Weinberger and Stephen Wershing, employees of an independent firm specializing in corporate communications, explain one such application:

> Animation can portray processes not normally observable. A recent assignment required us to map gas and liquid flow patterns through a fuel injection system. Sawing the fuel pump in half and pointing a camera inside would, in all likelihood, have not produced satisfactory results. The client would not have appreciated getting his injectors back in pieces, either. Our solution was to reproduce engineering drawings in the computer and cycle colors along the paths of fuel and air. The viewers saw an accurate representation of the system they could not have seen in person, with memorable and easily distinguished pathways of brightly colored fuel and air.[2]

Regardless of the subject, be it a fuel pump or an earnings report, graphics can clarify an image and make that image more interesting to the viewer. That communication is often said to occur on two levels: the foreground and background. The foreground level is the actual communication of the message. The background is the overall "image" projected by the organization, the "style" of the presentation.

One graphics designer, Chris Venne, notes that the background level is important and that "images" can backfire, especially when the graphic gives an inconsistent or contradictory message:

> An obvious example would be to use a dated style and technique in graphics about a company that markets state-of-the-art products. Or to create opulent looking electronic graphics to explain to employees the need to make wage concessions in their company. The mixed message between foreground and background levels of communication cannot help but undercut the effectiveness of the program.[3]

STANDARD GRAPHICS HARDWARE

Venne's point is well-taken: Glitz cannot be substituted for common sense. An additional factor must be considered: Glitz costs money, and because all budgets are finite, that money must usually come from another production area.

Today's television studio and postproduction editing suite are, without doubt, money-intensive. Rental of facilities can cost several hundred dollars an hour, an expensive proposition when a graphics effect is used because of the so-called Mount Everest syndrome (because it's there).

But graphics certainly should be used when needed, *if* they genuinely communicate a message both in foreground and background. The producer has a powerful arsenal at his or her fingertips, which when used correctly can add explosive power to the thrust of the production.

Those standard tools can be placed in many categories, but for the sake of description let's classify them as devices for *character generation*, *illustration*, *animation*, and *image manipulation*.

CHARACTER GENERATION

To briefly review some of the standard equipment available, consider the growth of the humble *character generator*, a device to produce titles, credits, and other graphics on screen. Originally a mere video typewriter, the CG can now store hundreds of pages of text as well as certain types of artwork.

The most modern character-generation devices produce a large variety of *fonts*; a font is a style of print, and the word is somewhat analogous to *typeface*. High-tech character generators are *antialiased*, meaning that they smooth out the "sawtooth" effect in digitally created images. Incidentally, it is interesting to note that one of the more popular new character generators, manufactured by Dubner Computer Systems, has an election-coverage graphics system built into it.

ILLUSTRATION SYSTEMS

Illustration mechanisms allow the user to create a drawing through various means. Sometimes, an electronic pen is used on a touchscreen or separate drawing tablet. Computerized commands also allow the operator to bring images together or create curves, lines, and other geometric shapes. Such systems can allow very impressive visuals, such as the translucent "airbrush" effects produced by devices such as the Quantel PaintBox. Illustration systems are often called "paint systems" because they allow the artist to use "brushes." Those brushes create soft edges, hard edges, and multicolored patterns.

Today, we're seeing an increase in so-called vector systems. *Vector systems* store descriptions of the created artwork via mathematical formulas, which the computer "memorizes" in three dimensions. Most traditional paint systems are two-dimensional.

ANIMATION SYSTEMS

Animation systems make images move on the screen. Unlike the traditional "cel" animation, which required artists to painstakingly draw thousands of individual frames, a modern animation apparatus creates the illusion of motion. High-end video-animation gear is capable of rotating "objects" in three dimensions. A less expensive option is known colloquially as "pseudo 3-D," in which the device does not really compute all dimensions but creates the illusion that it has done so.

Until recently, video animation did resemble traditional cel animation in that most of it was produced a frame at a time. Although frame-by-frame animation is still in widespread use, the top-of-the-line modern animation systems create movement in "real time"; that is, the computer rolls the scene in its entirety while the producer records.[4]

Note that there is no neat line between many illustration systems and animation systems. Some paint systems do allow animation, but some do not. In fact, many character generators offer very basic animation options.

IMAGE–MANIPULATION SYSTEMS

Sometimes called digital-effects systems, image-manipulation devices do not create images per se, as paint and animation systems do. Rather, they split, stretch, compress, flip, and rotate images. One of the more impressive images you may have seen in various television commercials and promotional spots — falling down an animated "tunnel" while the walls speed by you — was probably produced on the popular Quantel Mirage. Research and development engineers are constantly working on ways to increase the resolution of such devices as well as the ways in which images can be manipulated.

DESKTOP VIDEO

So how could anyone improve on this technology? To an institutional user on a limited budget, the answer is simple: *Make it affordable*. It is virtually impossible for most institutional operations to have this sophisticated equipment in house. A high-end image-manipulation system can cost $300,000, which is more than the initial price of some studios. Paint systems frequently have price tags topping $100,000.

Renting time on video graphics equipment at postproduction houses is a logical alternative, but it is quite obvious that a house that has paid more than a quarter of a million dollars for a piece of equipment must charge a hefty hourly rate just to pay off its loans. Postproduction can cost many hundreds of dollars per hour; and since effects take some time to create, the bill can add up quickly and stunningly.

But while the quiet revolution of institutional video was taking place, there was an even quieter revolution going on. Computer-savvy producers realized that the "brain" of expensive video equipment was essentially, in some cases *exactly*, the same brain as that in a personal computer. That brain, of course, is the microprocessor. Producers now realize that expensive video effects — character generation, animation, illustration, and, to an extent, image manipulation — can be approximated by the personal computer and specialized software.

Note the use of the word *approximated*. At this time personal computer-driven effects, known colloquially as *desktop video*, cannot duplicate the clarity and flexibility of the high-end video systems. However, desktop video can produce good-quality effects, and for simple graphics situations the results may be virtually indistinguishable.

THE BASICS OF DESKTOP VIDEO

In essence the "personal computer" is simply a small computer meant for the nonexpert user. Although you do not need a degree in computer science to operate a personal computer, some general knowledge is essential if you're going to use a PC in video applications.

First, recognize that video is not your computer's first language. A computer uses digital signals for producing graphics and doing all of its calculations. A video signal, however, is not in the simple on-off digitized format recognized by computer circuitry. As you are probably aware, a television production system mixes the three basic colors (red, green, and blue), information about the levels for whites and blacks, and the sync signal. This is called *composite video*, or *NTSC video*. (NTSC is an acronym for National Television Standards Committee.)

Most computers, though, cannot recognize or use a composite video signal. Computer visual images are usually produced by an RGB (red, green, blue) system, which creates an image by activating digital points of light on the monitor.[5] This is called a *component* signal.

Desktop video equipment handles this incompatibility problem with a genlock device. Genlock can not only synchronize video with video; it can, in desktop applications, synchronize video signals and computer-generated effects. One application of this mixing process allows you to mix RGB video and composite video and record the synthesis on tape.

Another useful device is the *frame grabber* or *video digitizer* (not exactly the same thing, but close enough for the purposes of this discussion). Either device stores a frame of video as a digital image. This allows you to use the power of the computer to manipulate the digitized video frame.[6]

In either case your desktop video system will provide you with a composite signal (usually at the output of a genlock device) that is patched to the input of the video tape recorder.

APPLICATIONS

There is a plethora of programs that produce video-usable titles, drawings, and animation. Programs such as Video Titler are popular for producers who want simple letter graphics for video productions. Video Titler, as well as the popular Deluxe Paint II, are especially appropriate for the Amiga computer line, which has become one of the most well-liked personal computers used in video production. In fact, the Amiga 2000 personal computer recently generated a great deal of interest at a National Association of Broadcasters convention. Observers noted that the entire realm of so-called low-end computer graphics equipment was a focus of much attention.[7] Amiga computers, at the time of this writing, were even gaining acceptance at broadcast outlets for producing weather graphics.

Apple is gaining acceptance in "low-end" video graphics, too. Philip Palombo, production chief at Greater Media Cable Advertising Sales in North Oxford, Massachusetts, has created an entire system driven by an Apple (Figure 12.1), a system about which he has lectured to industry groups. "The momentum for desktop video is tremendous," he says.[8]

FIGURE 12.1

The latest generation of computers can produce images that appear to rotate in three dimensions. The image on the screen has been digitally scanned and fed into the memory of the computer. Now it is being "modeled," or cast into "three dimensions."

Palombo feels that the Macintosh will gain rapid acceptance among institutional video users. (The Macintosh is extremely popular among Hollywood filmmakers and is catching on in broadcast and cable. Institutional video, Palombo feels, will be the next logical frontier.) Palombo uses the Mac to create some surprisingly complex animation (Figure 12.2) and graphics. In addition, he uses it to keep track of editing points on videotape and to maintain inventories of video effects.

(a)

FIGURE   12.2

Computer animation done via desktop video, such as this image produced at Philip Palombo's Greater Media facility (a), can produce startling effects. Also worth noting is that animation, such as the example
shown from a Boston Edison production (b), can produce effects that
make technical presentations more visual and understandable.

A variety of software is available for video-effects production on the Apple.
Studio 8 is a popular paint program; another program useful for institutional applications is Storyboarder, which produces storyboards as well as other effects.

IBM personal computers are not as well accepted by visually oriented users as
are the Apple and Amiga, but that situation is changing as additional software is
developed for the IBM. The Apple IIGS also is useful in some applications; its
program called Home Video Producer is functional for very low-budget productions on consumer-type gear.

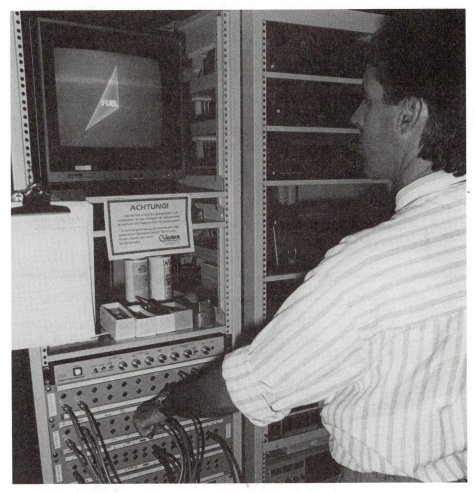

(b)

THE FUTURE OF DESKTOP VIDEO

No one can predict trends with certainty, but there does seem to be burgeoning interest in this emerging technology. Figure 12.3 contains one expert's perspective on the growth of the personal computer.

Perhaps one reason why computers are gaining such acceptance is the increasing "user friendliness" of the programs. You need not be a professional artist to use

THE PERSONAL COMPUTER AND THE FUTURE OF TELEVISION
by Philip J. Palombo

Prior to the personal and micro-computer's emergence, specialty hardware and software was the norm in television. With the PC establishing a foothold in many facets of production, what will it change? What is its future? While both audio and video equipment have enjoyed tremendous upward developments, so has the personal computer. The computer has had significant involvement in guiding major industries into the information age. We can now get an accurate glimpse of our future through the use of it. Projections of visionaries such as Nicholas Negroponte, Director/Cofounder of MIT's Media Lab, are becoming reality. The major premise of the work at Media lab is that the industries of broadcasting, publishing, and computing are merging to formulate a larger and richer direction. The lab's concern is how this research and development interface with the individual and that ergonomics are applied into this crossover craft of information technology. It's the computer industry that has facilitated this movement and it has become the source for better tools. We've experienced a span of four generations in microelectronic development to get us to the small, sleek and compact

Philip J. Palombo.

personal computer as we know it. The first was heralded before World War I with the introduction of the vacuum tube. The tube was the size of a light bulb and used as an amplifier and controller in much of the electronic equipment to come. In 1947 the first electronic digital computer, however unreliable, was invented. The ENIAC used 18,000 tubes, ran very hot and weighed thirty tons.

In 1948 Bell Telephone Laboratories baptized the second stage with the invention of the transistor. Still performing many switching functions of the tube, it used little current to control a larger one. With the dimensions of a pencil's eraser it performed more reliably and cooler.

FIGURE 12.3

The personal computer is making continuing inroads into television production. Here, one of the nation's leading experts on the subject, Philip Palombo, of Greater Media Cable Advertising Sales, gives his perspective. Palombo has written, lectured, and consulted extensively in this field. (Courtesy Ivan Shaw)

With the introduction of the transistor the first reliable, smaller and cool-running computer appeared in the l950s.

The 1960s ushered in the third step of the progression with our discovery of the silicon chip. It now became possible to etch electronic circuits onto a chip of silicon fitting thousands of transistors in an area no larger than a button. In 1969 the chips released from production accommodated a thousand or more transistors which introduced us into the fourth generation which became designated as very large-scale integration, or VLSI. Intel corporation designed the first computer on a chip and the microprocessor encompassed many of the functions of a computer. From here we can more clearly see the enormous contribution of the personal computer.

Recent introductions to the developing trend in computer assisted video are being applied to the production and post-production phases of television and film. Production workstations have been developed on the Macintosh platform by Seehorn and Avid Technologies. The Seehorn developers are not new comers to the field, they are Larry Seehorn and Steve Michaelson. Seehorn is a designer who has specialized in video technology and Michaelson founded "One-Pass Video," one of the country's premier production facilities. Earlier developments for Seehorn were the "'Epic," an advanced editor for its time, the "Light Finger," a touch sensitive multiple screen controller and "Editdroid." The last was produced by Lucas Film but utilized Seehorn's engineering prototype and tributary concept for video machine control. Seehorn's distributive intelligence concept for controlling editing machines is having individual controllers for two VTRs, each of which acts as a tributary to the main edit controller. Seehorn and Michaelson's newest introduction is the MIDAS (Multimedia Interactive Database Authoring System) which is quickly becoming a significant contribution to the industry. Believing that the editor was one portion of the post-production process, Seehorn set out to develop "spreadsheet" software that would fulfill the producer's needs in scripting, budgeting, and cataloging footage. With the emphasis on the database as the most prominent element of the MIDAS the producer dramatically increases their control over the project. Every facet of the production and post-production can now be identified through the database and starting as early as scripting and budgeting, enlightened decisions can be made.

Avid Technology's, Avid/1 Media Composer is also a workstation providing change to linear video editing. The Avid/1's major difference from the MIDAS is in the way it handles tape. Compression techniques permit the Media Composer to store two hours of motion video to CD-ROM. The two hours of footage includes two channels of 16-bit digital sound and requires 5 hard disks totaling 4.2 Gigabytes of storage. Full motion video editing is accomplished in the 8 bit color mode [256 available colors]. The MIDAS does not store the footage, instead it uses black-and-white frames digitized from the original tapes and uses them to represent the open and close of the edited sequences. Edit points are selected by clicking on an image; the image then drops into a lower position and its corresponding SMPTE time code becomes calculated as part of the edited sequence. This method on the MIDAS represents more of the traditional approach of film editing, while in contrast the Avid's screen display renders the buttons on a VTR.

The important thing to note about these newest contributions is that they differ from the traditional linear edit controllers in the way we interface with the machine and finally the program. Rather than choosing numbers (SMPTE data) from a CRT you are choosing visual images that are transparently associated with those numbers, representing a shot or a scene. The "in and out" points of your edit can now mean more than how each shot "cuts," they are more closely associated with the storyboarded images. In fact your rough cut can be a series of still frames "grabbed" from your footage. You begin to identify with the visual product much earlier in its development, providing you the ability to shape that product earlier into it. From conception to completion you have a clearer perspective of your direction. With the abundance of information introduced to the process creative decisions can be made more effortlessly.

These developments demonstrate similar patterns in the graphic arts and publishing industry. Just as desktop publishing has become a common term associated with producing graphics for print with a computer, we're now hearing the term applied to video. Conceptualizing on the desktop of a computer gives visual designers tremendous control and latitude in the processing of their work. It's this control that is referred to as the greatest advantage of all. To have the concept formulated into a tangible early in the process is a tremendous advantage. Another advantage is scaling cost and the production time line. Hyperscripting provides storyboard and animatic capabilities to aid in visualizing a TV commercial that previously would have been described in drawings.

There are now a number of ways to use video information in print. The user can "grab" (digitize) a video image and store the information in an exchange format for use later in desktop publishing. It wasn't too long ago that the only solution was a proprietary high resolution system such as those developed by Scitex, Crossfield, or Hell Graphics with a price tag of nearly a million dollars. Now several lower resolution but lower cost solutions are available on the desktop. These solutions will give you the abilities of the higher cost system, from capturing a video image to placing it in a page layout program. One company, Data Translations, provides complete hardware and software solutions for the Macintosh and PC with the ColorCapture digitizing board, a 24 bit retouch/color separation program, PhotoMac, and VideoQuill, an anti-aliased text application for keying graphics over your frame or genlocked dynamic video.

FIGURE 12.3, continued.

PostScript is a page description language that is established in the print industry as a de-facto standard to provide a method of describing and transferring images. Developed by Adobe Systems it assures the same quality on laser printers and high resolution imagesetters, using the same computer system and software. PostScript can transfer instructions about a page via telephone lines to film recorders, slide makers and high resolution prepress systems such as those developed by Scitex. Just as the print industry responded to consistency needs with PostScript there's been discussion in video about establishing a comparable standard. RenderMan Interface for 3-D Scene Description, has been introduced by Pixar as a potential way to define color 3-D images, complete with lighting and texture.

The personal computer, and with great speed, is moving toward a much needed interactive and intuitive interface. The graphical point and click interface is what propelled the Macintosh's early acceptance by visually oriented television producers and advertising directors. To not have to memorize obtuse codes is an advantage but also there's interformat compatibility through an application standard which means not having to "re-learn" each application's menus and functions. This accordingly increases productivity and leaves one to concentrate more on the work at hand, not on the application which also frees up the creative process.

Apple and NeXT Computers have been the trend setters in establishing the graphical desktop metaphor.

Active third party support programs also direct feedback from users regarding developments toward a more seamless interface. If there are advantages of a point and click interface, what are the associated disadvantages? Constant awareness of the point and click mechanism would probably be the most frequent response. The "mouse" is a step closer to a seamless interface than the keyboard but it's still not the solution. The graphical interface doesn't require learning the obscure codes of the command line interface (CLI) and becomes more of an intentional act. When you pick up a hammer you know what you're about to do with it, pounding nails is an automatic act. The user eliminates the notion of the act, freeing up vital creative instincts.

While the PC currently enjoys the power of digital processing, television will too become a totally digital medium. As we acquire more digital processing there will be an increase in the interactive capabilities; currently it's the personal computer that provides these capabilities. Interactivity will soar with the screen becoming a more intelligent display. HDTV is television that has computing capabilities.

Before discussing HDTV (high definition television) and ISDN (integrated services digital network), we must first understand some important theoretical concerns lurking behind accomplishing transmission of these technologies. Only then will we perceive the importance that calculates as a leap in accomplishing such a feat.

Bandwidth has been a major issue.

Bandwidth as described in *The Media Lab* by Stewart Brand: "The bandwidth bottleneck is the eternal bugaboo of communications technology: it governs the amount of data a medium can transmit per second." Think of bandwidth as an electronic conduit, a channel of sorts, through which information is pumped. Bandwidth determines fidelity and resolution; the higher the fidelity of a medium, the more bandwidth it requires to deliver the information. FM requires ten times per station more than AM. Television stations require thirty-three more times than FM stations. Graphic information is memory and disk space intensive and higher resolution even more so. What this currently means for the PC in television is that further resolutions in compression techniques are required and developing them is a challenging direction. To resolve this challenge, however, will mean momentous gains in processing information for business and entertainment.

Fiber-optic cable has become a solution for transmitting vast bandwidths of information. Fiber-optic can deliver millions of bits of information per second. Fiber has become the cable of choice over coaxial for both the telephone and cable TV industry. Eventually this could be introduced to every home, and ISDN would become a reality.

ISDN integrates voice, data and image for communications on one line. With ISDN, everything is transmitted as a digital signal allowing a phone call, data transmission, and visual images at the same time. Gone will be the day when a TV production company faxes over a storyboard to a client; audio and video images will be sent through an individual line instead. Bell Communications Research, Inc., predicts the U.S. will be rewired in the next 20 years, permitting voice, data and video to be delivered at up to 150 megabytes a second. With this transmission capability, we can consider delivering high-definition television.

Current National Television Standard Code (NTSC) for scanning is 525 lines per 30th of a second. The TV screen traces and retraces (refresh) at a rate that our eyes do not perceive flicker. However, if you were to position a monitor next to an Advanced Television display the scan lines become perceptibly slow. Standards have been proposed for HDTV for scanning rates of 1125 lines per 60th of a second. There is much debate and interest regarding this. Looking back at our bandwidth issue, 1125/60 will necessitate a spectrum of 5 television stations. In other words, a market now has frequency carriers for 5 TV stations, with 1125/60 there will be one. Every effort should be exhausted toward achieving the optimum system, when standards are adapted they tend to linger.

There are numerous examples demonstrating the merging of technologies with overlapping information activity. The personal computer has put us on a perfect course for the information age we've entered, when everything seems to approach the speed of light.

FIGURE 12.3, continued.

REFERENCES

Brand, Stewart. *The Media Lab; Inventing the Future at MIT*. New York: Viking Penguin, 1987.

Singleton, Loy A. *Telecommunications in the Information Age*, 2nd ed. Cambridge, MA: Belanger Publishing, 1986.

Rice, John, and McKernan, Brian. "Conversation with Nicholas Negroponte: Inventing the Future of Video." In *Videography*. New York: PSN Publications, 1988.

"Conversation with Larry Seehorn: The MIDAS Touch." In *Videography*. New York: PSN Publications, 1989.

a paint program, for example, although it helps if you are. Shapes are "stored" in the program, and if you are among the many who cannot draw a straight line, the paint program will present a grid that draws the line for you. The same process can be followed for drawing various regular and irregular shapes. Many fonts and letter sizes are available from computer programs.

Although the tools of computer paint and animation programs can serve as a partial substitute for mechanical skills, they cannot take the place of taste and discretion. A practiced eye is still the best judge of whether a graphic is balanced and effective. Should you have the opportunity to pursue training in basic graphics design, you may find it well worth the time and effort. In a relatively short period the producer, coupled with his or her computer, may be inheriting additional duties in the areas of layout and design.

SUMMARY

≡ Graphics fulfill a basic need in video: They present information that is not as easily grasped or as powerfully presented in a written or drawn presentation. We need graphics to represent locations, numbers, and abstract concepts not easily demonstrated by actual props or actions.

≡ Although many graphics effects are absolutely stunning, they should not be used just for the sake of using them. In fact, graphics can sometimes detract from the basic message of the program. Be sure that your graphics communicate the intended message on both the foreground and background levels.

≡ The video graphics equipment in current use can usually be classified either as devices for character generation, illustration systems, animation systems, or image-manipulation systems.

≡ The problem with much of the standard video-effects equipment is cost. Prices can be breathtaking, and even if you rent time on graphics-effects devices, your bill can still be enormous.

≡ One answer to the cost problem is desktop video, a process whereby a personal computer is used to imitate the effects of sophisticated video graphics equipment.

≡ Graphics effects produced via personal computers and special software cannot match the quality of those produced in a high-end studio or postproduction suite. However, the technology is continually improving, and much desktop video is perfectly adequate for simple titling.

EXERCISE

1. Computer or video-effects exercises must be designed and assigned by your instructor, since facilities and resources vary from institution to institution. However, here is an exercise that can be valuable even if you do not have access to a computer. Any large library contains books on printing. Look through some of these books and select typefaces (we'll call them *fonts*, because that is an accepted term in the video industry, but be aware that there is a slight technical difference in meaning between *typeface* and *font*) that you would consider appropriate in a logo for the following hypothetical firms:

   a. a high-tech computer firm that prides itself on manufacturing state-of-the-art hardware (Hint: Check the font called Helvetica)

   b. a midtown Manhattan furniture store that sells very trendy, very expensive modern pieces

   c. an old-fashioned saloon called the Four Aces

   d. a bank catering to very large businesses

   e. a bank catering to very small businesses

   f. a symphony orchestra

   g. a recording studio

   Photocopy samples of the fonts, and attach them to a paper in which you give a brief explanation of why you think a particular font reinforces the message. (You do not need to actually make the logo.) One strategy that may be helpful is to search through magazines and newspapers to find actual advertisements for the types of firms listed above. Note how the choice of lettering and other graphics elements communicates a foreground and background message.

NOTES

1. Alan Carter, "Graphics a Vital Tool, Users Say," *TV Technology* (April 1988): 12.

2. Tanya Weinberger and Stephen Wershing, "Corporate Communications Come to Life with Animation," *Educational and Industrial Television* (March 1986): 41–44.

3. Chris Venne, "Graphic Capabilities for Corporate Video," *Video Manager* (February 1987): 18, 19, 34.

4. One of the best summaries of animation systems and related technology was written by Bruce Hurn, "Developments in Imaging Programs Will Greatly Enhance Your Program Quality," *International Television* (September 1984): 38–50. The same issue carries an excellent article on creative image-making: David Hosansky, "New Options Offer You Endless Creative Possibilities": 52–58. Although they are becoming dated, articles from this issue offer succinct but complete explanations. If you want in-depth information, there are, of course, worthwhile books on the subject; some are listed in the suggested readings at the end of this book.

5. Steven Anzovin, "How Desktop Video Works," *Compute!* (December 1988): 28.

6. Ibid.

7. See Seven M. Davis, "Stations Improve Graphics Gear," *TV Technology* (April 1988): 21.

8. Interview, May 22, 1989.

CHAPTER 13

SATELLITES AND

DISTRIBUTION

NETWORKS

Item: Store managers at various branches of the J. C. Penney Corporation can now view the new season's fashions — by satellite. The fashion show is distributed nationwide, eliminating the cost and inconvenience of having store managers travel to a central location.

Item: The U.S. Army Material Command saves time by communicating with video through a hub at the Aberdeen Proving Ground in Maryland. Through special security measures even classified information can be discussed. An army commander estimates that two hours of airtime, bringing together as many as 10 different locations, saves 15 days of travel time for a conference.

Item: In Iowa a consortium of community colleges has joined forces with area businesses, hospitals, and other institutions to provide training via a private TV network. The institutions supply the training personnel and subject matter; the consortium supplies the hardware, presentational expertise, and technical know-how.

This is a small sampling of the applications of a satellite technology, a burgeoning area that promises to revolutionize corporate communications. Although distribution by satellite is not a new idea, the communications industry was, at the time of this writing, poised to move into new dimensions of satellite accessibility. The ease with which programming can be distributed is literally changing the way the United States does business. Firms today are able to market products, distribute training material, and hold corporate meetings by satellite-transmitted video.

This chapter focuses on distribution systems, in general, and satellites, in particular. Although satellites are not the only method of distributing corporate and institutional television, they are assuming preeminence, for reasons that will be explained. In fact, it is undoubtedly safe to predict that any institutional video producer will deal extensively with orbiting "birds" during his or her career; the impact of the evolving technology is, indeed, that pervasive. A cohesive base of knowledge concerning satellites and their workings will be essential. This chapter is intended to demystify the seeming magic of earth-to-space-to-earth transmission. Familiarity with satellite technology is an increasingly common prerequisite in institutional communications, and if nothing else, this chapter may prove valuable for future reference.

BACKGROUND OF DISTRIBUTION TECHNOLOGY

"Moving" information from one point to another, or to a number of points simultaneously, by some means other than physical transportation became a reality with the invention of the telegraph, circa 1832. That technology was refined into the telephone, an interactive device first demonstrated in 1876. Both used strung wires — "land lines," in more up-to-date communications parlance — to transmit information.

But the necessity of land lines made certain communications applications cumbersome or impossible; even the most inventive of innovators could not find a way to string wires to a ship at sea. The relentless efforts of Guglielmo Marconi produced a wireless telegraph by which the dots and dashes of Morse code could be sent through the air, a system patented in 1897; by the early 1900s a workable "radiotelephone" could transmit voices.

Researchers then worked to discover a method to include pictures in a radio-wave transmission. The first commercial applications of television were developed in the 1940s, although research into TV had been carried on during previous decades.

By the middle of the 20th century another important facet in moving information had been developed, bringing a portion of the communications industry full circle back to the era of physical transportation: practical methods of storage. Videotape and audiotape became the "film" of TV and radio, and programs could be mailed or sent by messenger.

Meanwhile, microwaves—very-high-frequency electromagnetic radiation—were becoming a new method of choice for moving information. Ground stations located on high hills and mountains could transmit data quite efficiently over long line-of-sight distances.

The capability of a microwave to produce a tightly focused beam held promise for extremely long-range transmission, and in 1960 an experimental balloon satellite was placed in a low orbit within the earth's atmosphere. Signals bounced off its metallic surface could be picked up when they returned to earth, and a new era was born. By 1974 the first satellite used for domestic U.S. communications, Westar I, was orbited.

Even though airborne signals, be they microwaves or the standard broadcast spectrum, were convenient, the communications industry found that this convenience had a price. That price was fueled by short supply. Because only a limited amount of information could be transmitted over electromagnetic spectra before those spectra became overcrowded (and the cost of spectrum space concomitantly increased because of supply and demand), attention was once again focused on the humble land line. Cable television, for example, was developed to the point at which a community could import an abundance of signals.

Physical distribution became easier through advancing technology. In the 1960s, for instance, only television stations and major TV facilities could make use of videotapes, since the tape of the time was spooled on a cumbersome reel and could be played back only on a gigantic, incredibly expensive machine that had to be operated by a trained engineer. Today, however, videocassette recorders are ubiquitous in businesses, organizations, and homes; distributing video information by mail has become a practical reality.

This brief history was presented to illustrate that methods of distributing program information change in light of new technologies and that in some cases those technologies bring about a rebirth of old methods. Advancing technology creates new options, and apparently outmoded methods exhibit previously unrealized potentials.

To the producer of institutional video, all the options presented in the history above have relevance. Although this chapter deals mostly with satellites, other still common — and, depending on circumstances, still perfectly viable — distribution mechanisms are discussed. Those mechanisms include *physical transportation of tapes, in-house closed-circuit distribution, standard broadcast or cable*, and *microwave transmission systems*.

PHYSICAL TRANSPORTATION

Mass duplication of videotapes has become reasonably cost-efficient in recent years, especially with the increased availability of consumer-oriented 1/2-inch VCRs. Some organizations that desire higher quality video or intend to distribute tapes to news organizations for public relations use broadcast-standard tape, such as the 3/4-inch cassette.

Although duplicating and mailing can be quite convenient, there are some disadvantages. First of all, there is no practical method for immediate feedback; a viewer cannot talk back to the tape (at least, in such a way as to elicit a response). Secondly, duplication and mailing involve an inherent time lag. Finally, expenses can be considerable if the number of individual tapes to be duplicated and mailed is high.

An option for physical transmission is to "bicycle" tapes, a method common to commercial television, although increasingly less so. Bicycling means that a station will play a tape and ship it to another station, which will then play the tape and mail it to yet another station. This method saves duplicating costs but involves a considerable time lag for the last destination on the list and also increases the possibilities of shipment problems.

IN–HOUSE CLOSED–CIRCUIT DISTRIBUTION

Television master-control centers in institutions such as colleges and major office buildings can easily route signals via cable to various locations in the building. In most cases all an instructor need do is call by telephone or intercom to cue the operator to begin transmission.

Closed-circuit television systems were considered a major innovation when many educational institutions incorporated them in the 1960s and '70s, but the concept has lost some of its luster. For one thing, the availability and ease of use of videocassette decks make many closed-circuit applications somewhat obsolete. Secondly, closed circuit has the disadvantage of lack of user control. An instructor cannot stop or rewind the tape if a point needs clarification.

STANDARD BROADCAST OR CABLE

An institution seeking to transmit video information to a widely dispersed group of viewers has the option of buying time on a commercial cable or broadcast television station. Broadcast TV is quite expensive; cable is less so. But both have the inherent disadvantage of offering a largely unfocused audience, whereas institutional television producers typically want to reach a highly specific group. The exception is when a tape is produced for public relations with the general public being the target.

MICROWAVE LINKS AND NETWORKS

A microwave gets its name from the fact that the wave is of an extremely high frequency and, therefore, has a very small *physical length*, virtually microscopic in the higher ranges of the frequency. (As you probably remember, the greater the frequency of an electromagnetic wave, the shorter the wavelength.) High-frequency waves such as microwaves travel in a line-of-sight beam and stay very focused. Low-frequency AM radio waves are not beams at all; they radiate and bounce every which way.

Microwaves are very useful for point-to-point communication. They can be emitted in a tight beam, usually focused by a parabolic dish, and received by a dish-shaped antenna. Microwaves are therefore excellent for *private* communications; they do not radiate in all directions and generally do not cross paths and interfere with one another. The microwave spectrum covers a range of about 1 gigahertz — meaning 1 billion hertz, with *hertz* being a frequency of one cycle per second — to 300 gigahertz, abbreviated gHz.[1]

Microwave installations are commonly used to transmit data, including phone calls. (The *M* in MCI, the private telephone company, stands for *microwave*.) Television can be transmitted by microwave, which is one way in which cable stations and broadcast stations pick up feeds of program material. Microwaves are essential for satellite distribution. But they are also used for ground transmission of television. The Instructional Television Fixed Service (ITFS) pioneered the use of private microwave transmission for distributing educational programming. The frequency at which ITFS operates, in the 2-gHz range, is ideal for low-power, short-range transmission.

Commercial applications of the same technology include the Multipoint Distribution Service (MDS). MDS transmits pay television to facilities such as hotels.

MDS became so popular, in fact, that the Federal Communications Commission took away some ITFS frequencies and allotted them to MDS.

The area where microwave transmission has made the most profound impact is in communicating with orbiting relay stations. These spaced-satellite relays receive the tightly focused beam and send it back to earth, eliminating the need for many regularly spaced ground-based relays to retransmit the signal. More than 60 relays would ordinarily be needed to transmit a signal from coast to coast; spanning the ocean offers obvious problems.

However, land-based transmission is still necessary. "Last-mile" systems often transmit microwaves from the receiving satellite to the actual reception location.

HOW A SATELLITE WORKS

Unlike a ground-based microwave relay, which transmits from point to point, a communications satellite can send a signal to any number of receiving dishes within the area on the earth where the signal falls. This area is known as the "footprint." A footprint can be as large as a third of the surface of the earth.

Because of the aforementioned cohesiveness of the microwave signal — its propensity to travel in a strict line of sight and not wander off — it can travel long distances and stay focused. And since the receiving antenna for microwave transmission points directly toward the source, interference from other signals (coming from other directions) is reduced.

The modern communications satellite (there are, of course, many other types of satellites, but the discussion here is limited to those that retransmit communications signals) typically operates in the following fashion.

The signal to be transmitted is sent from a ground dish called the *uplink earth station*. The orbiting satellite, which is in a fixed position relative to the earth (exactly how it stays in position is explained in a moment), picks up the signal on its antennas and transmits it back to the predetermined footprint area. Note that satellites transmit back to earth on a different frequency than the signal sent up; this is done to avoid interference. The device that receives, converts, and retransmits is called a *transponder*. Modern communications satellites typically carry 24 transponders. Each transponder operates on a different set of frequencies to avoid interference. The transponder signal is received by the *downlink earth station*, which uses a dish aimed at the satellite to pick up the signal. Most downlink stations are built only to receive a signal, and those used for reception of video are known as *television receive-only earth stations*, or TVRO earth stations.

Note that some microwave antennas can receive a certain type of data and send another. VSAT systems (an acronym for *very-small-a*perture satellite *t*erminal) can receive video and other data signals but can transmit only simple signals, such as computer data transmissions. VSATs are becoming popular in England and Japan for direct reception of satellite broadcasting, and they are often used in the United States for transmission of computerized data.

That is the essence of satellite operation. Some other concepts are useful for understanding the current status of satellite technology: geostationary orbits, limitations in orbital and spectrum space available, transmission bands, and how the user logs on to a satellite transmission.

THE GEOSTATIONARY ORBIT

Communications satellites operate most efficiently when they are "parked" in orbit 22,300 miles above the equator and circle the earth at a speed that keeps them over the same spot on the earth's surface. This way, they can "see" their targets at all times and remain in the same position relative to the uplink and downlink. Such a satellite is said to be in "geostationary" orbit.

THE CROWDED SKY

The seemingly limitless area above the equator is nevertheless a limited resource, at least in terms of current technology. Satellites must have some distance between them to avoid interference. Early U.S. satellites required about 4 degrees of distance; modern satellites can operate with 2 degrees of separation. The orbital slots are determined, of course, by dividing up the 360 degrees that constitute a complete circle around the earth. In space, 1 degree of separation translates to about 470 miles.

The problem is that many countries and private firms want a slice of that orbital pie, a pie that is diminishing as technologically advanced nations orbit new birds. Third World countries frequently complain that they are denied satellite space.[2]

TRANSMISSION BANDS

Communications satellites use specific portions, or bands, of the microwave spectrum. The C-band is made up of frequencies from 4 to 6 gHz, and the Ku-band satellites operate in ranges of 11 to 15 gHz. Most systems currently operate in the

FIGURE 13.1

A satellite dish "farm" at the Pittsburgh International Teleport. Although you cannot always distinguish C-band from Ku-band dishes by size alone, note that C-band dishes are usually bigger. The three front dishes, 30 feet in diameter, are C-band. The dishes on either side of the vertical antenna are Ku-band; they are 12 feet in diameter. The teleport serves a variety of clients, including CBS, CNN, and NASA.

Courtesy Pittsburgh International Teleport.

C-band, although the Ku-band is gaining increasing acceptance. One advantage of the Ku-band is that Ku transmitters generate higher power, meaning that ground-based reception stations can be smaller and less expensive. Ku-band dishes are sometimes only 2 or 3 feet in diameter. The smaller C-band dishes can be shrunk to a diameter of about 6 feet. High-performance installations usually use bigger dishes, though. The Pittsburgh International Teleport, for example, whose clients include CBS News, Cable News Network, and the National Aeronautics and Space Administration, utilizes 30-foot C-band dishes and 12-foot Ku-band dishes (Figure 13.1).

FIGURE 13.2

Here is where satellite signals are received and processed. The unit being adjusted is tuned to receive and decode the signals.

For the institutional video producer, the Ku-band is less subject to interference from existing ground-based microwave units, most of which operate on the C-band. But the extremely small wavelength of the Ku-band does make it susceptible to "rain fade," a phenomenon in which raindrops actually block the waves during heavy downpours.

Although predictions relating to satellite technology are risky, it is probably safe to assume that new developments, such as the growth of Ku-band technology and the ability to compress satellite-borne signals into a smaller bandwidth, will accommodate institutional video's continued expansion into satellite transmission.

HOW TO LOG ON TO A SATELLITE TRANSMISSION

The process of receiving a satellite feed has become relatively simple. The party transmitting the programming will inform you in advance of the logistics. Certain networks publish regular schedules.

In either case you will be given the beginning and ending time of the feed, the name of the satellite, the number of the transponder to which to tune your equipment, and other tuning coordinates. A reception unit (Figure 13.2) will allow you to key in the information and will automatically make the proper adjustments for the connection.

APPLICATIONS

Availability of satellite time allows institutional video producers a number of options. Renting time on a transponder is no longer prohibitively expensive for a small organization. Ku-band satellite video uplink time can be rented for as little as $700 per hour, with further discounts for those who buy in volume.[3]

Nor are frequency time and space difficult to come by. Expansion of the frequencies available and the two dozen or so American communication satellites now parked in orbit have made transponder time a less precious commodity, and there are often deals to be had from cable networks, such as certain regional sports channels, which rent out their transponder availability.

Businesses, schools, and nonprofit institutions are using imaginative approaches to exploit this new technology, including dedicated networks and video conferencing. Large-scale hookups are producing gigantic networks; General Motors, at the time of this writing, was designing a network with more than 10,000 sites. In addition, satellite applications hold great promise for reaching remote or widespread areas. India, a vast land with many communications problems, is turning to satellite transmission as a method of reaching learners across the nation. Learn Alaska, reputed to be the world's largest instructional satellite network, provides the same function for that sprawling state.

DEDICATED NETWORKS

Organizations that offer regular programming find that with proper production values organizational communications are streamlined, morale is boosted, and the costs of travel and tape duplication are cut considerably. Setting up these networks is greatly simplified by a new type of vendor: the private network services firm, which often arranges what might best be termed an ad hoc network. One such organization, Private Satellite Network, Inc., has brokered network time and space for such organizations as IBM, Aetna Life Insurance, and the Social Security Administration.[4]

FUTURE POTENTIAL

Like many other technological innovations, satellite transmission is rapidly becoming easier. Although a comprehensive knowledge of the technical details of satellites is certainly useful, it is becoming less of a necessity. Today's user need not know the intricacies of orbital parking spaces and transponder polarities; he or she can simply telephone an outside vendor and summon up the time. The lexicon is becoming less threatening, too. The names Satcom, Westar, and Telstar have moved into the general vocabulary.

There is a chance that satellite dishes may become as common as home VCRs. Although home satellite dishes are certainly not a rarity even now, technology may advance to the point at which extremely small and technically simple dishes for receiving signals from direct broadcast satellite (DBS) are commonplace. DBS is in its infancy, and although most observers see it primarily as a potential entertainment service, the evolving technology could find educational and corporate uses. But DBS has never really generated much enthusiasm, at least not in the United States.

Finally, it is worth noting that preeminence in communications technology may come full circle and return to the humble land line. Fiber-optic cables under development could eventually handle an enormous amount of video information, but that potential is still developing. It is unlikely, though, that satellites will lose any of their luster as the sky-borne stars of the communications empire.

SUMMARY

≡ Satellites have simplified long-distance transmission of institutional video to such an extent that they are changing the way the United States does business.

≡ Satellites are not the only method of distribution available to the institutional television producer. Other methods include physical transportation of tapes, point-to-point ground transmission, and in-house closed-circuit distribution.

≡ Microwaves have the ideal physical properties for satellite transmission: They stay tightly focused and therefore do not dissipate over long distances.

≡ A typical satellite feed begins from an uplink ground station and is transmitted to the satellite transponder, which amplifies the signal and feeds it back to a downlink station.

≡ Satellites operate in the C-band and the Ku-band. Ku-band applications are now undergoing new development, and they hold a great deal of promise for institutional users.

≡ Satellite systems are becoming much more accessible, and equipment and time are becoming less expensive.

≡ Although some organizations have full-time dedicated networks, others choose to rent isolated blocks of transponder time. Outside vendors often handle the entire process of arranging a satellite feed.

EXERCISES

1. Interview a local institutional video manager concerning his or her use of satellites. Describe, in a three- to four-page paper, the specifics of local use of satellite technology.

2. Assume that you are the manager of an in-house video department. Think of distribution technology(ies) you would use for this application: a training program illustrating maintenance procedures for a new piece of equipment manufactured by your company. Ten technicians, each of them at a different location across the country, need access to this demonstration. (One hint: Would one viewing of the presentation be enough? Wouldn't the technicians benefit from seeing portions several times?) Write a brief response.

3. Making the same assumption as in exercise 2, how would you distribute a demonstration of a new piece of equipment to department store product buyers for a nationwide chain of 700 stores?

NOTES

1. The official Federal Communications Commission classifications are based on frequency and not wavelength, so *microwave* is not always a precisely defined term. Microwaves are considered to be part of the superhigh-frequency (SHF) spectrum of 3 to 30 gHz, and the extremely high-frequency spectrum, 30 to 300 gHz. Microwave applications also utilize portions of the ultrahigh-frequency (UHF) range. UHF extends from 300 megahertz to 3 gHz, but the microwave portion of UHF is considered to begin at about 1 gHz. So for most purposes, the word *microwave* can be taken to mean radio frequency energy from 1 to 300 gHz.

   Two of the most understandable explanations of the electromagnetic-frequency spectrum can be found in George E. Whitehouse, *Understanding the New Technologies of the Mass Media* (Englewood Cliffs, NJ: Prentice-Hall, 1986): 2–120, and Sydney W. Head and Christopher H. Sterling, *Broadcasting in America*, 5th ed. (Boston: Houghton Mifflin, 1987): 127–191. The table of electromagnetic spectrum allocations, which lists microwaves as ranging from 1 to 300 gHz, is on page 130 of Head and Sterling.

2. "Satellite Slots," *Fortune* (June 24, 1985): 88. For an interesting view of the incredible complexities involved in allotting satellite space, see "Space WARC '85: A Look Back," *Satellite Communications* (November 1985): 67, 68, 70.

3. "Satellite Slots," 88.

4. "Growth of Private Networks Continues," *Video Manager* (April 1987): 1, 29.

CHAPTER 14

TELECONFERENCING

Once the exclusive domain of Fortune 500 firms, teleconferencing is becoming a reality for a wide spectrum of organizations. Schools, physicians, even churches meet electronically, sharing information and solving problems in what may be the next best option to face-to-face communication. Indeed, some communications professionals, as we'll see later in this chapter, feel that teleconferencing improves the quality of a meeting.

Although acclaim for the process of teleconferencing is virtually unanimous, definitions of what exactly constitutes a teleconference differ. This attempt to define terms, incidentally, is not entirely an academic exercise. It has been the experience of many video professionals that disputes over the feasibility of teleconferencing are often hindered by the fact that none of the negotiating parties knows what the other party believes a teleconference is.

Jan Sellards, president of the International Teleconferencing Association, defines the term this way:

> Teleconferencing is the meeting between two or more locations and two or more people in those remote locations, where they have a need to share information. That does not necessarily mean a big multimedia event. The simplest form of teleconferencing is an audioconference. Modern telephone systems let you connect two or more locations simply by pressing your switch hook and calling those locations; that is in effect a teleconference.[1]

Teleconferencing is a technology in transition, with frequent new developments. So be aware that some of the technical details in this chapter are doomed to be obsolete within a short time. Regular reading of trade journals, such as those listed in the suggested readings, will keep you up to date. This chapter also deals with the basics of how a video conference can be effectively organized to communicate ideas, and it examines the principles of planning and structure that contribute to a successful conference. Three areas will be stressed:

1. why a teleconference may or may not be a good option
2. options in teleconferencing
3. how an electronic meeting functions

WHY TELECONFERENCE?

At the same time that options in communications technologies were starting to shrink distances, the cost of physically traveling those miles was growing.

THE GROWING COST OF BUSINESS TRAVEL

A communications researcher, Frederick Williams has noted that from 1976 to 1980 (an active period in the growth of communications technologies) the cost of travel increased an estimated 30 percent while the dollar figure attached to communications costs for a computer terminal, audio line, and facsimile machine (an early ancestor to full-fledged video conferencing) was dropping 30 percent.[2]

Beyond the cost of transportation and lodging, face-to-face meetings create other problems. Among the most nettlesome is the physical and emotional toll that traveling takes on executives. People simply do not work well when they are exhausted from travel and stressed from worrying about whether their planes will be on time.

Another hidden problem inherent in business travel is the logistical complications created by corporate hierarchies. Businesspeople typically assert their status by the clothes they wear and the furnishings of their office. Such impositions of status, and the time and money spent constructing and reinforcing levels of status, could be better allocated to the business at hand. Even the site of a meeting is a logistical factor drastically complicated by status. It is obligatory that lower ranking executives travel to the offices of the higher ranking executives, even if that means rearranging the schedules of dozens of employees to accommodate one high-ranking man or woman.

Telecommunications, though, are largely "destatusing," and although communicating via audio and video does not solve all the problems of human interaction, many of the logistics relating to status are simplified.[3]

AVAILABILITY OF NEW TECHNOLOGY

Today, the technological capabilities of communications equipment make those of the early 1980s appear primitive by comparison; in addition, the options are accessible to almost everyone. No advanced training is necessary, for example, to arrange a telephone conference call or to hook up two computers to transmit text and data. Although linking meeting sites by video is more complex, it still is within the ability of organizations with even the most modest of budgets.

Using new communications technologies may not be overwhelmingly complex, but sorting through the terminology can be. One problem confronting the in-house video specialist who wants to teleconference is simply sorting through the inexact lexicon related to the process. Next, he or she must deal with the complexities of choosing the technological options to employ.

First, a primer in teleconferencing itself. *Teleconferencing* is a form of *telecommunications*. Telecommunications is a recently invented word with a long heritage. *Tele* is Greek for "distant" and is the root of words such as *telescope*. *Communicate* derives from a form of a Latin word meaning "to share."

Sharing information over a distance is what telecommunications is all about, and teleconferencing adds a new dimension: holding a conference among many people over a long distance. A teleconference, as the term is popularly used, often involves sharing information with video. Some practitioners prefer to call conferences using video "videoconferences" and conferences using audio "audioconferences." The terminology is not yet quite standardized, but the categories just listed are good ones to remember.

For many firms and organizations, sharing such information is vital. Consider these situations:

≡ A savings bank is going public and needs a mechanism by which to give details of its stock conversion to depositors and loan holders and to obtain their reactions. Teleconferencing is a superb alternative, and that's exactly the strategy followed by the Buffalo-based Empire of America Savings Bank, which held 20 nationwide video conferences. Fifty million dollars in stock was eventually sold.[4]

≡ Managers of a nationwide chain of stores need a way to reach, on a reasonably personal level, employees who are literally scattered across the country. Stores including J. C. Penney and K mart use teleconferencing regularly to meet this exact need.

≡ Experts in remote locations need to view a technical drawing and iron out design problems in a new assembly. Many high-tech firms find teleconferencing invaluable for this task. Samuel Long, teleconference coordinator for the General Dynamics Corporation's Convair Division, in San Diego, feels that teleconferencing is now indispensable for his group, for more reasons than simply saving on travel costs:

> We like to stress that now we can have all the experts on a particular project sit in on a meeting instead of just a few. When a question or problem comes up, the engineer involved can immediately come up to the mic and address the issue. It's a very efficient use of time and personnel, especially when dealing with complex engineering problems and far-flung company divisions.[5]

OPTIONS IN TELECONFERENCING

Keeping in mind that teleconferencing does not necessarily mean a multiscreen video extravaganza, let's examine the range of available options. Be aware that, as in any emerging technology, vocabularies are not precise across the entire range of users. But the following definitions are what appear to be the most accepted usage among knowledgeable leaders in the profession.

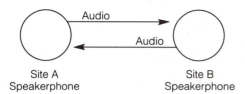

FIGURE 14.1

Two-way communication in an audioconference. The same model could be used for point-to-point audio with video.

TELECONFERENCING FORMATS

There are two fundamental types of conferences: interactive, in which there is two-way communication, and what for lack of a better term might be called a broadcast, a one-way transmission to many points. The following are variations on these two fundamental categories.

Point-to-Point Conference, Audio Only   The first option involves nothing more than a group of people at point A communicating with a group of people at point B. The groups at each end commonly use speakerphones (Figure 14.1).

Point-to-Point Conference, Audio and Video   In the second option the group at point A is able to hear *and* see the group at point B, and vice versa. Sometimes, a point-to-point audio and video conference is called a teleconference even if there is only one person at each end; when the same scenario occurs with audio only, the communication is obviously termed a telephone call.

   Although sometimes arranged on an ad hoc basis, facilities for point-to-point and point-to-multipoint teleconferences are often dedicated facilities, built specially for the task at hand.

Point-to-Multipoint Conference   A point-to-multipoint conference involves a program originating from a central production stage. The program is then sent to various locations. This is essentially a private broadcast (Figure 14.2).

Point-to-Multipoint Conference with Feedback   In the fourth arrangement the program originates from a central production stage and is sent to multiple locations, but viewers at those locations have the opportunity to talk back to

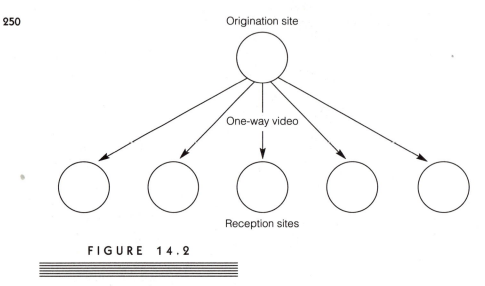

Origination site

One-way video

Reception sites

FIGURE 14.2

A point-to-multipoint conference without feedback.

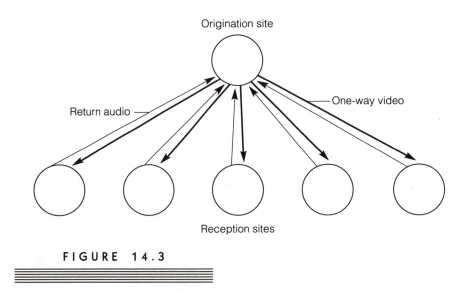

Origination site

Return audio

One-way video

Reception sites

FIGURE 14.3

A point-to-multipoint conference. Bold lines represent video (with audio, of course); fine lines represent return audio. Point-to-multipoint can also be accomplished with return video.

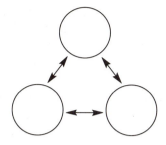

FIGURE 14.4

A multipoint-to-multipoint conference. All sites are origination sites and can receive audio and video from the other sites. The same model could be applied to audio only.

the original point, sometimes through video and commonly through audio (Figure 14.3).

Multipoint-to-Multipoint Conference Whether they involve audio only or audio and video, conferences can be held at several different sites, with each site being able to communicate with the rest. This is by far the most complex method of teleconferencing (Figure 14.4).

A variety of technologies is available to the producer who plans to use any of the above teleconferencing formats.

TRANSMISSION OPTIONS

Satellites, described in the previous chapter, provide the most common path for transmission of a teleconference signal, although land-based microwave units, telephone transmission lines, and fiber-optic cables are also options. Unfortunately, any transmission medium involves expense. A high-quality video signal takes up about as much transmission bandwidth as 2,000 telephone calls, meaning that the full-video option uses a high amount of limited resources and therefore involves a relatively high cost.

The transmission method most closely approximating the resolution (picture quality) of standard television is known in teleconferencing terminology as *full-motion video*. To understand why full-motion video requires a large amount of bandwidth, remember that a television picture contains a huge amount of information compressed into a short period of time. In the United States we see 525 lines of information scanned onto the screen at the rate of 30 frames per second. The scanning rate cited for standard broadcast television refers to how often the screen must refresh itself in order to properly recreate, let's say, the motion of a running back in a football game. This is known as *temporal resolution*.

It became apparent to developers of teleconferencing equipment that coverage of meetings does not require the same temporal resolution as a football game. CEOs giving speeches don't move that much; scientific drawings don't move at all. A device was needed to save the amount of bandwidth needed and therefore save money in the transmission of video teleconferences.

That device is known as a codec, a coder-decoder camera or TV mixing console to a digital signal, meaning a signal composed of the binary on-off language of the computer. A codec on the other end reconverts the digital signal to video.

The codec has an additional capability that results in a quite miserly use of the bandwidth: It digitally stores and "freezes" parts of the picture that do not change rapidly. A codec-translated picture often appears somewhat unnatural if the transmission rate is low. Lips may move, but the face may stay frozen, for example. A speaker walking across the stage may blur. Such blurring is a result of the low temporal-resolution capability of a codec-encoded picture moving at a low transmission rate. Remember, low transmission rates are utilized because they use less bandwidth and therefore save money on the rented transmission channel.

The highest range of information-carrying capability generally available to teleconferences is known as DS-3 (digital service Level 3; digital service is a reference to an industry standard). Information is transmitted at about 45 million bits of data per second. *Bit* is a computer term for a unit consisting of binary digits. Forty-five million bits per second is abbreviated 4.5 megabits per second, *mega-* meaning million, or simply 4.5 mbps. Codecs transmitting at 4.5 mbps produce a picture that, for most applications, is almost indistinguishable from standard broadcast TV.

Level DS-2 operates at a little less than 7 mbps. This level provides reasonable video fidelity for almost all videoconferencing applications.

Level DS-1, also called T-1, operates at approximately 1.5 mbps. This level of transmission can be handled by a good-quality specialized land line. It produces a blurrier picture than does DS-2, although it's still appropriate for talking heads.

The lowest level, DS-0, sends signals at about .056 mbps. This produces a low-quality signal but one that can still transmit some motion while occupying no more space than a standard telephone call.[6]

It is difficult to describe with precision the quality of pictures available at each transmission level because the capabilities of the codecs play a major role in determining quality. Additionally, the picture quality must be judged by its suitability to the task at hand. Some codecs are better at transmitting graphics but produce poor motion; the reverse can also be true.

Remember, too, that different makes of codecs, by and large, are not compatible with one another. You generally need identical models at both ends. There is promise of eventual standardization, just as basic computer modulator-demodulator (modem) transmissions have been largely standardized in recent years.

While we're on that subject, don't forget that other technologies are useful in teleconference communications, and the computer is one of them. Personal computers can share information by modem. In fact, recently developed programs allow users on distant ends of the connection to work on the same document simultaneously. High-resolution graphic devices (basically, souped-up facsimile machines) transmit hard copy with excellent detail. The telephone company can hook you up with videophones, too, an easy way to break into teleconferencing. In addition, remember that you do not need a satellite to transmit video. Locally available microwave service, such as Instructional Television Fixed Service, is useful for educators whose teleconferencing needs do not exceed a 25-mile radius.

CHOOSING AMONG OPTIONS

How does the person in charge of video arrangements choose from among the myriad options available? The following guidelines have gained widespread acceptance among teleconferencing professionals.

First, define the need, and then choose the hardware. Don't design the facility first and attempt to invent ways to use it. Consider whether most of your transmission needs will be, out of necessity, two way, or mostly transmission of simple graphics, or among large groups, and so forth.

Second, establish the success or failure of teleconferencing experimentally. It is a mistake to squander capital on a system that won't be used to full advantage. Likewise, a video department may not be able to secure the backing of top management unless executives have a chance to see teleconferencing in action. Many firms lease equipment on a long-term basis. Many production companies specialize in teleconferencing design and will provide you with a one-time setup or a long-standing turnkey operation.

The first two guidelines both relate to the idea that research is necessary in order to maximize the potential of teleconferencing. Firms that have experienced the greatest success with teleconferencing, such as the Atlantic Richfield Company and the Xerox Corporation, conduct extensive investigations into communications needs before installing equipment. These two firms documented earlier methods of communication and investigated employees' expectations about teleconferencing. Today, both companies enjoy high usage of their teleconferencing systems.[7]

A fourth guideline is not to be reluctant to use the minimum setup required. Surprisingly good results can be obtained from modest installations, and expansion is often relatively simple if demand warrants. Conversely, elaborate and expensive setups that fall into disuse erode confidence in the in-house communication department's professional and fiscal judgment. By the way, if teleconferencing is a rare occurrence in your organization, there really is no need for a dedicated net. Many firms arrange ad hoc networks and transmissions. That is often a good option, because these firms have the right hardware *and* the practical experience.

Finally, keep in mind that you will want to be able to measure the success or failure of your teleconferencing innovations after they are in place. Records on usage and research into the effectiveness of the setup are essential. You will need to evaluate the content of the meeting, the technical performance of the equipment, and how well participants understood and retained the subject matter.

HOW AN ELECTRONIC MEETING FUNCTIONS

The corporate video department member's responsibilities during a videoconference are as varied as the conference structures themselves. In the case of a meeting where the particular institution is on the receiving end of a point-to-point conference with audio feedback, the department's responsibilities may involve little more than aiming the satellite reception dish to the bird's coordinates, moving a television monitor to the appropriate room, and arranging for the phone line, such as a speakerphone, to be placed in the room.

In the case of a full-video, multipoint-to-multipoint conference, the person in charge of the arrangements has a task that can reasonably be judged to be as complicated as directing a live television variety show. In addition to switching among the various sources, the producer has the unenviable job of determining whose image will go on top if the conference is a multiscreen affair. Corporate egos, it might be noted, are sensitive to such matters.

Although scenarios for such conferences differ hugely, we will see that there is some common ground. First, the protocol of a meeting, the way in which it is planned and executed, will be described. Secondly, the chapter will conclude with a summary of methods by which experienced telecommunicators ensure that the medium does not obscure the intended message.

PROTOCOL OF A VIDEO TELECONFERENCE

Realize from the start that most of the substance of a successful teleconference — the planning that made it work — is invisible. Choosing the technical options has been discussed above, and in fact those options may have been decided for you in advance by department management. Some questions about the format of the conference might remain, though, as well as a host of logistical details.

Individual circumstances will obviously differ vastly, so no common prescription is possible or practical. However, many video professionals do agree that the following points relate to virtually any circumstance.

First, if you have a choice of the format of the teleconference, consider the format's impact in human terms. For example, a private one-way broadcast without provision for feedback may be appropriate for a company news program. But if the teleconference is intended to reach stockholders, they certainly may feel offended if there is no provision for feedback.

Evaluate the enormous communications problems involved in teleconferencing's tendency to produce "information overload," and determine if and how you can avoid them. Communications scholars note that we humans have a marvelous capability to invoke the "cocktail party effect," meaning that we're able to filter out extraneous noise and concentrate on one speaker, even if we're in a roomful of people speaking at full volume. Audio equipment, though, has no such filtering effect, as anyone who has tried to record in a crowded, noisy environment has learned through experience. From the standpoint of a teleconference planner this means controlling the amount of sound sources that will be on the air at one time. A good deal of this problem can be resolved by common sense. If you are sending a panel discussion to five points and inviting questions, for instance, don't open up all five lines at once. Have a producer screen the questions and choose which line to air. (An even more selective method is to have an operator record and relay the questions; this also eliminates duplicate questions.) When it is necessary to have many lines open, an audio producer can often kill the mics of those who are not expected to be responding so that ambient noise (which is usually considerable) can be reduced. For a more innovative solution, the Shure Corporation markets a mic that shuts itself off when no one is speaking into it. (Note that this tends to "clip" off people's words if they make an inordinately long pause; inform them of this factor.) Various other audio options, specifically designed for teleconferencing, can alleviate many of the difficulties. A "master of ceremonies" can also simplify the communications overload by keeping close tabs on who talks when and inviting those responses at appropriate times. In other cases, presentations may be so tightly scripted that overlapping of speakers is not a problem.

A third suggestion is to keep it simple. Caroline Laden, director of the America Law Network, advises first-time teleconferencers that any additional complications beyond the bare essentials can scuttle a show. "The detail is enormous," she contends. "You just can't keep all those threads going."[8]

Meet with everyone involved well in advance of the teleconference. Find out what they want to do and who intends to do it. By "well in advance" most pros mean several months, possibly even a year. In addition to content, the person in charge must worry about logistics, including the rental of facilities and satellite transponder rental. (For an explanation of transponders, see the previous chapter.)

Nail down any technical problems. Are videotapes part of the presentation? Make sure you have an adequate method of playback. How about facsimile machines? If they're needed, be sure that the proper equipment is on hand. Will the teleconference include an overseas destination? Brace yourself, because you may be in for some major compatibility predicaments. Also, you may find that the information being discussed is of a proprietary nature, and you may have to arrange with the communications carrier to have the signal scrambled.

Don't forget that you're planning a *meeting* as well as a teleconference, with all its attendant intricacies. You may have to arrange lodging for people who come to a regional teleconference site and even orchestrate food service. (Bear in mind that there are time-zone problems, too; lunch in New York is breakfast in Los Angeles.) In sum, remember that the event is a meeting first and a teleconference second. The meeting may fail (and so will you) if its objectives are not met — and this can happen even if the teleconference is a dazzling technical success.

Identify and put in writing as many of the presentational details as possible, including the date and time of the meeting, speakers, who is responsible for scripting, and timetables for production of script and collateral material, such as charts, artwork, and brochures.

Finally, be sure that you have answered the paramount question: Why is this teleconference being planned in the first place? If the meeting could be handled in a more appropriate fashion, the preliminary stage is the time to make that determination. Likewise, use the planning stage to determine the prospective audience and gear the presentation accordingly.

EFFECTIVE COMMUNICATIONS

Now comes the final responsibility of an in-house video professional managing a teleconference: making sure that communication is effected smoothly and, to put it bluntly, that participants perform well. Suggestions for clothing and on-air demeanor were discussed in Chapter 8. However, here are some points unique to teleconferencing.

In general, coach speakers to look into the lens of the camera. It is more comfortable for a nonprofessional speaker to look at the monitor showing video from the other end of the hookup or to look at someone physically in the same room who has just asked a question. But those viewing such a speaker who is not looking at the lens find it disconcerting, to say the least. Some teleconferencing organizations overcome this problem by using prompting devices similar to those used by TV anchors. Instead of a news script being shown on the half-silvered mirror, though, the image projected is that of the party on the other end of the video hookup. Some technically adroit teleconferencers simply jury-rig their own systems.

Second, when choosing talent, it may be wise to give preference to those people who have experience and skill in running a meeting. Managing meetings is a different skill from television announcing. In the best of all possible worlds you'll find a staffer with skills in both areas.

Be certain to warn participants of the delays involved in a satellite-transmitted teleconference. Satellites are parked more than 22,000 miles above the earth, and, as explained in the previous chapter, their footprints are sometimes not large enough to cover intercontinental transmissions in one hop. So even with messages transmitted at the speed of light (which is the speed at which electromagnetic waves travel), response time can be thrown off by almost a full second when two birds are involved in the transmission. That's enough to cause some very distracting lapses in normal communication patterns. (This is a phenomenon that really must be experienced to be appreciated.)

Finally, it must be explained that the teleconference has to end at the scheduled time. If only one hour of transmission time has been leased on a carrier, the transmission will end after one hour, regardless of whether the conference has reached its conclusion.

This last point leads to an important concluding item: Because teleconferencing must be meticulously planned, it usually reduces time-wasting to a minimum. Experienced teleconferencers feel that the extra preparation businesspeople give to a television appearance makes electronic meetings more efficient than face-to-face meetings, even though personal encounters do provide more interpersonal cues than electronic interaction can.

Teleconferencing need not be highly complex, although it certainly can be, given the right circumstances. Many of the facets of this rapidly changing field are beyond the scope of this chapter, and it would be advisable for anyone interested in the area to pursue additional readings. Trade journals, such as *Video Manager, Corporate Television, Videography,* and *Audio-Visual Communications,* carry regular features updating technologies and techniques. In addition, new books are giving this emerging area in-depth coverage; one such book is Georgia A. Mathis's *How to Produce Your Own Video Conference* (White Plains, NY: Knowledge Industry Publications, 1987).

SUMMARY

- Teleconferencing is becoming viable — some say indispensable — for business because it results in substantial savings. While travel costs have been rising communications costs have generally declined.

- There are several formats for teleconferencing. The most common are point-to-point video with audio and video feedback and point-to-point video with only audio feedback.

- Several standards exist for transmission of teleconference images. The higher the amount of transmission information per second, the better the picture; but this improvement also results in higher costs.

- When choosing among options, make them suit the needs of the organization, not the other way around.

- Because teleconferencing presents so many logistical challenges, it is critical to begin planning as far in advance as possible.

- Coach speakers to look into the lens of the camera whenever possible. When choosing speakers, it is wise to select people with experience in running meetings.

- Teleconferences are bound by strict time limits. The fact that teleconferences in general require more precise planning than does a standard face-to-face meeting often results in more efficient use of time.

EXERCISES

1. Individual class members or small groups can prepare reports on how local firms use teleconferencing technology. Call the public relations departments of area firms. If you do not know the major firms in your area, local chambers of commerce almost always provide lists. Failing this, ask the reference librarian at the main branch of your local public library. Write a two- or three-page report about each firm.

2. The class can give a presentation on Teleconferencing in the City of _____, which will be planned and presented during class time. Split up into two groups, each group handling a different angle on the topic. (For ex-

ample, one group could report on the current state of teleconferencing; the other could report on plans for the future.) But here's the hitch: All communication between groups must be done by telephone. One group can meet in an office equipped with a phone and speak with the other group in a similarly equipped office. Logistics are up to you.

3. The presentation can be given to the class or, better yet, via television if a studio is available. One suggestion: Half the class could meet in the control room, simplifying viewing of those in the studio. A camera and mic(s) could be moved into the control room and wired to transmit to the studio. If there is a window between studio and control room, draw the curtains or tape backdrop paper over the window. Now you are free to structure the presentation in any form you wish. You may want to videotape it for review.

NOTES

1. "Conversation with Jan Sellards," *Videography* (November 1987): 68.

2. Reported in Frederick Williams, *The Communications Revolution* (New York: New American Library, 1983): 135.

3. For a discussion of telecommunications and the destatusing effect, particularly as it applies to audio conferencing, see Everett M. Rogers, *Communication Technology: The New Media in Society* (New York: Free Press, 1986): 51.

4. Figures cited in "Corporate AV: Videoconference Calls," *Audio-Visual Communications* (March 1987): 42.

5. Samuel Long, "Teleconferencing Matures," *Videography* (March 1986): 56.

6. Note that the transmission rates are rounded off and that the values given are those that apply to North America. For more precise summaries of standardized transmission rates here and abroad see "A Teleconferencing Primer," *Videography* (November 1987): 56–64; and "Teleconferencing Matures," *Videography* (March 1986): 56–59.

7. For further guidance on how large and small firms have created teleconferencing setups, see "Meeting with Success," *Audio-Visual Communications* (September 1986): 28, 29, 36, 37.

8. Quoted in "Videoconferencing: Planning and Preparation," *Video Manager* (November 1987): 12.

CHAPTER 15

RELATED

AUDIOVISUAL

TECHNOLOGY:

THE MERGING MEDIA

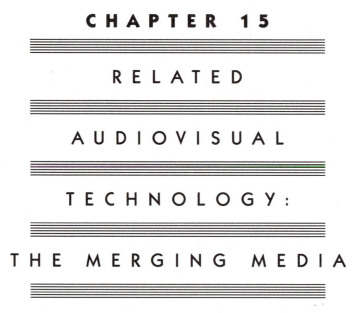

Divisions among institutional media are blurry nowadays. For example, the multi-image slide show was once within the domain of the photography department; today, many of those slides are produced *on video* and transferred to slide by a specialized scanning camera.

The situation can be reversed. Images on paper or film can now be scanned and digitally encoded. The digital pattern can then be altered and manipulated and the results transferred to video.

Once, the computer was the sole domain of the folks who carried pocket calculators on their belts and spoke what to the uninitiated was a foreign language. Well, the language is still arcane, but the computer is now inextricably linked to AV functions, including video. The computer is now a design center that allows production of printed (or digitized and video-transferred) materials, including illustrations, animation, and training manuals.

In fact, those of us in the business of producing instruction materials often find clients asking for an entire package: video, slides, overhead projections, and a printed manual. And indeed, the new merging technologies do allow a small group of people to produce all those elements. It's not unrealistic to think that in certain applications the AV department might soon become a one-man or one-woman shop.

The purpose of this chapter is not to provide a quick audiovisual course. Instead, this concluding portion of the book presents something of a jumping-off point, offering a very brief glimpse of some of the technologies that are merging with video production. We'll specifically examine the use of the computer in audiovisual production, computer-generated audio, multi-image, hybrid technologies, and desktop publishing.

THE COMPUTER IN AV

No single tool has had more effect on the institutional producer than the computer, and it promises to become an ever-more-dominant factor in all areas of audiovisual production.

APPLICATIONS OF THE PERSONAL COMPUTER

Some of the applications of computer technology have been discussed in appropriate chapters of this book, and for the sake of keeping this work smaller than the Manhattan phone directory, many applications must be omitted. But the most important point — and this really cannot be stressed too strongly — is that as a video or AV producer *you must become computer-literate*. A time will come when your function is irretrievably tied to the computer. In fact, if you are now involved in any type of video editing, that time is probably already upon you. Soon, an increasing number of functions will be directly tied to the personal computer. In some cases entire editing suites and control rooms are computer-driven (Figure 15.1).

This growth is primarily due to the tremendous increase in computing power available to the user of a PC. Until very recently complex operations requiring high memory (such as the production of graphics) were possible only on

FIGURE 15.1

Entire production facilities can be controlled by computer. The computer command center, far left, not only stores and adapts editing decision lists but also digitally processes audio signals to produce an assortment of special effects.

high-power and high-price industrial units. But the past several years have seen huge increases in the available memory, processing speed, and flexibility of desktop machines. That's why video practitioners, slide-show producers, AV art directors, and even music composers are finding the PC indispensable in day-to-day operations.

A personal computer means anything that is customarily sold to consumers, is meant for nonexpert use, and can sit on your desk top (although some PCs do have stand-alone units that are floor-mounted). PC is an acronym for personal computer, but the abbreviation has come to be synonymous with personal computers that are compatible with the operating system used by IBM.

Apple, which makes the popular Macintosh as well as other computers, uses a different operating system than does IBM. The two cannot use the same computer disc or run each other's programs, although specialized conversion utilities and hardware can accomplish that. It is likely that within the next few years programs and hardware to convert between Apple and IBM will become commonplace, although for the present it is wise not to count on the ability to translate all programs and program output.

We'll look at some of the applications of PCs in the remainder of this chapter. The next section, though, will briefly focus on the fundamentals of computer operation.

A BRIEF HISTORY OF THE COMPUTER

The technicalities may differ, but computers all do essentially the same thing. Although those operations are undeniably complex, at their root they are reasonably easy to comprehend. Hardware (the computer itself) and software (the programs that run on the computer) are different, but the operations all follow the same strategy.

To illustrate just how simple that strategy is, consider that the direct ancestor of the computer was a weaving loom. The first example of "digital" control was a punched piece of paper (later replaced by a card) that determined the position of a certain part of the loom. If there were a hole in the paper, the loom would perform a certain operation. No hole? That operation would not be performed.

This concept, which dates back to the 1700s, was the basis of digital technology, which operates by a series of on-off switches. This principle was first used to "program" the loom to produce a certain pattern of cloth, and later it was used in a wide variety of applications for manufacturing and calculation.

Calculation, of course, is the computer's strong suit, and this enormous power became available to the consumer when printed circuits were developed. Printed circuits are direct descendants of the vacuum tube, a hot, fragile, and bulky device that was used in the earliest computers, such as the UNIVAC. The UNIVAC, more than 10 feet long by 6 feet wide by 7 feet high, was developed in the early 1950s. It used about 20 times as much power as an electric stove with four burners in operation, and, according to an engineer who worked on the computer's development, was "a pygmy compared to a modern computer."[1]

The UNIVAC had only a fraction of the computing power of currently available laptop units that run for several hours on a battery. What accounts for the change? Basically, the microchip, a solid-state device that can perform the same function as a vacuum tube. (The microchip had one intermediate ancestor, the transistor.) Chips are the brains of the computer and perform the on-off tasks, the manipulation of digits, that add up to the digital calculating process. This on-off process, the presence or absence of an electrical signal, is known as *binary coding*. It is by the binary process that the computer understands information. For example, the letter *A* can be represented in binary terms by the pulses "off . . . off . . . off . . . off . . . on."

These pulses can be generated, manipulated, and tabulated with lightning speed — literally, lighting speed, because the pulses move with the speed of electricity. That is why computer calculations can be made with such inhuman rapidity. Thousands of calculations are performed in an instant.

All this calculation takes place deep in the brain of the beast, that part known as the central processing unit, or CPU. The CPU is generally accessed via commands entered through a keyboard, and the functions generated are displayed on a monitor.

The computer stores information in two places, random-access memory (RAM) and read-only memory (ROM). ROM information was plugged into the computer at the factory, cannot be changed, and, barring disaster, is permanent. RAM is usually where software is loaded; it is volatile, meaning that the information in RAM is usually lost when the power is turned off.

A computer that loses information when the power is shut off obviously has drawbacks, which is why computers are equipped with a storage mechanism, usually a device to transfer the information to a disc. Discs come in a variety of sizes, including the standard floppy (it bends), the microfloppy (which is in a hard case and doesn't bend), and the hard disc, which is encased within the computer. The above are all magnetic methods of storage. The compact disc and video disc are optical methods of storage. Huge advances in storage capabilities are taking place. Computer engineers are just now beginning to tap the potential of the optical storage disc. For example, one compact disc could hold all the information currently contained in a multivolume encyclopedia.

But it is not the amount of storage that is important so much as the computer's ability to *manipulate* what it has stored. For example, 2,000 recipes might just as easily be stored on index cards and arranged by category in a metal box. This would be cheaper, take less room, and probably be more convenient in the long run than putting the recipes into a computer's memory. But if you were under doctor's orders to remove eggs from your diet, how would you sort those recipes out? A computer can do this easily by using its digitally based brain to scan every recipe in its memory and sort for the word *egg*. You could, if you wished, also sort out only the recipes that used eggs, olives, and garlic in the same dish.

FIGURE 15.2

The computer can manipulate sound by producing a visual depiction of the sound signal. The keyboard and "mouse" can then modify the sound to produce creative effects. As computer memory increases, so do the possibilities for computer control of sound. Soon, much sound editing may be done digitally; the days of audio-splicing tape appear to be numbered.

Courtesy Philip Benoit, *Modern Radio Production*, Wadsworth Publishing Company, 1990.

COMPUTER–GENERATED AUDIO

The ability of a computer to manipulate information has many applications in the audiovisual field. For example, audiovisual producers are now often composing their own music and creating sound effects by computer and a device known as the musical instrument digital interface, abbreviated MIDI and pronounced "middy." It allows the producer to synchronize any number of electronic musical instruments and other sound-production devices, including standard tape recorders, with a computer.

HOW SOUNDS ARE MANIPULATED BY COMPUTER

Often, the main link in the audio chain is the synthesizer, sometimes called an "electronic piano." It is more than a piano, though: It can reproduce a wide variety of sounds and, in some cases, can "invent" new sounds by digitally sampling, storing, and manipulating audio sources.

The computer gives a visual readout of sound (Figure 15.2), commonly referred to as a "sound envelope." The computer and MIDI allow the producer to shape and reshape the sound — say, to a "laser beam" tone for a science-fiction-like special effect. This level of control allows a producer to automatically actuate a drumbeat, for example, and then add many layers of music. You do not have to be a musician to produce the simplest music beds, although musical ability is necessary for real composition.

WHO USES COMPUTER AUDIO?

Although AV producers are making increasing use of this equipment, it is not yet a staple in most production suites. It *is*, however, commonplace among audio specialists who provide the musical background for institutional pieces. Many firms now undertake original composition for institutional videos. Because of the advancing technology, the individual composition may not be much more expensive than "canned" music, for which a needle-drop fee must be paid. But individually tailored music is usually much more useful to a producer than beds from music libraries, and custom-produced music can make a presentation infinitely more effective.

"Our clients demand sophistication," notes Matt Kaplowitz of New York's Onomatopoeia Productions. "Today, corporate communicators realize that the impact of effective music can be significant. Music takes the visuals and restates them in sound. It doubles the impact of the production."[2]

MULTI–IMAGE

Thanks in part to the computer, the slide show has remained a healthy part of the audiovisual scene. Today, the slide program is usually referred to as multi-image, since it is just that: collections of slide images that mesh, contrast, and create the illusion of motion.

THE NEW TECHNOLOGY OF MULTI–IMAGE

First, note that new technology has changed some of the fundamental precepts of multi-image. As mentioned, scanning devices that operate by computer control are now capable of printing high-resolution slides from video images. This capability is something of a godsend to production facilities that have invested heavily in

FIGURE 15.3

Photographic slides are still valuable tools for institutional communications. For one thing video cannot produce a large image as sharply as slides. Also, slides are easily handled and viewed.

illustration systems based on video or desktop computers. Specialized units such as the Aztek StudioSystem provide extra flexibility in producing charts and graphs useful for slide presentations; their output can also be transformed to video.

Multi-image, by the way, has continued its healthy growth despite the rising popularity of institutional video. One reason is that no truly satisfactory method has been devised to project video clearly and inexpensively. Slides, though, produce a brilliant image that can be viewed from a distance by a large audience. They can also be easily viewed and sorted by the producer planning the production (Figure 15.3).

In addition, multi-image is not merely a substitute for video or motion picture film; it is an art form in itself. Certain effects are unique to multi-image and, of course, to multimedia (in which motion picture film, video, and just about anything else can be incorporated). It is difficult to describe these effects, so if you are not already a connoisseur of multi-image, it would be worthwhile to view some presentations to gain an understanding of the strengths of this particular medium.

COMPUTER PROGRAMMING OF MULTI-IMAGE

Although multi-image has its own unique powers, it certainly has its own difficulties, too. Modern programs involve many slide projectors directed by computer. Programming and design of multi-image shows are extremely complex. To begin with there are many variations not only in the number of projectors but also in how those projectors place their image on the screen. In some cases the images overlap, often in the center of the screen. It is not uncommon for banks of projectors to be focused on entirely different screens.

The people who plan this complexity and the physical units that control the computers are both known as *programmers*. Many of the more popular programming machines are plugged into personal computers, either IBM-type PCs or Apples. A device called a *dissolve unit* controls the actual motion of the slide projector. The human programmers list when an individual projector will come on, for how long it will stay on, and when it will be instructed to change.[3]

HYBRID TECHNOLOGIES

Just as creating a slide via video technology has become standard practice, other hybrid technologies are also becoming part of the producer's repertoire.

PRINT AND VIDEO IMAGE TRANSFER

The new technologies offer tremendous flexibility to a producer who becomes involved in the merging media. And such technology is not beyond the reach of many institutions. For example, a relatively inexpensive (under $2,000 at last check) device known as the Polaroid FreezeFrame Video Recorder produces prints of video or computer images. It is a convenient tool for using video to generate, among other items, photos for archival purposes or the company newsletter.

Merging media create video from printed materials, too. A work on paper can be scanned into a digitized format that can be altered by computer illustration programs or even animated.

ELECTRONIC CINEMATOGRAPHY

But don't think that advancing technology is a death knell for traditional media, because it need not be. Motion picture film, for example, is making something of a comeback. People who were originally trained on film know that the medium has some inherent advantages over video. For example, film is not as susceptible to what TV news people used to call the "prisoner being led from the courthouse syndrome." Those of us who worked in TV news during the era when stations were changing from film to video news gathering remember the problems that arose when the only shot we could get of a notorious criminal came during the few seconds when he was led from the courthouse to the sheriff's van. Inevitably, crews would wait for an hour or more to catch the elusive shot. The film crews always got it. But the video-equipped crews would sometimes miss the shot because they were trying to power up or figure out why their battery had died.

Although video gear has improved in portability and reliability, it can still be more complex than a motion picture camera. Film cameras don't get damaged if they are accidentally pointed toward the sun. They are tolerant of heat and cold. And though it is not recommended practice, you can drop them occasionally without disastrous results.

But more importantly, film just *looks* better to many people. It has a depth and a richness that cannot be matched by videotape, and that difference is apparent even when the film is shown on television.

Unfortunately, film is an absolutely hellish medium on which to edit. Various pieces of film, along with the audio track, must be cut and spliced and synchronized with a multiwheeled device. The obvious compromise would be to shoot on film and dub the processed film onto videotape, which could be edited with comparative ease. That was done, with some success, but not without initial problems. Picture and sound quality were often eroded.

But modern computerized systems allow for clearer dubs, accurate color correction, and improved synchronization. Many firms are now producing high-quality entertainment and institutional film-video. This technique is often known as "electronic cinematography," although the term is also applied to shooting with video while using film-style techniques.

DESKTOP PUBLISHING FOR THE VIDEO PRODUCER

Finally, we'll consider a topic that is within the immediate realm of audiovisual production but not typically associated with video. Desktop publishing is, however, becoming an important adjunct to many types of institutional video and audiovisual production, and it is rapidly changing the complexion of modern corporate communications. It is a corollary to the desktop video technology described in Chapter 12.

DESKTOP PUBLISHING AND CORPORATE COMMUNICATIONS

One reason why a video producer should know something about desktop publishing is the increasing recognition that instruction is more effective when various media are used. A workbook, for example, typically makes a videotape much more memorable. Another factor that makes desktop publishing of at least marginal concern to the television producer is that many of its technologies are used in the creation of graphics, which can, in turn, be transferred to video.

A final element has to do with the corporate culture: Those seeking to rise in a company's media hierarchy will inevitably encounter publication production and design as part of their job duties. Understanding the production process and philosophy of publications is a necessity for anyone looking to advance in the field of corporate communications.

HOW DESKTOP PUBLISHING WORKS

The convergence of media production functions again stems from advancing computer technology. The personal computer uses page-layout software and high-quality printers, usually laser-driven, to produce printed material that, although not indistinguishable from typeset matter, nevertheless comes pretty close.

Desktop publishing allows you to create artwork (even if you are not an artist), set headlines, "dump" text into columns, and lay out entire printed pages. To do this, you will typically need to run your desktop publishing software on a high-speed, high-memory computer.

High speed relates to how quickly the computer can construct and reconstruct items in its memory. In the desktop publishing lexicon, this ability is referred to as the time it takes the screen to "refresh" itself after you have made a change in the graphic. Slow computers take an agonizingly long time. As a general rule you will want to do desktop publishing on a high-power-level Macintosh, such as the SE or Macintosh II, or a PC with at least a 286 processor. (The designation of 286 refers to the computer's central processing unit; the number is sort of a model number and has no intrinsic meaning.) A PC with a 386 processor is even faster but is also more expensive.

In addition to speed, you will also need a great deal of *memory*. Graphics gobble up huge chunks of storage space, so anyone contemplating desktop publishing should opt for at least a 20-megabyte hard drive.

Note that many of the software packages useful for desktop publishing are similar in function to those used for low-end video graphics. Paint programs allow even the nonartist to produce striking effects. However, it should be noted that whether the ultimate product is on paper, film, or video, hardware and software cannot substitute for good taste. Bad graphics and layouts are produced by fine equipment in the hands of mediocre operators.

CONCLUSION

This chapter and, indeed, this entire book, have dealt with principles of *communication*. After all, getting the message across is what the game is all about—not hardware, not glitzy graphics, not tricky camera shots.

A related concept, the merging of the media, has been dealt with in only a superficial manner, but it does point to a deeper issue that has a direct impact on the producer involved in any type of mass medium. For many years it appeared that we had irrevocably entered the world of the specialist. Things in general, and media in particular, became so complex that only specialists could understand them. Computers, for example, were not tools but enemies, malevolent creatures plotting to crash our data. In audio recording, how could anyone manage 32 digitally encoded tracks and a console that looked like the control panel to a spaceship? Worst of all, the new generation of production and postproduction equipment seemed all but incomprehensible, and it offered so many different hues, palettes, and effects that we were tempted to slink back into a quiet state of option-shock.

But things are changing, and the emergence of the institutional video "specialist" is changing all that. Why? Because that "specialist" is really a generalist. He or she is not a cog in a wheel but a creator who must knit together the contributions of technicians, educators, business managers, artists, scientists, writers, and videographers.

Much has been made of the corporate and institutional world's affection for the "bottom line." But the phrase does not necessarily carry negative connotations for the institutional producer. The bottom line, in terms of video, is a program that *works*, that serves a specific purpose: It motivates, informs, and inspires. Meeting that bottom line is a goal for a broadly educated person, a man or woman with curiosity and a wide range of general knowledge, someone with an open and flexible mind. That, for lack of a better term, can be a valuable "specialty."

SUMMARY

≡ The boundaries between various media are blurring. Computer technology allows for the transfer of one medium to another, meaning that the producer has many more options from which to choose.

≡ Anyone wishing to advance in the world of institutional video or AV probably has no choice but to become computer-literate. Computers are a link in many AV functions right now, and they promise to be an important factor in many others in the future.

≡ One particularly intriguing aspect of the computer is its ability to drive devices that create original music or sound effects. Original audio can be an extremely powerful element in a production.

≡ Multi-image, too, is profiting from the power of the computer. Many projectors can be programmed in synchronization much more easily than they could be in the past.

≡ The ability of computer technology to cross boundaries of media results in many hybrid technologies, such as devices to produce film from video and vice versa.

≡ Desktop publishing promises to significantly alter the face of corporate relations. While only an adjunct to a television producer's job, the technology promises to be extremely important to anyone who wishes to advance to upper levels of corporate communications management.

NOTES

1. Interview with Richard Spencer, an engineer on the original UNIVAC project, May 25, 1989.

2. Quoted by Stephen Friedlander in "AV Communications: They Write the Songs," *Audio-Visual Communications* (June 1981): 22–26.

3. For a good introduction see Clint Wallington, "Programming, Part I," *AV Video* (August 1986): 30–33. This is an extremely complex field, and the technology is changing rapidly.

GLOSSARY

Above-the-line cost A budgetary term indicating nontechnical production personnel. See *below-the-line cost*.

A-B rolling The practice of using two rolls of film simultaneously during the process of editing film. Filmmakers manufactured dissolves by placing one scene on a roll of film marked "A" while the corresponding portion of film on the reel marked "B" was black leader. When scenes were to be changed, the relationship of the two reels was changed accordingly, with a scene on "B" and black leader on "A." Both reels were run at the same time, and the output was printed onto a third reel. In video, A-B rolling refers to alternating between shots on two different reels or cassettes of videotape.

Address A particular location on a videotape, usually indicated via a *time code*.

Aesthetics The artistic elements of a production.

Affective learning That type of learning primarily involving emotions, motivation, and attitudes.

AFTRA   The American Federation of Television and Radio Artists; a union representing, among others, on-air broadcast performers.

Antialiased   Of video graphics, having their sharp edges smoothed.

Applications software   Software designed to achieve a specific purpose, such as word processing or desktop publishing. Compare *programming language* and *authoring language.*

Assemble editing   The process of editing shots onto a videotape consecutively, from beginning to end. Compare *insert editing*.

Authoring language   A term primarily used in interactive technology, referring to the user-friendly computer program that allows you to program the computer.

Battery memory   A problem associated with batteries that are not completely discharged before recharging. Such batteries tend to "remember" their previous level — say, half discharged — as the point at which they stop functioning.

Below-the-line cost   A budgetary term referring to technical production staff. Compare *above-the-line cost*.

Boom   A long device that holds a microphone. Many booms have operator controls at one end to allow pointing the mic.

Branching   In interactive technology, the ability of a program to follow various paths as directed by the viewer.

Camera registration   The technical adjustment of the three primary colors coming from cameras, so that the colors are exactly matched and overlapped to produce a quality picture.

C-band   Those microwave frequencies from 4 to 6 gHz. See *gigahertz*.

CD ROM   A compact disc with read-only memory. See *ROM*.

Cel animation   The older system of animation (as opposed to computer animation) in which an artist drew the moving image frame-by-frame onto transparent sheets.

Character generator   A device for creating video letters and graphics; abbreviated CG.

Characterization   A scriptwriter's term indicating the process by which characters are fully fleshed out in a program and given a believable personality.

Charge-back system   The budgetary process whereby a media department bills client departments for some or all of the work done.

Close-up   A tightly framed shot. The term is often modified, as in "extreme close-up" or "medium close-up."

Codec   Acronym for a coder-decoder, a device that converts video into a more easily transmittable digital signal; used in *teleconferencing*.

Cognitive learning   The type of learning associated with remembering facts, figures, and concepts.

Color bars   A series of bars of various colors, electronically generated, that allow engineers to adjust video equipment so that colors from all sources are consistent.

Component video   Computer visual images produced by activating digital points of light on the monitor.

Composite video   A television production system that mixes the three basic colors (red, green, and blue), information about the levels for whites and blacks, and the sync signal into a composite signal. This is the standard type of television signal, as contrasted with *component video*.

Continuity   The quality of having all aspects of a production match despite the fact that shooting may have spanned more time than shown in the particular scene. As one example, an actor may appear in a half-hour program that was shot over four days. It is important that he or she wear exactly the same clothing and hairstyle for each day's shooting in order to preserve continuity.

Control group   In research, a group that has not been exposed to a particular effect and therefore provides a baseline against which the effects of an experiment can be measured. A control group in video might be the people who did not see a tape that is supposed to increase workers' capabilities to perform a certain task; their performances are measured against those of people who did see the tape.

Control-track editing   A system using the area of the tape that holds the *synchronization track*.

Control unit   A device that controls two or more edit decks.

Cost per minute   A method of calculating or estimating costs of a production by determining the costs per running minute of the final tape.

Cost per program   A method by which costs are estimated for each individual program; useful primarily for departments that produce many programs or programs in series.

Cost per viewer   A method of calculating the overall costs of a production by estimating how many people will see it and pegging that cost to an individual viewer.

Cover shot   A wide shot used to establish a scene; also used to indicate a shot used to cover editing points in video.

Critical path structure   A dynamic system that ties together tasks and the times at which those tasks must be completed.

Cross-networking   Renting or providing time for one organization on another organization's network.

Cut   An abrupt change from one shot to another. Also, a term indicating that the take must come to an end.

DBS   Direct broadcast satellite, a term usually used to indicate a form of broadcasting from the satellite to home viewers.

Desktop publishing   Using computers and specialized *applications software* to do typography and page layout.

Desktop video   Using computers and specialized *applications software* to produce video effects, including graphics and animation.

Dissolve   A gradual transition from one shot to another, during which the two shots are briefly overlapped.

Dissolve unit   In *multi-image*, the device that creates a *dissolve* between slide projectors.

Documentary   A program with a news orientation, usually presented as a narrative and imbued with a certain point of view.

Dolly   To physically move the camera forward toward the object or person being shot.

Downlink earth station   A device to receive a signal beamed down from an orbiting satellite.

Dramatic script   A script that has the name of the character centered and dialogue written full across the page; also called a Hollywood script or a film-style script.

Edit deck   See *editing control unit*.

Editing control unit   A device to control two or more video recorders, synchronizing them and making possible the process of editing.

Edit interface   See *editing control unit*.

EFP   Electronic field production; gathering and producing a program entirely from a remote location.

Electronic cinematography   A method whereby cinematic values are used in video; sometimes taken to mean shooting on film and then dubbing the film to video for editing.

Fade   Going to black. Do not confuse with *dissolve*.

Fishpole   A colloquial term for using any long device to hold a microphone so that it can be maneuvered closer to the speaker but still be kept slightly out of camera range.

Flat budget   An accounting method in which a department is given a certain amount of money for a specified period and expected to field all reasonable requests.

Floor director   The crew member who directs operations on the studio floor; he or she is the director's link to the studio.

Focus group   Individuals who join to examine a particular problem or issue; used by producers and advertisers to gain perspective.

Foldback system   A method whereby audio going out on the air is fed back into the studio. By using foldback, as one example, talent on the set can hear the theme music playing. Foldback systems are carefully adjusted not to produce feedback, meaning that they do not allow the sound fed into the studio to be picked up strongly enough by studio mics to be reamplified over and over until the sound becomes a loud squeal.

Font   A variety of print; often used synonymously with *typeface*, although there are certain differences in the precise definitions of the two terms.

Footprint   The area of the globe covered by a satellite signal as the signal returns to earth.

Frame grabber   A device that holds a still frame of video, storing it as digital information.

Full-motion video   Video that shows complete action; the highest grade of video used in *teleconferencing*.

Genlock   A system that locks together the sync signals of differing video equipment, allowing switching from source to source without a breakup or roll in the picture.

Geostationary   Of satellites, remaining in the same position relative to the earth.

Gigahertz   A unit of frequency, abbreviated gHz; a gHz is 1 billion Hz; 1 Hz means one cycle per second.

Headroom   The amount of space between the top of the subject's head and the top of the video frame.

Hollywood script   See *dramatic script*.

Industrial   A term sometimes used to refer to an institutional production. Actors and producers often use this term even if the institution is not an industry per se; the term also refers to productions by businesses, nonprofit institutions, and educational organizations.

Insert editing   An editing method whereby video or audio is inserted at any point within a program.

Interactive program   A style of video or computerized presentation in which the viewer is allowed to choose various paths for the program.

Ku-band   Those microwave frequencies from 11 to 15 gHz. See *gigahertz*.

Lavaliere   A microphone, originally hung from the neck like a pendant but now almost always clipped to clothing.

Likert scale   A graduated series in which the respondent to a question chooses from among various levels of agreement.

Looking space   The room left in front of the subject's eyes in the video frame. Allowing proper looking space creates a more natural-appearing frame.

Magnetic storage   The use of computer discs or videotape for retaining magnetic impulses.

Microchip   The "brain" of the computer; a highly miniaturized collection of circuitry.

Microwave   Extremely high-frequency waves, which tend to stay tightly focused.

MIDI   Musical instrument digital interface, a device for linking a synthesizer with a computer.

Mixed field dominance   A problem that arises when videotape is dubbed onto video disc. The fields — odd and even frames — must be consistent in order for the program material to be correctly dubbed onto the disc master.

Moving-coil mic   A rugged and durable microphone in which a coil, attached to a diaphragm, is moved through a magnetic field to create an audio signal.

Multicamera production   A production method in which the outputs of several cameras are fed into a switcher, a device that the director uses to select shots.

Multi-image   A sophisticated presentation using several slide projectors and, occasionally, other media.

NTSC   National Television Standards Committee. Often used as a designation for standard television video — the interlaced scanning pattern used on American TV.

Off-line editing   Editing done on a basic system of two VCRs and an interface. The term is typically used to indicate the practice of using simple editing equipment to provide a rough cut (without such elements as graphic effects or *dissolves*) that will be used as a guide for the final cut.

On-line editing   *SMPTE* time-code editing done through a video switcher, the same device used in studio directing; allows the use of *dissolves*, introduction of special effects, and sophisticated *A-B rolling* with dissolves.

Operating budget   The document that describes and projects expenses for a department over a period of time, usually a fiscal year.

Overhead   The price of "keeping a roof over one's head"; basically, all the costs involved in a project, including heat, space, telephones, and the like.

Overlay   A term usually used to refer to a computer-generated graphic display that appears over video.

Paint, or painting system   A device to electronically create artwork for the video screen.

Pedestal   To move a camera higher by raising the pedestal that holds the camera head. Compare *tilt*.

Phasing   The interaction of sound from various sources. Usually used in the context of mic phasing, often referring to problems resulting when multiple microphones pick up the same sounds at slightly different times, causing audio distortion.

Pot   Short for potentiometer; a knob or vertical sliding device that controls the microphone levels of sources being fed into an audio console.

Programming language   The most basic method of communicating with a computer. Many computer operators who run *applications software* do not see or use programming language.

Project budget   A budget drawn up for one particular program; compare *operating budget*.

Prompting device   A unit with a one-way mirror that fits over the camera lens; the script is projected onto the mirror so that performers can read the lines while looking into the camera.

Psychomotor learning   That type of learning dealing with developing physical skills.

RAM   Acronym for random-access memory; the type of computer memory that can be accessed and changed without restriction.

Rate card   A list of equipment and studio rental prices; also widely used in broadcasting to indicate the cost of advertising on a station.

Reel   A videographer's collection of samples of his or her best work; still used even though videographers place their samples on a cassette.

Remote   A production done away from the studio.

ROM   Acronym for read-only memory; memory stored optically or magnetically that cannot be changed. It can only be "read" by a scanning device such as a compact disc reader (a laser) or a computer disc reader (a magnetic head).

SAG   The Screen Actor's Guild, a union primarily representing film actors.

Segue   A transition from one part of a program to the next.

Semantic differential scale   A measurement technique whereby a respondent chooses from various points between two extremes, such as "good" and "bad."

SFX   Sound effects.

Shotgun   A type of microphone designed to pick up sound from long distances; named for its shape.

Single-camera video   A technique in which all of a program is taped with one camera and edited together.

Slate   An identifier of the take number or other relevant information about a production. The slate used to be a chalkboard on which the information was written; today, it is likely to be made of plastic or may even be electronically generated. Sometimes crews will "slate" a take orally, such as by saying, "This is take two of the second scene, rolling in five, four, three, two . . ."

SMPTE   Society of Motion Picture and Television Engineers. This organization prescribed the *time code* used in sophisticated editing, often called SMPTE time-code editing.

SOT   Sound on tape; usually used in a script to indicate the taking of audio and video from a tape.

Storyboard   A series of drawings that approximate the video scenes in a program or commercial.

Synchronization track   A series of pulses that keeps all components of a video signal in proper alignment.

Talent   On-air performers.

Teleconferencing   Linking two remote sites with audio and, sometimes, video.

Teletext   Projection of printed words onto the video screen in a form meant to be read as text. Also called videotext or videotex, although the terms are not always considered to be precisely synonymous.

Temporal resolution   A term referring to how well motion (action over time) is reproduced on a video picture.

Tilt   To move the nose of a camera up or down while keeping the center relatively stationary. If the entire camera is raised while keeping the lens pointed at the same object, the movement is known as a *pedestal*.

Time-base corrector   A device that stabilizes playback of a videotape.

Time code   An editing method whereby precise timers are recorded on a portion of the videotape not seen by the viewer. See *SMPTE*.

Transduction   Changing one form of energy into another. For example, a microphone transduces the motional energy of sound into electrical energy, known as audio.

Transponder   A device on a satellite that receives a signal from the earth and transmits it back.

Treatment   A capsulized description of a program.

Truck   To physically move a camera from side to side.

Two-column script   A script that indicates video in the left-hand column and audio in the right-hand column. Sometimes called a video script.

Uplink earth station   A mechanism that transmits a signal from the ground to an orbiting satellite. Compare *downlink earth station*.

VCR   Acronym for a video cassette recorder. A VCR is a type of *VTR*, although video tape recorders can also use other formats, such as reel-to-reel.

Vector systems   Computerized video components that allow images to be manipulated in what appear to be three dimensions.

Verisimilitude   Having the appearance of truth throughout the presentation. It is important for a scriptwriter to ensure that what happens on the screen squares with reality.

Video digitizer   A device that translates standard video into a digital computer-type format.

Video disc   A disc imprinted with video signals generated by a laser beam. Discs are particularly useful when random access to the program material is required.

VO   Voice-over, meaning that an announcer reads over the video.

VSAT Very-small-aperture terminal, a type of relatively inexpensive satellite receiver.

VTR Acronym alternately used for video tape recorder or video tape recording.

XLR A frequently used type of three-pin audio connector.

Zero-based budget A budget built from scratch each year rather than being based on historical information.

Zoom To move in on a subject by narrowing the field of view by magnification.

SUGGESTED

READINGS

GENERAL VIDEO PRODUCTION

Alten, Stanley. *Audio in Media*. 2nd ed. Belmont, CA: Wadsworth, 1990. Very useful for the video producer who wants high-quality audio.

Burrows, Thomas D., and Woods, Donald N. *Television Production Disciplines and Techniques*. 4th ed. Dubuque, IA: Wm. C. Brown, 1988. Good basic text, especially appropriate for the producer who needs in-depth technical details.

Mathias, Harry, and Patterson, Richard. *Electronic Cinematography*. Belmont, CA: Wadsworth, 1985. An important manual for producers who want those all-important "cinematic values" in their video productions.

Millerson, Gerald. *TV Lighting Methods*. Stoneham, MA: Focal Press, 1982. Exhaustive guide to solving one of the most nettling production problems.

Millerson, Gerald. *The Technique of Television Production*. 11th ed. Stoneham, MA: Focal Press, 1985. Venerable work with generous attention to technical details.

O'Donnell, Lewis, Hausman, Carl, and Benoit, Philip. *Announcing: Broadcast Communicating Today*. Belmont, CA: Wadsworth, 1987. Although designed primarily for broadcast announcers, it will be useful for any performer, especially nonprofessionals who need a crash course in on-camera performance or directors who need to coach those nonprofessionals.

Rabiger, Michael. *Directing the Documentary*. Stoneham, MA: Focal Press, 1986. Practical book, important for the institutional producer involved in the popular "documentary" format for in-house work.

Utz, Peter. *Video User's Handbook*. 4th ed. White Plains, NY: Knowledge Industry Publications, 1989. Primer for producer and operator; starts from ground zero.

Zettl, Herbert. *Sight-Sound-Motion: Applied Media Aesthetics*. Belmont, CA: Wadsworth, 1990. Deep study of the factors that make video a communicative medium.

Zettl, Herbert. *Television Production Handbook*. 4th ed. Belmont, CA: Wadsworth, 1984. Definitive reference on most aspects of TV production.

SPECIALIZED PRODUCTION GUIDES: TRAINING, NEW TECHNOLOGIES, AND TELECONFERENCING

Blank, Ben, and Garcia, Mario R. *Professional Video Graphic Design*. Englewood Cliffs, NJ: Prentice-Hall, 1985. Blank, a network graphics designer, effectively conveys the principles of communication with video graphics.

Cartwright, Steve R. *Training with Video: Designing and Producing Video Training Programs*. White Plains, NY: Knowledge Industry Publications, 1986. Complete guide, with special attention paid to planning.

Gayeski, Diane. *Corporate and Instructional Video*. Englewood Cliffs, NJ: Prentice-Hall, 1983. Broad treatment of the field; somewhat dated, but new edition expected soon. Gayeski's company, Omnicom of Ithaca, NY, also publishes *Interactive Toolkit*, a combination workbook and software collection. *Interactive Toolkit* is distributed through Knowledge Industry Publications, White Plains, NY: 1987.

Hansell, Kathleen, ed. *The Teleconferencing Manager's Guide*. White Plains, NY: Knowledge Industry Publications, 1988. Up-to-date book with very precise details regarding planning and budgeting.

Iuppa, Nicholas V., with Anderson, Karl. *Advanced Interactive Video Design*. Stoneham, MA: Focal Press, 1988. Up-to-date and highly detailed reference.

Percival, Fred, and Ellington, Henry. *A Handbook of Educational Technology*. New York: Kogan Page, Nichols, 1988. Comprehensive discussion of how people learn; good theoretical base.

Wershing, Stephen, and Singer, Paul. *Computer Graphics and Animation for Corporate Video*. White Plains, NY: Knowledge Industry Publications, 1988. Workable reference with special attention paid to personal-computer user.

SCRIPTING, BUDGETING, AND BUSINESS ASPECTS

Drucker, Peter F. *Managing for Results*. New York: Harper & Row, 1986. Classic guide to management and motivation; useful skills for any producer.

Hilliard, Robert. *Writing for Television and Radio*. 5th ed. Belmont, CA: Wadsworth, 1990. Comprehensive guide to writing for media, including much fundamental material adaptable for institutional producers.

Matrazzo, Donna. *The Corporate Scriptwriting Book*. 2nd ed. Portland, OR: Communicom Publishing Co., 1985. Although basically a book on scripting, this work is valuable for learning techniques of thinking *visually* and putting those thoughts on paper.

Singleton, Ralph S. *Film Scheduling/Film Budgeting Workbook*. Beverly Hills, CA: Lone Eagle Publications, 1984. Some useful hints for producers of films, much of it adaptable to corporate video.

Stokes, Judith Tereno. *The Business of Nonbroadcast Television*. White Plains, NY: Knowledge Industry Publications, 1988. Authoritative guide that provides extensive information about the nation's institutional video industry.

Sweeny, Allen, and Wisner, John N. *Accounting Fundamentals for Nonfinancial Executives*. New York: McGraw-Hill, 1977. The title says it all, and it's a perfect guide for video professionals suddenly charged with preparing budgets.

Wiese, Michael. *Film and Video Budgets*. Stoneham, MA: Focal Press, 1984. Very practical guidebook; many workable formulas.

PERIODICALS

The world of magazine and journal publishing is volatile, and by the time you read this, many publications may be out of print, and, of course, new periodicals will be in circulation. But even periodicals no longer produced are frequently kept in libraries, and they are often excellent references when dealing with subjects other than new equipment.

Audio-Visual Communications. Media Horizons, Inc., 50 W. 23rd St., New York, NY 10010. Strong emphasis on scripting and development.

AV Video. Montage Publishing, 25550 Hawthorne Blvd., Suite 314, Torrance, CA 90505. Heavily oriented toward the art of production; also good regular features on facility construction, operation, and management.

BM/E (Broadcast Management/Engineering). 820 2nd Ave., New York, NY 10017. A very technical but still comprehensible publication for people involved in engineering management. Most articles are understandable by the nontechnical professional, and it is a good guide to developing technologies.

Broadcasting. Broadcasting Publications, 1705 DeSales St. NW, Washington, DC 20036. Although not geared to the nonbroadcast video specialist, it contains many items of use to the institutional producer.

Business Marketing. Crain Communications, Inc., 740 Rush St., Chicago, IL 60611. Devoted to many aspects of marketing and provides an interesting overview of the relationship between media and business.

Corporate Television. ITVA, 50 West 23rd St., New York, NY 10010. Official publication of International Television Association.

EITV (Educational and Industrial Television). Broadband Information Services, Inc., 295 Madison Ave., New York, NY 10017. Updates on equipment and good articles on techniques.

International Television. Now defunct but found in the stacks of many libraries; succinct and insightful accounts of how business uses video.

Post: The Magazine for Post Production Professionals. Testa Communications, 25 Willowdale Ave., Port Washington, NY 11050. Technical but readable guide for postproduction workers; also provides interesting insights into editing in the entertainment industry.

Television Broadcast. P.S.N. Publications, 2 Park Ave., New York, NY 10016. Although geared primarily to television station operations, it contains very valuable updates on equipment and production trends.

Training. Lakewood Publications, Inc., 50 S. Ninth St., Minneapolis, MN 55402. Offers insights into the techniques of training, with due attention paid to video strategies.

TV Technology. Industrial Marketing Advisory Services, Inc., 5827 Columbia Pike, Suite 310, Falls Church, VA 22041. Wide range of news and information on new trends and products, including computers, high-definition television, and computer uses.

Videography. Media Horizons, Inc., 50 W. 23rd St., New York, NY 10010. Offers particularly strong sections on new technologies and their applications.

Video Manager. Knowledge Industry Publications, Inc., 701 Westchester Ave., White Plains, NY 10604. Excellent magazine aimed directly at the institutional producer. Good information, good writing.

Video Systems. Intertect Publishing Corp., 9221 Quivira Rd., Overland Park, KS 66212. For professionals in nonbroadcast video who have purchasing authority. In-depth coverage of new equipment.

INDEX